WISCONSIN GAZETTEER,

CONTAINING THE

NAMES, LOCATION, AND ADVANTAGES,

OF THE

COUNTIES, CITIES, TOWNS, VILLAGES, POST OFFICES, AND SETTLEMENTS,

TOGETHER WITH A DESCRIPTION OF THE

LAKES, WATER COURSES, PRAIRIES, AND PUBLIC LOCALITIES,

IN THE

STATE OF WISCONSIN.

ALPHABETICALLY ARRANGED.

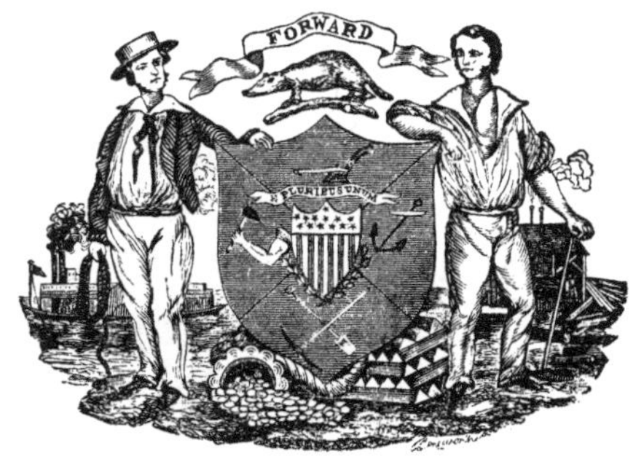

BY JOHN WARREN HUNT.

MADISON:
BERIAH BROWN, PRINTER.

1853.

Entered according to Act of Congress, in the year 1853.
BY JOHN WARREN HUNT,
In the Clerk's Office of the District Court of the United States for the District of Wisconsin.

22452.

PREFACE.

The utility of a Work, like the one now presented to the public, will not be questioned. The State of Wisconsin has grown into importance with unexampled rapidity, and is now so far advanced in settlement and improvement that some compilation of correct and authentic information, in relation to its natural features and advantages, seems to have become of the highest interest and necessity—to the citizen as a detailed description of his State—to the immigrant as a Guide Book in the selection of a home.

As this is the first publication of the kind which has ever appeared in relation to Wisconsin, its preparation, from materials scattered and undigested, has necessarily been attended with many difficulties and great labor. No pains, however, have been spared to make it, as far as possible, a correct and complete description of the State, historical and geographical, and of the peculiar characteristics of its different districts.

Through circulars, and otherwise, the author has consulted every Postmaster in the State, as well as a large number of other residents, known to be familiar with the portion in which they reside, and from them he has derived much of the information for his descriptions of cities, villages, and post offices. The notices of the legal history and situation of counties and towns, are the result of the most careful examination of the laws, journals, and records of the Territory and State. The description of lakes, rivers, &c., and of the face of the country, to a great extent has been compiled from maps and documents of the General Government and from other authentic publications, and from reliable sources furnished directly for this Work. Much valuable information has also been received from conversation and correspondence with the members of the legislature, and others, from every section of the State, for the past three years. By the method pursued a knowledge has been acquired of every portion of Wisconsin which it would not have been possible to have gained in any other manner. Perfect accuracy in all cases is neither claimed or expected, but it is hoped that these means have insured as great a degree, as is possible, in a new State of which much remains unoccupied and undeveloped, and but little settled long enough to be described with that certainty and complete familiarity that would be expected in an older State.

Notwithstanding great care has been taken in perfecting this Work, several mistakes have been discovered in the printed edition, a list of which will be found in the Errata. Many omissions were necessarily made in the body of the Work, which are inserted in the Appendix, but mostly prepared in such a manner as not to give that accuracy of description that is desirable. It is not supposed that it is free from other errors and omissions. Should such be discovered, the Author will consider it a great favor to have them pointed out to him, by letter or otherwise, as it is his wish to make any future editions, if called for, as full and exact as may be.

With these introductory and explanatory remarks the WISCONSIN GAZETTEER is submitted to the public, confidently trusting that it may receive sufficient patronage to render a reasonable compensation for the labor and money expended in its compilation and publication.

In conclusion, the Author desires to tender his sincere thanks to all who have aided him; and to extend his grateful acknowledgments to Governor Farwell, General Smith, Chancellor Lathrop, I. A. Lapham, and Lyman C. Draper, for their kindness and courtesy, and the valuable assistance he has received from each of them, in the prosecution of this undertaking.

MADISON, WIS., June 1st, 1853.

WISCONSIN.

Situation, Bounds, Extent and Area.—History of Territory and State.—Face of the Country, Soil, &c.—Antiquities.—Climate and Health.—Productions.—Manufactures.—Trade.—Education.—Government.—Civil Divisions.—Improvements.—Public Lands.—Miscellaneous.

SITUATION, EXTENT, BOUNDS AND AREA.—The State of Wisconsin embraces all of that portion of the Northwestern Territory lying north of the parallel of latitude 42° 30′ and west of Lake Michigan, excepting a portion of said Territory north and east of the Menomonee River of Green Bay, belonging to and forming the Upper Peninsula of Michigan; and another portion lying west of the River St. Croix, included in and constituting a portion of the Territory of Minnesota. Its greatest extent from north to south is two hundred and eighty-five miles, and from east to west two hundred and fifty-five miles.

Wisconsin is bounded on the north by Minnesota and Michigan, on the northeast, and east in Lake Michigan by Michigan, on the south by Illinois, and on the west by Iowa and Minnesota; or according to the Constitution, as follows, to wit: "Beginning at the northeast corner of the State of Illinois, that is to say, at a point in the centre of Lake Michigan, where the line of forty-two degrees and thirty-nine minutes of north latitude crosses the same; thence running with the boundary line of the state of Michigan, through Lake Michigan, Green Bay, to the mouth of the Menomonee river; thence up the channel of the said river to the Brule river; thence up said last mentioned river to Lake Brule; thence along the southern shore of Lake Brule, in a direct line to the centre of the channel between Middle and South Islands, in the Lake of the Desert; thence in a direct line to the head waters of the Montreal river, as marked upon the survey made by Captain Cram; thence down the main channel of the Montreal river to the middle of Lake Superior; thence through the centre of Lake Superior to the mouth of the St. Louis river; thence up the main channel of said river to the first rapids in the same, above the Indian village, according to Nicollet's map; thence due south to the main branch of the river St. Croix; thence down the main channel of said river to the Mississippi; thence down the centre of the main channel of that river to the northwest corner of the state of Illinois; thence due east with the northern boundary of the state of Illinois, to the place of beginning, as established by 'an act to enable the people of the Illinois territory to form a constitution and state government, and for the admission of such state into the Union on an equal footing with the original states,' approved April 18th, 1818."

The area of Wisconsin in land is 53,924 square miles, or 34,511,360 square acres.

History.—Wisconsin was first visited by French Missionaries in 1660, in October of which year Mesnard reached Che-goi-me-gon, on Lake Superior. In 1672, Aloues and Dablon visited Green Bay, and the country between the Fox river and the south end of Lake Michigan. In the year following, on the 13th of May, Marquette, a Jesuit Missionary, and Joliet, an agent of the government of France, with five other Frenchmen, embarked from their Mission, near Mackinac, and arrived at Green Bay, where they found an Indian village and procured guides to accompany them up Fox river to the Portage with the Wisconsin. They descended this river to its mouth, where they arrived on the 17th of June, 1673, and made the first discovery of the Upper Mississippi river. The Territory remained under the government of the French, who claimed it, until 1763, when, at the treaty of Paris, it was ceded to Great Britain, who retained it until the Independence of the United States was acknowledged by that county in 1783, when it was claimed by Virginia, as a part of the Illinois country conquered by Col. George Rogers Clark. It however remained in the possession of Great Britain until 1796, when it was surrendered in accordance with Jay's treaty, ratified the previous year. On the first day of March, 1784, it was ceded by Virginia to the United States. By the celebrated ordinance passed the 13th of July, 1787, a government was provided for the Territory northwest of the Ohio river, which territory was divided into two separate governments, the western called Indiana, by an act passed May 7th, 1800. An act dividing the Indiana Territory and organizing Illinois, was passed and approved February 3d, 1809. By the act of Congress to enable the people of Illinois to form a State government, approved April 18th, 1818, all that portion of said territory north of the parallel of latitude 42° 30′ west of the middle of Lake Michigan, was attached to the Territory of Michigan, which had been set off from Indiana in 1805.

In 1835, Michigan having assumed a State government, John S. Horner, Secretary and Acting Governor, convened a session of the legislature, at Green Bay, from the remainder of said Territory. No business was transacted, except the passage of several Memorials to Congress, among which was one asking for the organization of the Territory of Wisconsin, with the seat of government at Cassville, on the Mississippi.

An act establishing the Territorial government of Wisconsin, was passed and approved April 20th, 1836, and the Territory fully organized July 4th, 1836.

On the 12th day of June 1838, an act was passed dividing the Territory of Wisconsin, and establishing that portion on the west side of the Mississippi (which had been attached to Michigan in 1834,) into a separate government, under the name of Iowa.

In 1836, Governor Dodge, by proclamation dated September 9th, convened the legislature at Belmont, now in Lafayette county, on the 25th day of October in that year. The second session was held at Burlington, now in the State of Iowa, Nov.

6th, 1837, at which session the seat of government was located at Madison, where the first session of the 2d Legislative Assembly of Wisconsin was held Nov. 26th, 1838.

A Convention was held at Madison, October 5th, 1846, for the purpose of drafting a State Constitution, which was adopted in Convention, December 16th, 1846, but rejected by the people at the election held on the first Tuesday in April, 1847. A second Convention was held December 16th, 1847, and a Constitution agreed to February 1st, 1848, which was approved of by the electors at the election held April, 1848, and Wisconsin was admitted into the Union, on an equal footing with the other States, on the 29th day of May, 1848.

At the dates given below, the gentlemen named were appointed by the President of the United States, to the offices designated:

GOVERNORS.

Henry Dodge	April	13th, 1836.
Henry Dodge, re-appointed . . .	March	9th, 1839.
James Duane Doty, ...	September	30th, 1841.
Nathaniel P. Tallmadge	June	21st, 1844.
Henry Dodge	April	8th, 1845.

SECRETARIES.

John S. Horner		1836.
William B. Slaughter	February	16th, 1837.
Francis J. Dunn		1841.
A. P. Field		1841.
George R. C. Floyd		1845.
John Catlin	February	24th, 1846.

SUPREME COURT.

Charles Dunn	Chief Justice.
—— Frazier	Associate.
David Irwin, Jr.	Associate.
Andrew G. Miller.	Associate, in place of Frazier, deceased.

The following is a list of the several State Officers, from the organization of the State:

GOVERNORS.

Nelson Dewey	May	8th, 1848.
Nelson Dewey, re-elected	November,	1849.
Leonard J. Farwell	November	4th, 1851.

LIEUTENANT-GOVERNORS.

John E. Holmes	May	8th, 1848.
Samuel W. Beall	November,	1849.
Timothy Burns	November	4th, 1851.

SECRETARIES OF STATE.

Thomas McHugh	May	8th, 1848.
William A. Barstow	November,	1849.
Charles D. Robinson	November	4th, 1851.

STATE TREASURERS.

Jairus C. Fairchild	May	8th, 1848.
Jairus C. Fairchild, re-elected . .	November,	1849.
Edward H. Janssen	November	4, 1851.

ATTORNEYS-GENERAL.

James S. Brown	May	8th, 1848.
S. Park Coon	November,	1849.
Experience Estabrook	November	4th, 1851.

STATE SUPERINTENDENTS.

Eleazer Root	May	8th, 1848.
Eleazer Root	November,	1849.
Azel P. Ladd	November	4th, 1851.

BANK COMPTROLLER.

James S. Baker, appointed by Governor, November 20th, 1852.

JUDGES OF THE SUPREME COURT.

Edward V. Whiton,	Judge of	1st	Circuit	1848.
Levi Hubbell,	"	2d	"	1848.
Charles H. Larrabee,	"	3d	"	1848.
Alexander W. Stow,	"	4th	"	1848.
M. M. Jackson,	"	5th	"	1848.
Wiram Knowlton,	"	6th	"	1850.
Timothy O. Howe,	"	4th	"	1850.
Levi Hubbell,	"	2d	"	1851.
M. M. Cothren,	"	5th	"	1852.

SEPARATE, OR NEW SUPREME COURT.

Edward V. Whiton,	Chief Justice	1852.
Abram D. Smith,	Judge	1852.
Samuel Crawford,	"	1852.

Face of the Country, Soil, and Geological Features.—The natural features peculiar to Wisconsin, is the uniformity of its elevation, and shape of its surface, which is neither mountainous, hilly or flat, but gently undulating. The country west of Sugar river and south of the Wisconsin, is somewhat broken, principally by the dividing ridge upon which the road from Madison to Prairie du Chien passes. In this section, known as the Mines, are several peculiar elevations called Mounds. West of the Wisconsin river, are a range of high hills, being the only elevations in the State, either deserving or assuming the dignity of mountains. The southeastern portion of the State is marked by ravines at the streams but little depressed below the surrounding level. Its prominent features are the Prairie, destitute of tree or shrub, covered only by a luxuriant growth of grass, interspersed with flowers of every hue; the Oak Opening; the Lake; the woodland, on the border of streams, and the natural meadow. Proceeding north, to the Fox and Wisconsin rivers, and Green Bay, the timber increases, and the soil gradually changes from the vegetable mould of the prairie to a sandy loam. The surface also becomes somewhat depressed and uneven, diversified with timber, rolling prairie, large marshes and extensive swamps, having an abundant growth of cranberries and wild rice. Still north, and west, the surface becomes more uneven, and the streams rapid, affording an abundance of water power for the manufacture of lumber from the immense forests of evergreen, scarcely surpassed on the western continent.

The soil of the prairie consists of a dark brown vegetable mould, from one to two feet in depth, very mellow, and entirely destitute of stone or gravel, and for fertility and agricultural properties, cannot be surpassed. The sub-soil is a clayish loam, similar to the soil of the timbered lands, and is also suitable for cultivation. The soil of the timbered land is less rich than the prairie, not so deep, and contains less carbonate of lime, which enters into the composition of the latter in the proportion of from 20 to 40 per cent. The mining region, unlike that of any other mineral district, promises a liberal reward, as well to the farmer as to the miner. The soil of the evergreen district is mostly sandy, and not so rich as in other portions of the State. It is nevertheless, well adapted to agriculture and grazing.

The prairies of Wisconsin are not so extensive as those of other states, and are so skirted and belted by timber, that they are well adapted to immediate and profitable occupation.

The openings, which comprise a large portion of the finest land of the State, owe their present condition to the action of the annual fires which have kept under all other forest growth, except those varieties of oak which can withstand the sweep of that element.

This annual burning of an exuberant growth of grasses and of under-brush, has been adding, perhaps for ages, to the productive power of the soil, and preparing it for the plough-share.

It is the great fact, nature has thus "cleared up" Wisconsin to the hand of the settler, and enriched it by yearly burnings, and has at the same time left sufficient timber on the ground for fence and firewood, that explains, in a great measure, the capacity it has exhibited, and is now exhibiting for rapid settlement and early maturity.

There is another fact important to be noticed in this connection. The low level prairie, or natural meadow, of moderate extent, is so generally distributed over the face of the country, that the settler on a fine section of arable land, finds on his own farm, or in his immediate neighborhood, abundant pasturage for his stock in summer, on the open range; and hay for the winter, for the cutting—the bounty of Nature supplying his need in this behalf, till the cultivated grasses may be introduced and become sufficient for his use.

The limestone, underlying the coal fields of Illinois, forms the immediate basis of the alluvion of Southern Wisconsin. This geological district, in addition to that portion of the State which lies southerly of the valley of the Wisconsin river, comprises the whole of the slope towards Lake Michigan.

In many portions of this district, the lime rock disappears, and the out-cropping sand stone furnishes a fine material for building.

The lead bearing rock of the mineral region, is a porous lime stone, prevailing throughout Grant, Lafayette and Iowa Counties, comprising four-fifths of the "Lead District" of the upper Mississippi; the remaining one-fifth being in the States of Illinois and Iowa.

Deposites of iron ore, water lime stone, and beds of gypsum, together with other varieties of minerals, are found in localities more or less numerous, throughout the lime stone region.

All of that section of the State, which lies between Lake Superior on the North, and the falls of St. Anthony on the Mississippi, and the falls of the other rivers flowing southerly, is primitive in its prevailing geological character; and it is within this primitive region, that the copper mines of Lake Superior are found—probably the richest in the world, and apparently inexhaustible.

In all that portion of the State, lying between the primitive region just described, and the lime stone formation of the South and East, the transition sand stone prevails ; interspersed with lime stone, and more sparsely, with rock of a primitive character. This formation comprises that section of the country drained by the Wisconsin and other rivers tributary to the upper Mississippi, and below the falls of those streams. Within this Geological District, are found quarries of white marble, which promise to be abundant and valuable.

ANTIQUITIES.—The mounds and antiquities of this State are similar to those in other Western States. I. A. LAPHAM, Esq., who has made this subject his study for several years, in speaking of them in his work on the Geography and Topography of Wisconsin, says :

"Wisconsin does not fall behind the other portions of the western country in the monuments it affords of the existence of an ancient people who once inhabited North America, but of whom nothing is known except what can be gathered from some of the results of their labors. The works at Aztalan, in Jefferson County, are most known and visited, but there are many other localities which are said to equal them in interest and importance. The substance called brick at this place, is evidently burned clay, showing marks of having been mixed with straw, but they were not moulded into regular forms. There is a class of ancient earth-works in Wisconsin, not before found in any other country, being made to represent quadrupeds, birds, reptiles, and even the human form. These representations are rather rude, and it is often difficult to decide for what species of animal they are intended ; but the effects of time may have modified their appearance very much since they were originally formed. Some have a resemblance to the buffalo, the eagle, or crane, or to the turtle or lizard. One representing the human form, near the Blue Mounds, is, according to R. C. TAYLOR, Esq., one hundred and twenty feet in length : it lies in an east and west direction, the head towards the west, with the arms and legs extended. The body or trunk is thirty feet in breadth, the head twenty-five, and its elevation above the general surface of the prairie is about six feet. Its conformation is so distinct that there can be no possibility of mistake in assigning it to the human figure.* A mound at Prairieville, representing a turtle, is about five feet high; the body is fifty-six feet in length; it represents the animal with its legs extended, and its feet turned backwards. It is to be regretted that this interesting mound is now nearly destroyed. The ancient works are found in all parts of the Territory, but are most abundant at Aztalan, on Rock river, near the Blue Mounds, along the Wisconsin, the Neenah and the Pishtaka rivers, and near Lake Winnebago.

"The mounds are generally scattered about without any apparent order or arrangement, but are occasionally arranged in irregular rows, the animals appearing as if drawn up in a line of march. An instance of this kind is seen near the road seven miles east from the Blue Mounds, in Iowa County. At one place near the Four Lakes, it is said that one hundred tumuli, of various shapes and dimensions, may be counted—those representing animals being among others that are round or oblong.

"Fragments of ancient pottery of a very rude kind are often found in various localities. They were formed by hand, or moulded, as their appearance shows evidently that these vessels were not turned on a 'potter's wheel.' Parts of the rim of vessels usually ornamented with small notches or figures, are most abundant.

"A mound is said to have been discovered near Cassville, on the Mississippi, which is supposed to represent an animal having a trunk like the elephant, or the now extinct Mastodon. Should this prove true, it will show that the people who made these animal earthworks, were contemporaries with that huge monster whose bones are still occasionally found; or that they had then

* The reader is referred to the "Notice of Indian Mounds, &c., in Wisconsin," in Silliman's Journal, vol. 34, p. 88, by R. C. Taylor; and to the "Description of Ancient Remains in Wisconsin," by S. Taylor, vol. 44, p. 21, of the same work, for more detailed descriptions and drawings of these interesting animal mounds.

but recently emigrated from Asia, and had not lost their knowledge of the elephant."

Climate and Health.—The climate of Wisconsin is similar to that of the interior and western counties of New-York. The winters for the past four years have for the most been mild, and without much snow. The mean temperature of nine different localities in the State, in 1851, was 45° 54'. Mr. Lapham, in the work above referred to, says:

"The salubrity of the climate, the purity of the atmosphere, and of the water, which is usually obtained from copious living springs; the coolness and short duration of summer, and the dryness of the air during winter, all conspire to render Wisconsin one of the most healthy portions of the United States. The wet meadows, marshes and swamps, are constantly supplied with pure water from springs; and as they are not exposed during summer to a burning heat, they do not send forth those noxious and deleterious qualities so much dreaded in more southern and less favored latitudes. Many of our most flourishing towns and settlements are in the immediate vicinity of large swamps, and partially overflown meadows, yet no injurious effects upon the general health are produced by them.

It has usually been found, in making new settlements in the western wilderness, that as the forests are cleared away and the surface thereby exposed to the direct influence of the sun and winds, a deleterious effect is produced on the general health—the decaying vegetable matter being thus suddenly made to send forth its malarious qualities. But in Wisconsin no such result is apprehended, or can be produced, for a large proportion of the country consists of oak opening and prairie, and may therefore be considered as already cleared. The removal of the few remaining "burr oaks" cannot have the same effect upon the soil as the cutting down of the dense forests of the other States. And besides this, the fires that have annually raged over the surface, often kindled purposely by the Indians, on their hunting excursions, have prevented that rapid accumulation of vegetable matter which is always found in deep shady woods where the fires do not so often penetrate.

It is believed that the facts here stated will be sufficient to satisfy the reader of the truth of the opinion expressed by our most intelligent physicians, that Wisconsin is, and will continue to be, one of the most healthy places in the world."

PRODUCTIONS.—The productions of Wisconsin may be divided into four classes, the Forest, Animal, Vegetable and Mineral. The comparative amount belonging to each will be shown by the statement given below, which is mainly compiled from the United States census of 1850:

FOREST—

Bales furs and peltry	800
Feet sawed lumber, pine	150,000,000
Thousand shingles	30,000
Cubic feet timber	20,000,000
Number staves	10,000,000
Cords tan bark	2,000
Tons ashes, pot and pearl	25
Pounds maple sugar	610,976
Gallons molasses	9,874
Pounds wax and honey	131,000
Bushels cranberries	2,000

ANIMAL—

Value of live stock, June, 1850	$4,879,385
Number of horses	30,335
" milch cows and cattle	183,434
" sheep	124,892
" swine	159,276
Pounds of cheese	400,283
" butter	3,633,750
" wool	253,963
" fish	10,000
Dozen of eggs	100,000
Value of animals slaughtered	$920,178

VEGETABLE—

Bushels wheat	4,286,131
" rye	81,253
" corn	1,988,979
" barley	209,602
" oats	3,414,672
" peas and beans	20,657
" potatoes, Irish	1,402,077
" " sweet	879
Pounds flax	100,000
Bushels flaxseed	6,000
Pounds hops	15,930
" tobacco	4,000
Bushels buckwheat	79,876
" grass seed	3,000
Tons hay	275,662
Value of orchard products	$8,000
" garden products, market	$32,142

MINERAL—

Pounds lead	40,000,000
" copper	
Tons of iron	5,000

The amount of lead shipped from Galena, during the last year was 40,000,000 pounds, nine-tenths of which was raised in Wisconsin. Considerable more than the remaining one-tenth of the amount above stated has been shipped from ports in this State, from which it will be seen that this estimate is small.

To the practical miner, as capitalist or operative, the lead region of the Upper Mississippi offers the most substantial inducements to settlement. The exceeding abundance and richness of the mineral; the comparative ease with which it may be mined; and the high price it commands the moment it is brought to the surface, open to the industrious and prudent operator a highway to wealth.

New leads of the richest promise, have been recently discovered in the mineral district, and an increasing emigration to that section of the State, promises to replace the California draft, and to meet the growing demand for the mineral.

The steady advance in the price of lead, which has prevailed for five years past, is indicative of a gradual but decided extension of its uses in the arts. There is no ground for apprehension that the supply will outrun the demand, or be able to work a reduction of the wages of labor and profits of capital in this industrial occupation, for some years to come.

The copper mines of Lake Superior are of established celebrity throughout the world, and open an inviting field for enterprise. The mining interest in that region is fast losing its character of adventure, and is attracting the attention of the prudent capitalist and the practical miner, as a remunerative branch of business.

The iron mines of Wisconsin have not yet been opened to any extent, but are worthy the attention of the immigrant. There are rich localities of ore near the head waters of the Rock, and on the Upper Mississippi and its branches.

The following statement exhibits the shipment of lead from Galena from the year 1841 to 1852 inclusive, and the value of the same at four dollars per hundred weight:

Years.	*Number of Pounds.*	*Value.*
1841	29,749,909	$1,189,996
1842	29,424,329	1,176,973
1843	36,878 797	1,475,151
1844	41,036,293	1,641,451
1845	51,144,822	2,045,792
1846	48,007,938	1,920,317
1847	50,999,303	2,039,972
1848	49,783,737	1,991,349
1849	45,985,839	1,839,433
1850	41,485,900	1,659,436
1851	34,500,384	1,380,015
1852	40,000,000	1,600,000

Total valuation of exports at the ports of Kenosha, Racine, Milwaukee, Port Washington, Sheboygan, Manitowoc and Green Bay, for 1851	2,079,060
Total valuation of lead exported in 1851	1,380,015
Total exports	$3,459,075

There are also large quantities of lead shipped at different points along the Wisconsin and Mississippi rivers, the precise amount of which no data has been furnished upon which an intelligent estimate can be made.

In reviewing the foregoing statement, it should be recollected that Wisconsin is rapidly increasing, not only in population and wealth, but in the amount and quality of its resources, manufactures and products.

MANUFACTURES.—The richness of the soil of Wisconsin, and its ability to produce in abundance all kinds of grain, as well as the facility by which the lands are brought under subjection, create a permanent demand for all kinds of agricultural implements and mechanical labor. Architectural elegance in public and private buildings, and elaborate perfection in complicated machinery, is not to be expected in new settlements; but many of them in Wisconsin compare favorably with those of the older States. The rapid growth of towns, and the great influx of farmers with their families, create a necessity for temporary buildings, soon to be superseded by comfortable dwellings and outhouses; and give constant employ for the mason, the carpenter, and all other mechanics. The immense flouring mills of the State already in operation, as well as those in progress of erection, provide labor for the millwright and machinist, and furnish not only their respective vicinities with all kinds of mill stuff, but more than 100,000 barrels of flour annually for exportation.

To the lumberman, the pineries of Wisconsin present inducements for investment and settlement, which can be hardly overrated. That of the Upper Wisconsin and its tributaries is the most extensive; and distinguished still more for the fine quality, than the inexhaustible quantities of its timber. The other localities of the white pine and other evergreens, are mainly on the Wolf, the great northern affluent of the Fox, the tributaries of Green Bay, and on the La Crosse, the Black, Chippewa, and the St. Croix, branches of the Upper Mississippi.

The rapids of these streams furnish abundant water power for the manufacture of lumber, and on the annual spring rise, and occasional freshets at other seasons of the year, the yield of the mills is floated from the Wolf into Lake Winnebago and the lower Fox; and from most of the other streams into the Mississippi.

Scarcely ten years have elapsed since the Alleghany pine of Western New York and Pennsylvania, had undisputed possession of the market, not only of the Ohio Valley, but of the Mississippi and its tributaries, above New Orleans, at which point it competed with the lumber of Maine and New Brunswick.

The course of the lumber trade may now be considered as permanently changed. The pineries of Wisconsin now control, and will hold exclusive possession of the market of the valleys of the Mississippi and its great western affluents.

The amount of pine lumber estimated to be sawed in Wisconsin annually, is as follows:

Black River	15,000,000	St. Croix	20,000,000
Chippewa	28,500,000	Wisconsin	58,500,000
Green Bay	21,000,000	Wolf	25,500,000
Manitowoc	24,500,000		
Total number of feet			183,000,000

Aside from the manufacture of pine lumber, reaching as it does nearly 400,000,000 feet per year, saw mills driven by both steam and hydraulic power, are now in operation in every section of the State where timber is found, and large quantities of oak scantling and plank, and basswood siding and lath, are yearly manufactured.

Considerable attention has of late been paid to the raising and culture of flax, and this has caused the necessity of oil mills, and machinery for breaking and manufacturing the straw into dressed flax.

Scattered over the State in different localities, are manufactures of various kinds, which are rapidly increasing both in number and respectability. Woollen, flax and cotton mills will soon become fixed facts in Wisconsin. The raw material for the two former will be among the more profitable home productions of her agriculture, while the supply of cotton will, through the channel of the Mississippi, be more direct, safe, and easy, than by sea to towns on the Atlantic border. Several paper mills are now in operation, and more than 300,000 pounds of paper was made in the State during the year 1852. For all of these operations there are abundant water powers in suitable localities.

The great number of railroads, in progress of construction in Wisconsin, have directed the attention of capitalists to the building of locomotives and other railroad fixtures.

During the past year more than 100,000 pounds of shot have been made in this State. For the year ending June 1850, over 130,000 bushels of grain was manufactured into spirituous and malt liquors; of the former there was made 127,000 gallons, and of the latter 31,300 bbls. During the same period, 14,900 skins and 59,600 sides of leather were tanned The value of agricultural implements was estimated at $1,641,568; fourteen hundred tons of iron cast and 1000 tons of pig iron made; 134,200 pounds of wool was manufactured into cloth.

Trade.—Bordered on three sides by navigable waters, every portion of the State has easy access to the ocean, and a complete command of the eastern and southern markets, which command will be greatly increased by the completion of the several railroads in progress of construction in this State. The small sums for which these can be built, owing to the uniformity of the surface and easy grade, which will also permit their construction to any desired point, together with the rapidity of transit upon them and their superiority in every respect over water conveyance for passengers and light freight, must bring them in successful competition with the lake and river business, and ultimately supersede it. Trade, then, instead of following arbitrary lines will run where business requires. The location of important depots of trade and market towns will also conform to the same necessity, and will consequently be built at the great central points of production.

EDUCATION.—The bounty of congress has set apart the 16th section of every township in the State for the support and maintenance of common schools. From this source, nearly 1,000,000 acres will accrue to the State, the proceeds of the sales of which are to constitute a permanent fund, the income of which is to be annually devoted to the great purpose of the grant.

This magnificent foundation has been widely enlarged by constitutional provisions, giving the same direction to the donation of five hundred thousand acres, under the act of 1841, and the five per cent. reserved on all sales of Government lands within the State. The donations for educational purposes to the State have now reached 1,004,728 acres. A still larger addition will accrue from the grant of the swamp and overflowed lands, which the settlement of the country, the lapse of time, and easy processes of reclamation, will convert into the best meadow land in the world, and a large portion, ultimately, into arable. It is estimated that this grant will amount to 5,000,000 acres, of which the selection of 1,259,269 acres has already been approved.

For the support of a State University, seventy-two sections of choice land, comprising 46,080 acres, have been already granted, and it is not improbable that this provision may be also enlarged by subsequent grants. If these trusts are administered with ordinary wisdom, the educational funds of Wisconsin, cannot be less, ultimately, than $3,000,000, and may reach $5,000,000.

The University is already chartered and in successful operation. The school system has been wisely designed, and the progress of organization, under the law, keeps pace with the progress of settlement. There are already not far from 3,000 school districts in the State.

The system contemplates, by the introduction of union schools, to extend academic instruction to each town in the State.

In addition to this munificent public provision for common and liberal education, there are, in different parts of the State, educational incorporations, both academic and collegiate, founded on private subscriptions. The most promising of these are the

College at Beloit, well endowed, and in successful operation: and similar Institutions at Milwaukee, Racine and Waukesha in Eastern Wisconsin, and at Appleton, in the North.

Indeed, in none of the new States, even in the Northwest, will the means of education be more ample; and in none is there a more rational appreciation of the importance of this paramount public interest.

In Wisconsin, as in the other States of the Union, there is, and ever will be, an entire freedom of ecclesiastical organization, and an equal protection of every religious institution and arrangement, conservative of good morals, and protective of the highest and most enduring interests of man.

In consideration of all these elements of prosperity, economical and social, such as have never, till now, gathered around the opening career of a new political community, there is little ground for wonder that the early growth of Wisconsin has been without a parallel in the history of States; and it may be very safely assumed, that the advent of men and capital to that favored portion of the Northwest, will continue, in increasing volume, for many years to come.

University Lands.—The following statement shows the counties in which the lands granted by Congress to the University of the State of Wisconsin, comprising two townships, or seventy-two sections, are located:

Counties where located.	*Acres.*	*Counties where located.*	*Acres.*
In Waushara county,	640	In Jefferson county,	2,720
In Walworth "	1,280	In Dodge "	2,960
In Racine "	640	In Fond du Lac "	2,400
In Rock "	2,560	In Winnebago "	3,239
In Columbia "	2,240	In Calumet "	1,920
In Dane "	4,320	In Manitowoc "	1,700
In Green "	4.160	In Richland "	2,560
In Lafayette "	5,920	In Washington "	640
In Iowa "	2,320	In other couuties,	13,880
			46,080

These lands are being offered for sale at their appraised value, at the office of the State Treasurer, in Madison; ten per cent. being required in advance, and the interest at seven per cent. in advance, annually, on the balance, upon which ten years time is given.

School Lands.—The following table exhibits so much of the sixteenth sections as have been appraised, and are now for sale on the same terms and at the same place as University Lands:

Counties where located.	*Acres.*	*Counties where located.*	*Acres.*
In Adams county	24,320	In Marquette county	9,960
In Bad Ax "	26,640	In Marathon "	25,600
In Brown "	3,200	In Milwaukee "	5,120
In Calumet "	6,400	In Outagamie "	13,800
In Chippewa "	45,440	In Portage "	28,800
In Columbia "	14,080	In Ra ine "	7,040
In Crawford "	8,960	In Richland "	10,240
In Dane "	21,760	In Rock "	12,800
In Dodge "	22,400	In Sauk "	17,280
In Fond du Lac "	13,440	In Sheboygan "	9,600
In Grant "	19,840	In Walworth "	10,249
In Iowa "	16,000	In Washington "	12,140
In Green "	10,240	In Waukesha "	10 240
In Kenosha "	4,480	In Waushara "	11,520
In Lafayette "	9,600	In Waupacca "	13,440
In La Crosse "	73,600	In Winnebago "	9,960
In Manitowoc "	10,880		
Total			539,060

The grant of section 16, in each town, by Congress, to the State of Wisconsin. for Common School purposes, estimated upon an area of 55,404 square miles, the one thirty-sixth part of which is 1,539 square miles or sections, at 640 acres each, amounts, in acres, to	984,900
Deduct amount already offered for sale	539,060
Leaving	445,900

Nearly all of which is yet among the unsurveyed lands of the State.

State Lands.—The following lands have been selected as a part of the 500,000 acres granted by Congress to the State of Wisconsin, and located in the following counties, to wit:

Counties where located.	*Acres.*	*Counties where located.*	*Acres.*
In Bad Ax county	41,806.86	In La Crosse county	45,314,23
In Brown "	10,773,35	In Lafayette "	15,475,02
In Calumet "	28,027,84	In Manitowoc "	22,321,92
In Columbia "	22,073,00	In Outagamie "	6,267,83
In Crawford "	4,517,20	In Richland "	17,538,76
In Dane "	16,760,96	In Sauk "	12,396,18
In Fond du Lac "	320,00	In St. Croix "	105,657,03
In Grant "	6.024,68	Rock River Canal grant, (Waukesha and Jefferson counties)	13,694,18
In Iowa "	7,075,87		
Total			375,994,99

and are offered by the State for sale, at the same place as school and University Lands, on a credit of thirty years, at prices varying from $1 25 to $3 00 per acre, with interest at seven per cent per annum, to be paid annually in advance.

By the reports of the State officers, it appears that the capital of the school fund, December 31, 1852, was $819,200 50; of which amount $681,931 71 was due from sales of school lands, $132,491 64 from loans made, and $4,776 15 then in the treasury subject to loan. The interest upon this sum, at seven per cent., amounts to $57,274 03, of which $56,128 31 was paid in and apportioned to the several towns in this State, in March 1853. The whole amount of money raised from all sources was $127,-718 42.

The Superintendent reports that for the year ending August 31st, 1852, 2,765 school districts and parts had made reports. In the districts reported, the average duration of schools was five and a half months; average monthly wages of male teachers $16 34; of female teachers $8 52. There are 66 school houses of brick, 74 of stone, 778 of logs, and 812 framed, all valued at $261,986 32. The highest valuation of any school house is $5,500, and the lowest $1 50.

Government.—The government of Wisconsin does not differ essentially from that of the other States of the Union—in many respects it is more liberal. The qualification for electors is, one year's residence in the State; and this applies as well to persons of foreign as native birth, subject only to the limitation that they shall have declared their intentions to become citizens, comformably to the laws of the United States, on the subject of naturalization. No distinction can be made, under the organic law, between aliens and citizens in reference to the possession, enjoyment, or descent of property. Imprisonment for debt is prohibited by the Constitution.

The legislative power is vested in the Senate and Assembly. The Senate consists of twenty-five members, who hold their offices for two years, and are chosen from single districts. Those from the odd numbered districts being chosen one year, and those from the even numbered the next.

The Assembly consists of eighty-two members, who are chosen annually, and hold their office for one year.

The executive power is vested in a Governor, who is elected by a plurality of votes, and holds his office for the term of two years. A Lieutenant Governor is chosen at the same time, and in the same manner. The usual executive powers are conferred upon the Governor; whose salary is $1,250. The Lieutenant Governor is President of the Senate, and receives five dollars a day, while in attendance, and the same mileage as members. In certain contingences he succeeds to the duties of the office of Governor.

The administrative powers are conferred upon the Secretary of State, salary $1,200; State Treasurer, salary $800; Attorney General, salary $800; and State Superintendent, salary $1,000. They severally hold their offices for two years, and are elected at the same time as the Governor.

Several offices for the performance of special duties have been established by law since the adoption of the Constitution.

The judicial power is vested in a Supreme Court, Circuit Courts, County Courts, and Justices of the Peace.

The Supreme Court, with few exceptions, has appellate jurisdiction. It consists of one Chief Justice, and two Associates, who are elected by the people, and will hereafter be chosen for six years. [The Judges of the several Circuit Courts have heretofore comprised the Supreme Court.] A majority of the Judges appoint a Clerk, who continues during their pleasure. This Court has two terms a year at the Capitol, in Madison. The salary of each of the Judges is $2,000.

Circuit Courts have original jurisdiction in all matters civil and criminal, except such as is otherwise provided, and an appellate jurisdiction from all inferior Courts and tribunals. The Judges are elected by districts, holding their office for six years, and having a salary of $1,500. Two terms of this Court are holden annually in each county organized for judicial purposes in the State. The voters of any county so organized, elect a County Judge, who holds his office for four years, and has certain civil, original and appellate jurisdiction. He is also Judge of the Probate Court of the county.

Four Justices of the Peace are elected in each town, two annually, and hold their offices for the term of two years; they possess the powers usually conferred upon such officers.

Civil Divisions.—The State of Wisconsin is divided into forty-four counties, with about four hundred towns ; three Congressional Districts, and six Judicial Circuits.

Counties—Adams, Bad Ax, Brown, Calumet, Chippewa, Columbia, Crawford, Dane, Dodge, Door, Fond du Lac, Grant, Green, Iowa, Jackson, Jefferson, Kewaunee, Kenosha, La Crosse, Lafayette, La Pointe, Manitowoc, Marathon, Marquette, Milwaukee, Oconto, Outagamie, Ozaukee, Pierce, Polk, Portage, Racine, Richland, Rock, St. Croix, Sauk, Shawana, Sheboygan, Walworth, Washington, Waukesha, Waupacca, Waushara and Winnebago.

Congressional Districts.—1st, Daniel Wells, jr., member; composed of the Counties of Kenosha, Milwaukee, Racine, Walworth and Waukesha.

2d. Ben C. Eastman, member; composed of the counties of Adams, Bad Ax, Chippewa, Crawford, Dane, Grant, Green, Iowa, Jackson, La Crosse, Lafayette, La Pointe, Marathon, Pierce, Polk, Portage, Richland, Rock, St. Croix and Sauk.

3d. John B. Macy, member; composed of the counties of Brown, Calumet, Columbia, Dodge, Door, Fond du Lac, Jefferson, Kewaunee, Manitowoc, Marquette, Oconto, Ozaukee, Outagamie, Shawana, Sheboygan, Washington, Waupacca, Waushara and Winnebago.

Judicial Circuits.—1st. Green, Kenosha, Racine, Rock and Walworth counties.

2d. Dane, Jefferson, Milwaukee and Waukesha counties.

3d. Adams, Columbia, Dodge, Marathon, Marquette, Ozaukee, Portage, Sauk, Waushara and Washington counties.

4th. Brown, Calumet, Door,* Fond du Lac, Kewaunee,* Manitowoc, Oconto,* Outagamie, Shawana,* Sheboygan, Waupacca and Winnebago.

5th. Grant, Iowa, Lafayette and Richland counties.

6th. Bad Ax, Chippewa,* Crawford, Jackson,* La Crosse, La Pointe, Pierce,* Polk,* and St. Croix counties.

Improvements.—Of the many railroads projected and chartered in this state, several are already under contract and rapidly progressing to completion. Plank roads have been constructed and are now in progress, connecting most of the leading towns of the interior with each other, and with the towns on the lake shore. A large grant of land has been made by Congress to aid in the improvement of the navigation of the Fox and Wisconsin rivers, and to connect the same by a canal. This work is under the immediate supervision of a board of Public Works, comprised of three Commissioners, and a Register and Treasurer, who are elected yearly by the legislature. The Governor has the general control and supervision of the work. A large portion of

* Not organized for judicial purposes.

the Improvement is let out by contract, while some parts are carried on by the Commissioners. This work, when completed, will open steamboat navigation nearly through the centre of the State from the Gulf of Mexico to St. Lawrence.

The construction of the canal and the improvement of the Lower Fox, has been under contract for several years, but owing to various causes is as yet unfinished.

Public Lands.—By a pre-emption law passed September, 1841, any person being the head of a family, widow, or single man over the age of twenty-one years, a citizen of the United States, or who has filed declarations to become so under the naturalization laws, who makes a settlement on any public lands in person, is entitled to enter, at the minimum price of $1 25 per acre, a quarter section, of 160 acres, or a less legal subdivision, at the district land office. Lands not entered by pre-emption are offered for sale, previous to which no person not having a pre-emption claim can purchase.

There has been granted to Wisconsin, by the General Government, for various purposes, the following amounts of public lands:

Improvements	858,400	acres.
Individuals and Companies	5,705	"
Public Buildings	6,400	"
Salines	46,400	"
Educational purposes	1,004,728	"
Swamp Lands	1,259,269	"
There is still undisposed of	24,506,295	"

Public lands are laid out by the rectangular system of surveys adopted for the first time in 1785, by the United States, and are so simple that the position of any surveyed section or township is known at once, by observing the letters and figures applied to each. Each township of six miles has a number different from every other; and to follow the directions here given, it is only necessary to take the *meridian* as a straight line, extending due north and south, when reckoning east or west; and the *base* extending due east and west, when reckoning north or south. Commencing at the base line, (which, in Wisconsin, is the south line of the State,) every six miles numbering to the north is called a town, and is numbered town one, town two, town three, &c. Commencing at the meridian, (which is the line separating Grant from Iowa and Lafayette counties,) every six miles is called a range, and is numbered range one east, range two east, or range one west, &c., as the case may be. It will be seen that this system divides the whole surface of the country into squares of six miles square, or thirty six square miles each. These squares are *townships*, and the figures are applied as follows: Madison is in town 7 N., range 9 E.; Fond du Lac, in town 15 N., range 17 E.; Lancaster, in town 4 N., range 3 W.; Hudson, in town 29 N., range 19 W., &c. Townships are divided into thirty-six squares of one mile each, called sections, and numbered as follows:

6	5	4	3	2	1
7	8	9	10	11	12
18	17	School 16 Section	15	14	13
19	20	21	22	23	24
30	29	28	27	26	25
31	32	33	34	35	36

Each section contains 640 ares of land, and is divided into four equal parts, called quarters, by a line through the centre each way, each quarter consequently containing 160 acres, thus:

N. W. qr.	N. E. qr.
S. W. qr.	S. E. qr.

Each quarter is again subdivided into four equal parts, after the manner of the division of sections, each subdivision containing 40 acres:

N. W. qr. of N. W. qr.	N. E. qr. of N. W. qr.	N. W. qr. of N. E. qr.	N. E. qr. of N. E. qr.
S. W. qr. of N. W. qr.	S. E. qr. of N. W. qr.	S. W. qr. of N. E. qr.	S. E. qr. of N. E. qr.
N. W. qr. of S. W. qr.	N. E. qr. of S. W. qr.	N.W. qr. of S. E. qr.	N. E. qr. of S. E. qr.
S. W. qr. of S. W. qr.	S. E. qr. of S. W. qr.	S. W. qr. of S. E. qr.	S. E. qr. of S. E. qr.

The subdivisions are designated as quarters of quarters, thus the northeast 40 acre subdivision is known as the N. E. qr. of the N. E. qr. Madison is situated at the corners of sections 13, 14, 23 and 24; it is therefore on the S. W. qr. of sec. 13, S. E. qr. of sec. 14, N. E. qr. of sec. 23, and N. W. qr. of sec. 24.

MISCELLANEOUS.—The District Court of the United States for the district of Wisconsin, ANDREW G. MILLER, Judge, holds one term at Madison, and one at Milwaukee, annually.

HENRY DODGE, of Dodgeville, Iowa county, and ISAAC P. WALKER, of Milwaukee, are United States Senators in Congress, from Wisconsin.

The following are the officers of the Wisconsin Militia:

LEONARD J. FARWELL, Commander-in-Chief, Madison.

BENJ. F. HOPKINS, Madison, C. C. WASHBURNE, Mineral Point, COLES BASHFORD, Oshkosh, CHARLES CLEMENT, Kenosha, Governor's Aids.

WILLIAM L. UTLEY, Racine, Adjutant General, salary $300; DAVID ATWOOD, Madison, Quarter-Master General; JAMES B. MARTIN, Milwaukee, Pay-Master General; JAMES RICHARDSON, Madison, Commissary General; JOHN W. HUNT, M. D., Madison, Surgeon General; N. BISHOP EDDY, Madison, Judge Advocate General; WILLIAM DUDLEY, Madison, Military Secretary.

ANDREW PROUDFIT, BENJAMIN ALLEN and LUCAS M. MILLER, are Commissioners; R. P. EIGHME, Register, and JAMES MURDOCK, Treasurer of the Board of Public Works.

H. S. ORTON, is Private Secretary of the Governor, also Reporter of the Supreme Court. WILLIAM DUDLEY, State Librarian.

The following are the names of members of the Legislature:

Senators by Districts.—1st. H. N. Smith; 2d. James. S. Alban; 3d. A. M. Blair; 4th. B. S. Weil; 5th. E. M. Hunter; 6th. D. C. Reed; 7th. J. W. Cary; 8th. J. R. Sharpstein; 9th. Geo. R. McLane; 10th. M. H. Bovee; 11th. T. T. Whittlesey; 12th. E. Wakeley; 13th. Charles Dunn; 14th. Alva Stewart; 15th. Levi

Sterling; 16th. Joel C. Squires; 17th. Ezra Miller; 18th. J. R. Briggs, Jr.; 19th. Benjamin Allen; 20th. Bertine Pinckney; 21st. Coles Bashford; 22d. Judson Prentice; 23d. David S. Vittum; 24th. Thos. S. Bowen; 25th. James T. Lewis.

Timothy Burns, President. John K. Williams, Chief Clerk.

Members of Assembly by Counties.—Adams and Sauk—Charles Armstrong.

Brown, Kewaunee and Door—Randall Wilcox.

Bad Ax and Crawford—H. A. Wright.

Calumet—J. Robinson.

Chippewa and La Crosse—A. D. La Due.

Columbia—O. D. Coleman and J. Q. Adams.

Dane—Matthew Roche, H. Barnes, H. L. Foster, P. C. Burdick and S. W. Field.

Dodge—Whitman Sayles, W. M. Dennis, P. Kelly, John W. Davis, Edwin Hillyer and E. N. Foster.

Fond du Lac—J. S. Tallmadge, Charles D. Gage, Querin Loehr and N. M. Donaldson.

Grant—J. E. Dodge, J. A. Barber, H. E. Block, H. D. York and T. Hayes.

Green—Thomas Fenton.

Iowa—H. Madden and P. W. Thomas.

Jefferson—Patrick Rogan, W. W. Woodman, D. Powers, J. E. Holmes and J. H. Ostrander.

Kenosha—J. McKisson and C. L. Sholes.

Lafayette—Eli Robinson, P. B. Simpson and Nathan Olmstead.

Marquette and Waushara—Ezra Wheeler.

Marquette—E. B. Kelsey.

Milwaukee—H. Haertel, E. McGarry, H. L. Palmer, Richard Carlile, H. C. West, J. Meyer, J. H. Tweedy, W. A. Hawkins, and E. Chase.

Manitowoc—E. Ricker.

Outagamie, Waupacca and Oconto—A. Resley.

Portage—G. W. Cate.

Racine—H. T. Sanders, W. H. Roe, T. West and P. Belden.

Richland—Henry Conner.

Rock—C. Stevens, H. Stebbins, W. D. Murray, and H. Holmes.

Sheboygan—C. B. Coleman and D. Taylor.

St. Croix and La Pointe—O. T. Maxson.

Walworth—John Bell, James Lauderdale, O. T. Bartlett, T. H. Fellows, Joseph W. Seaver and T. W. Hill.

Washington—C. E. Chamberlin, C. Schutte, W. P. Barnes and J. W. Porter.

Waukesha—Orson Reed, E. Lees, W. D. Bacon and E. Pearl.

Winnebago—Curtis Reed and Lucas M. Miller.

Henry L. Palmer, Speaker. Thomas McHugh, Chief Clerk.

The settlement in Wisconsin at the organization of the Territorial Government, will be shown by the following statement of the number of votes given at the first election under the organic law, in 1836:

Brown County—Green Bay, 118; Howard, 32; Mason, (Depere,) 34; Sheboygan, 36; Menomonee river, 15; Little Butte des Morts, 9; Manitowoc, 20; Portage of Fox and Wisconsin, 61.—325.

Crawford County—Prairie du Chien, 68.—68.

Iowa County—Elk Grove, 28; Van Buren, (Potosi,) 97; Diamond Inn, 35; New Diggings, 77; Platteville, 90; White Oak Springs, 106; Hamilton, (Wiota,) 64; Hardscrabble, (Hazel Green,) 48; Wingville, 57; Gratiot's Grove, (Shullsburg,) 43; Mineral Point, 226; Menomonee, (Jamestown,) 24; New Mexico, (Monroe,) 47; Cassville, 150; Paris, 12; Belmont, 76; Bois Prairie, (Lancaster,) 18; Dodgeville, 90.—1288.

Milwaukee County—Pike River, (near Kenosha,) 108; Milwaukee, 449; Louis Vieux, (Waukesha,) 60; Moses Smith's, (Rochester,) 13; Racine, 92; Rock River, (Watertown,) 23; Upper Fox River, (Waterford,) 25.—781. Total, 2,462.

The following Table shows the Census of Wisconsin, from 1825 *to* 1850.

COUNTIES.	1836.	1838.	1840.	1842.	1846.	1847.	1850.
Adams							187
Brown	2706	3048	2107	2146	2662	2914	6223
Calumet			275	407	836	1060	1746
Chippewa							615
Columbia					1969	3791	9565
Crawford	1220	850	1503	1449	1444	1409	2399
Dane		172	314	776	8289	10935	16654
Dodge		18	67	149	7787	14905	19140
Fond du Lac			139	295	3544	7459	14512
Grant		2763	3926	5937	12034	11720	16169
Green		494	933	1594	4758	6487	8583
Iowa	3218	5234	3078	5029	14906	7963	10479
Jefferson		463	914	1638	8860	11464	15339
Kenosha							10730
Lafayette						9335	11556
Lapointe						367	595
Manitowoc			235	263	629	1285	3713
Marathon							466
Marquette			18	59	986	2261	8642
Milwaukee	2893	3131	5605	9565	15922	22791	31119
Portage			1623	646	931	1504	1267
Racine		2054	3475	6318	17983	19538	14971
Richland							903
Rock			1701	2867	12405	14720	30717
Saint Croix					1419	1674	624
Sauk			102	393	1003	2178	4372
Sheboygan			133	227	1637	5580	8386
Walworth		1019	2611	4618	13439	15039	17866
Washington		64	343	965	7473	15447	19476
Waukesha					13793	15866	19324
Winnebago			135	143	732	2748	10167
Total	11,683	18,130	30,945	44,478	155,277	210,546	305,566

From the above census return, it will be seen that the population of Wisconsin has increased in greater ratio than any other State in the Union. In 1825, the population of the Territory was only 1,444.

An Abstract of the Census Returns of the Territory of the United States, from 1800 *to* 1850.

STATES.	1800.	1810.	1820.	1830.	1840.	1850.
Ohio	4,500	230,000	581,000	937,000	1,519,000	1,980,000
Indiana	4,000	24,000	147,000	353,000	685,000	988,000
Illinois		12,000	55,000	157,000	476,000	851,000
Michigan		4,000	8,000	31,000	212,000	397,000
Wisconsin					30,000	305,000

From the foregoing table, it appears that the greatest ratio of increase of Ohio was, from 1800 to 1810, 409 per cent.; Indiana, from 1810 to 1820, 506 per cent.; Illinois, from 1810 to 1820, 350 per cent.; Michigan, from 1830 to 1840, 570 per cent.; Wisconsin, from 1840 to 1850, 890 per cent.

WISCONSIN GAZETTEER:

CONTAINING THE

NAMES, LOCATION, AND ADVANTAGES OF THE CITIES, TOWNS, VILLAGES, POST-OFFICES AND SETTLEMENTS,

TOGETHER WITH A DESCRIPTION OF THE

LAKES, WATER COURSES, PRAIRIES, AND PUBLIC LOCALITIES IN THE STATE OF WISCONSIN—FOR 1853.

ALPHABETICALLY ARRANGED.

NOTICE.—Names and descriptions prepared too late for their proper place, will be found in the Appendix.

ABBREVIATIONS.—*C. H.*, Court House, or County Seat; *L.*, Lake; *Pr.*, Prairie; *P. O.*, Post Office; *P. V.*, Post Village; *R.*, River; *T.*, Town; *V.*, Village.

ABBOTT, *Town*, in county of Sheboygan, being town 13 N., in range 21 E.; located southwest from Sheboygan, the county seat. It has 9 school districts.

ADAMS, *P. V.*, in Walworth county, on section 18, town 4 N., range 17 E.; being in the town of Troy, 10 miles north from Elkhorn, and 60 miles southeast from Madison, in a good farming district, 8 miles southwest from the Milwaukee and Mississippi railroad depot at Eagle Prairie.

ADAMS, *Town*, in the county of Green, being township 3 N., of range 6 E.; located ten miles northwest from Monroe, the county seat. It has 5 school districts.

ADAMS, *County*, is bounded on the north by Portage, on the east by Waushara and Marquette, on the south by Columbia and Sauk, and on the west by La Crosse and a portion of Sauk. It was established March 11, 1848, from Portage; at which time it embraced the territory south and west of the Lemonwier and Wisconsin rivers, north of town 13, and east of range 1 E. By an act approved March 6, 1849, the territory was extended north and east, and so changed in the southeast that it embraced only about four townships of its original limits. At the session of the legislature of the winter of 1853, it was restored to its former southern bounds, and the seat of justice located at Kingsbury's Ferry, on the Wisconsin river. The county is attached to Sauk for legislative purposes. It is watered by the Wisconsin, Lemonwier, Yellow, Necada, and the two Roche a Gris rivers, with several other streams, the banks of some of which are covered by an excellent growth of pine timber. The first surveys of Adams county having been made so recently as 1851, but little is as yet known of its advantages and resources. The population in 1850 was 187, since which time it has been rapidly settling. Upon the Lemonwier are erected and in operation, four saw mills propelled by water, and one by steam, and are supposed to produce from four to six million feet of pine lumber per annum. The valley of the Lemonwier, so called, constitutes that part lying on the west and south of said river, is not easily surpassed in richness and fertility of soil; the timber being principally black and burr oak; numerous small streams and rivulets flow from the high lands across the valley, which already contain a numerous population. There is one steam saw mill, and one mill propelled by water, on the Yellow river, employed in the manufacture of pine lumber, producing from two to three million feet per annum. The country lying between the Yellow river and the Wisconsin, and the Yellow river and the Lemonwier, presents a flat and monotonous appearance; the soil in general being unfit for agricultural purposes, affording, however, many facilities for stock raising and dairy farming unsurpassed in the state. The features of the country are more varied in the east than on the west side of the Wisconsin river, presenting a more broken and undulating surface, and more elevated. This part of the country is fast being settled by a hardy and enterprising class of farmers, and is destined, at no distant day, to be one of the best grain-growing portions of the State. The southeast part of the county is the most densely populated, the country being diversified and much elevated, but not very well watered. At the first election held in the county, in April 1853, the following gentlemen were elected County Officers: County Judge, E. S. Miner; Sheriff, W. J. Sayre; Clerk of Court, S. G. Holbrook; Clerk of Board Supervisors, Wm. H. Spain; Register, Wm. H. Palmer; District Attorney, D. A. Bigelow; Treasurer, S. G. Holbrook; Surveyor, Caleb McArthur; Coroner, W. I. Webster.

ADDISON, *Town*, in county of Washington, being town 11 N., of range 18 E.; located 23 miles west from Ozaukee. The population in 1850 was 1,092. It has 9 school districts.

ADELL, *P. V.*, in county of Sheboygan, being on section 17, in town 13 N., (Abbott,) range 20 E.

AHNEPEE, *Creek*, rises in Door county, and runs southeast, entering Lake Michigan in town 25, range 25 E., in Kewaunee county.

AJASOWI, *River*, see Courterielle river.

ALBANY, *P. V.*, in Green county, on section 28, town 3 N., range 9 E.; 14 miles northeast from Monroe, 28 miles south from Madison. Population, 200; 26 dwellings, 8 stores, 2 hotels, 2 mills, and 9 manufactories. It has a large water power—in the midst of a good farming country, and has three regular mail routes passing through the village.

ALBANY, *Town*, in Green county, being township 3 N., range 9 E.; located 12 miles northeast from Monroe. The population in 1850 was 546. It has 6 school districts.

ALBION, *P. V.*, in town of same name, Dane county.

ALBION, *Town*, in county of Dane, being in town 5 N., range 12 E.; centrally located, 25 miles southeast from Madison, the county seat. It has 7 school districts.

ALBION, *Town*, in county of Jackson, being all of said county, north of township 22. It has 4 school districts.

ALCOVE, *P. V.*, in Fond du Lac county, on section 32 of the town of Empire, (town 15 N., range 18 E.,) 6 miles southeast from Fond du Lac, the county seat, and 75 miles northeast from Madison.

ALGOMA, *Town*, in county of Winnebago, south side of Fox river. The population in 1850 was 702. It has 7 school districts.

ALGOMA, *P. V.*, in town of same name, Winnebago county, on section 15, in town 18 N., range 16 E., on Fox river, between Lake Great Butte des Morts and Winnebago, 2 miles above Oshkosh.

ALLEN'S GROVE, *P. V.*, in town of Sharon, Walworth county, on section 6, in town 1 N., range 15 E.

ALMOND, *P. V.*, in county of Portage. It is 16 miles from Plover, the county seat, and 105 miles from Madison. Population, 150.

ALTO, *P. V.*, Fond du Lac county, on section 13, in town of same name, being town 14 N., range 14 E.; located 18 miles southwest from Fond du Lac city, and 55 miles northeast from Madison.

ALTO, *Town*, in the county of Fond du Lac, being town 14 N., of range 14 E.; centrally located, 10 miles southwest from Fond du Lac. Population in 1850 was 630. It has 9 school districts.

AMENECON, (Amican), *River*, a tributary of Lake Superior, next east of Sandy river, in La Pointe county.

AMHERST, *Town*, in county of Portage, being towns 21, 22, 23, 24 and 25, in range 10, and 24 and 25 in range 9 E.

APPLE, *River*, rises near the head of Duck Creek, and runs northeasterly into Fox river, 5 miles below Rapide de Croche, in Outagamie county.

APPLE, *River*, a tributary of St. Croix river from the east, in St. Croix county, enters the same from the east, near the line between townships 30 and 31.

APPLETON, *P. V.*, and *C. H.*, in Outagamie county, town of Grand Chute, on section 26, town 21 N., range 17 E. It is about 125 miles northeast from Madison. The Lawrence Institute is located at this place, and the surrounding country is very healthy and fertile. Population 800; 275 dwellings, 10 stores, 5 hotels, 4 saw mills, 1 flouring mill, 1 edge tool factory, 2 planing mills and a paper factory. It is situated on the Lower Fox river at the Grand Chute Rapids, 30 miles from Green Bay. Its hydraulic advantages are equal to any in the United States, the aggregate fall being 40 feet. It is in a direct line between Manitowoc on the Lake, and Stevens' Point on the Wisconsin, between which places a plank road is in process of construction.

ARENA, *Town*, in the county of Iowa, being townships Nos. 7 and 8 N., of ranges 4 and 5 E.; centrally located, 20 miles northeast from Mineral Point, the county seat. It has 3 school districts. It is in an agricultural district, containing bottom lands of the first quality, sandy, but well watered. Settled originally by the British Temperance Emigration Society.

ARENA, *P. V.*, in town of same name, Iowa county, on the Wisconsin river, town 8 N., range 5 E.

ARMITAGERS, *Rapids*, in Chippewa county, and on Chippewa river, in town 30 N., range 7 W.

ARMY, *Lake*, in town of East Troy, Walworth county, on section 16, town 4 N., range 18 E. It is named in compliment to the U. S. army, and is owned by Major H. W. Merrill, of the army. His farms, which includes the lake, contains 640 acres. The lake covers about 100 acres; is 28 miles southwest from

Milwaukee, and is on the northwest quarter of the section. Its form is oval, beautifully curved and indented with small bays and promontories, and being supplied by springs it has no visible inlet. Its shores are elevated by gently rising banks, and bordered on all sides with a fine growth of forest trees.

Ashford, *Town*, in county of Fond du Lac, being town 13 N., range 18 E.; centrally located, 15 miles southeast from the city of Fond du Lac. The population in 1850 was 546. It has 7 school districts.

Ashippun, *Town*, in county of Dodge, being town 9 N., range 17 E.; centrally located, 14 miles southwest from Juneau. It has 8 school districts.

Ashippun, *P.O.*, in town of same name, in southwest corner of Dodge county.

Ashwabena, *River*, in Brown county, a small tributary of the Fox, emptying opposite to Depere.

Attanwa, *River*, a tributary from the east of St. Croix river, a few miles above the Falls of St. Croix.

Attica, *P. V.*, in southwest corner of the town of Brooklyn, on Sugar river, Green county.

Attonowining, *River*, a tributary from the north of river St. Croix.

Auburn, *P. O.*, Fond du Lac county, on section 18, of town of the same name, 14 miles southeast from Fond du Lac, and 90 miles northeast from Madison. It is situated on the Rubicon, the head waters of Milwaukee river, and has 1 store, 1 hotel, and 1 church.

Auburn, *Town*, in the county of Fond du Lac, being town 13 N., range 19 E.; centrally located, 18 miles southeast from Fond du Lac. The population is 400. It has 8 school districts.

Avoca, *P. V.*, in Fond du Lac county, on section 13, town 14 N., range 16 E.

Avon, *P. O.*, in town of same name, Rock county, on section 8, town 1 N., range 10 E.

AVON, *Town*, in the county of Rock, being town 1 N., of range 10 E.; centrally located, 17 miles southwest from Janesville. The population in 1850 was 588. It has 7 school districts.

AZTALAN, *Town*, in the county of Jefferson, being town 7 N., of range 14 E.; centrally located, 5 miles north from Jefferson, the county seat. The population in 1850 was 429. It has 8 school districts.

AZTALAN, *P. V.*, in Jefferson county, and town of same name, 7 miles northwest from Jefferson, and 28 miles east from Madison. It is on both sides of the Crawfish, on the direct road from Madison to Milwaukee. It contains 1 Baptist church, 3 denominations of Christians, 2 blacksmiths, 1 waggon-maker, 1 shoe shop, 1 fanning mill shop, brick yard, 1 saleratus factory, 3 stores, 2 hotels, 1 steam mill, 1 nursery of 150,000 trees, and an extensive stone quarry. In this town is situated the renowned "Ancient City," which comprises 30 acres of land. The city is surrounded by a brick wall, and is an object of antiquarian research. Population 250.

BACHELOR'S GROVE, *P. V.*, in Rock county, on section 4, town 2, range 11 E., of the town of Plymouth; 10 miles west from Janesville, and 40 miles south from Madison. Population 70, with 12 dwellings, 1 temperance hotel, and a M. E. church.

BAD AX, *Town*, in county of Bad Ax. The population in 1850 (at which time it formed a portion of Crawford county,) was 630. It has 8 school districts.

BAD AX, *County*, is bounded on the north by La Crosse, on the east by Sauk and Richland, on the south by Richland and Crawford, and on the west by the Mississippi river, and was set off from Crawford and organized March 1, 1851. The county seat was established by a vote of the electors of the county on the 29th day of June, 1852, at Varoqua, near the centre of the county. It forms a part of the sixth judicial circuit, the second congressional, and the nineteenth senate district, and with Crawford sends one member of the assembly.

The streams are the Bad Ax, Kickapoo and Racoon rivers, with their tributaries, and small streams emptying into the Mississippi. A large quantity (41,807 acres,) of that portion of school lands known as the 500,000 acre grant, is situated in Bad Ax county, the soil of which is good, and produces good crops of wheat, oats, corn, &c. This county is comparatively new, and contained in 1850 less than 700 inhabitants. During the last two years the population has increased very fast.—County Officers: Judge, Henry J. Defrees; Sheriff, James Bailey; Clerk of Court, Wm. F. Terhune.

Bad Ax, *River*, in Bad Ax county, rises in town 14, range 4 W.; runs southwest, and empties into the Mississippi, in town 12. Its mouth is remarkable for being adjoining the site of the last battle field with Black Hawk, August 2d, 1832.

Bad Ax, *P. V.*, in Bad Ax county, on section 25, town 12 N., range 5 W.

Bad Fish, *Creek*, rises in Oregon, Dane county, and runs southeast, emptying into the Catfish river, in Porter, Rock county.

Bad, *River*, of Lake Superior. See Mauvoise.

Bailey's, *Harbor*, on western shore of Lake Michigan, in town 30, Door county, at Gibraltar.

Baker's Corner, *P. V.*, in Walworth county, on section 6, town 3, range 18 E., town of Spring Prairie, 10 miles northeast from Elkhorn, and 80 miles southeast from Madison, on the road from Janesville to Racine, at the junction of the highway to East Troy and Milwaukee. It is in a good farming district, well adapted to raising wheat, &c.

Bald, *Prairie*, in Winnebago county, in towns of Clayton, Vinland, Winneconne and Winchester.

Ball, *River*, see La Crosse river and Prairie La Crosse.

Baraboo, *P. V.* and *C. H.*, on both sides of river of same name, in Sauk county; it is mostly on section 2, in town 11 N., of range 6 E., and is about 50 miles northwest from Madison.

It now includes the village of Adams. It has 6 taverns, 7 stores, 5 mills, 26 mechanical shops, 1 carding machine, 1 tannery, and 1 printing office at which the Sauk County Standard is published weekly. Population, 2,000.

BARKER'S, *Lake*, is in the northwest part of the town of Sugar Creek, Walworth county. It is about one and a half miles in length.

BARK, *Point*, Lake Superior, near the mouth of Heron river.

BARK, *River*, rises in Richfield, Washington county, and running southwest through the towns of Merton, Delafield, Summit, and Ottawa, in Waukesha county, passes through the towns of Sullivan. Hebron, Cold Spring and Koskonong, in Jefferson county, emptying into Rock river at Fort Atkinson, five miles above Lake Koshkonong.

BARK RIVER, *P. O.*, Jefferson county, in the town of Hebron, 10 miles southeast of Jefferson, and 40 southeast of Madison.

BARTON, *P. O.*, Washington county. See village of Newark.

BASS *Lake*, a small lake on section 24, in the town of Rutland, Dane county.

BASS LAKE, *P.O.* in Rutland, Dane county, *discontinued.*

BATTLE, *Creek*, is a small stream having its source in two or three small lakes in Summit, Waukesha county, runs northwesterly, and empties into Oconomowoc river, in the town of Concord, Jefferson county.

BEACHWOOD, *P. O.*, in county of Sheboygan, being in Scott, town 13 N., range 20 E.

BEAR, *Creek*, Chippewa county, enters Buffalo Slough from the east.

BEAR CREEK, *P. O.*, in Richland county.

BEAR, *Creek*, rises in Sauk county, and runs southwest into the Wisconsin, in range 2 E.

BEAR, *Island*, in lake Michigan, near southeast corner of town 32, range 29 E., Door county. It is about a mile in diameter.

BEAR, *Lake*, in the town of Greenbush, Sheboygan county, on sec. 29, township 15, range 20 E.

BEAVER, *Creek*, a tributary from the north of Black river, entering the same near Dakorra Mound, La Crosse county.

BEAVER DAM, *Town*, in the county of Dodge, being township 11, of range 14, and south half of town 12, range 14, and south half of town 12, range 13, eight miles west from Juneau, the county seat. The population in 1850 was 1,830. It has 10 school districts.

BEAVER DAM, *River*, rises in Fox lake, and runs south, emptying into the Crawfish, in the southern portion of Dodge county.

BEAVER DAM, *P. V.* in town of same name, Dodge county, being on section 4, town 11 N., range 14 E. It is situated on a stream of the same name, at the outlet of a pond some 8 or 10 miles in extent, where stands a flouring mill, in which are constantly employed 4 runs of stone; where there is to be built the coming season another flouring mill and woollen factory, an oil mill, a saw mill, and a carding machine; with 5 more saw mills and 2 flouring mills with two runs of stone each, within 3 miles of the village, and yet the stream is considered sufficient for considerable improvement in the line of mills and machinery. A strip of excellent timber skirts its banks, rendering timber and lumber very abundant and cheap. In the village there are 3 hotels, 10 or 12 stores, 1 apothecary shop, 1 furnace, 1 cabinet, 1 tin, 1 saddle and harness shops, 2 livery stables, 3 churches, and two to be built immediately; 1 jewelry store, 6 doctors, 1 printing office, besides carpenter, tailor, blacksmith, waggon and shoe shops, &c., with some 400 dwellings, and a population of at least 1,500. This place possesses superior advantages. It has plenty of water power, and of timber to saw, thus reducing the price of lumber and rendering building easy. It is surrounded by one of the most fertile sections of the state, which naturally inclines to this point for a market; and its means of transit when the La Crosse and Milwaukee railroad is completed, will add another important feature to its prospects. With such natural advantages, and these evidences of prosperity, who can wonder that Beaver Dam should make such rapid strides in advancement and business facilities, while it requires no prophetic eye to discover that, ere long, she is to be ranked among the most populous, wealthy, and business inland towns in Wisconsin.

BEAVER, *Lake*, is near the centre of the town of Merton, a short distance east of Pine lake, in Waukesha county, into which it has its outlet. It is about a mile in length.

BEETOWN, *Town*, in the county of Grant, being townships 4 and 5 N., of range 4 W.; 6 miles west from Lancaster. It has 7 school districts.

BEETOWN, *P. V.* on section 30, in town of same name in Grant county, town 4, range 4 W.; is surrounded by rich lead mines and a good farming region of land, with timber on the east, and prairie on the north, west, and south. The population is about 300; with 55 dwellings, 9 stores, and 1 hotel.

BEETOWN, *Diggings*, a mining place on section 17, town 4, range 4 W., in Grant county.

BELFONTAINE, *P. O.*, in Columbia county.

BELGIUM, *Town*, in the county of Ouzaukee, being township 12 N., of range 22 E.; located 7 miles north from Ouzaukee. The population in 1850 was 1,154. It has 7 school districts.

BELMONT, formerly *P. O.*, in town of same name, in northwest corner of Lafayette county, at Platte Mounds. At this place the first session of the territorial legislature of Wisconsin was held. It is now the residence of Hon. Charles Dunn, chief justice of the territorial supreme court.

BELOIT, *Town*, in county of Rock, being township 1 N., of range 12 E.; located southerly, 10 miles from Janesville, the county seat. The population in 1850 was 2,750. It has 9 school districts.

Beloit and Madison Rail Road Company.—Directors: John B. Turner, W. L. Newberry, Edward J. Tinkham, and E. S. Wadsworth, Chicago, Ill.; L. G. Fisher, Hazen Cheney, and John Hackett, Beloit, Wis.; Volney Atwood, J. A. Sleeper, and Otis W. Norton, Janesville, Wis.; Simeon Mills, F. G. Tibbits, and Elisha Burdick, Madison, Wis.; John P. Turner, President; Benj. Durham, Secretary; Edward J. Tinkham, Treasurer; and John P. Ilsley, Chief Engineer. This company was incorporated by act of the legislature, approved Feb. 18, 1852. By the charter the company are authorized to create a capital stock of $1,200,000, and to locate, construct and operate a single or double track railroad, from the village of Beloit in the county of Rock, via Janesville in the county of Rock, to Madison, the capital of the State of Wisconsin, with power also to connect or consolidate with other railroad companies. The company was organized at Madison on the 1st day of July, the same year, by the election of officers as above stated. Preliminary surveys were immediately commenced, preparatory to the location of the line, and the attainment of the right of way. The report of the chief engineer shows the length of the line from Beloit to Madison to be 52,08 miles, and the estimated cost $790,000, or $15,027 per mile, laid with heavy T rail. Some portions of the work have already been contracted, and the engineer is now actively engaged in completing the surveys and procuring the right of way, and the whole line will soon be ready for contract, and it is confidently believed that the entire road will be completed to Madison by the 4th of July, 1854. By an amendment to its charter, passed February, 1853, this company are authorized to construct their road direct from Beloit to Madison, and by running about twelve miles west of Janesville, the line will be reduced in length something over four miles, and be entirely removed from competition with rival roads. The district of country through which this road passes to its present terminus, the capital of

Wisconsin, is equal, if not superior, in population, productiveness and natural beauty to any portion of the state; while its ultimate extension to the Wisconsin river at Portage city, and thence through the extensive pine regions of the north to Lake Superior, or the Upper Mississippi, insure for it an immense and constantly increasing business, as that interesting portion of the country becomes settled and more fully developed. The very favorable terms upon which this company have arranged with the Chicago and Galena railroad company, to run in connection with and operate this road as a branch of that already popular and profitable thoroughfare, added to the many other superior advantages already enjoyed by this company, warrant the belief that this will prove one of the most useful, as well as most profitable, railroad enterprises in the Great West. To Simeon Mills, Esq., of Madison, is due the credit of originating and largely contributing toward the successful prosecution of this enterprise.

Beloit, *P. V.*, Rock county, on sections 35 and 36, in town of same name, being town 1 N., of range 12 E., 12 miles south from Janesville, and 45 miles southeast from Madison. It is situated on the State line, at the junction of Turtle Creek with Rock River. Its commercial and manufacturing facilities are of a superior character, and the means of education are as great as in any other town in the State. It has a population of 3,000, with 400 dwellings, 1 baptist, 1 congregational, 1 methodist, 1 presbyterian, 1 episcopal, and 1 catholic church; 18 dry goods stores, 10 grocery and provision, 2 hardware and 3 drug stores; 3 stove and tin, 2 shoe, 4 clothing and 2 book stores; 2 cabinet, 2 barbers, 2 jewellers, 4 market and 2 paint shops; 3 saddle and harness, 4 blacksmiths and 2 coopers shops; 1 tobacco factory and store, 3 hotels, 3 flouring, 1 oil, and 1 saw mill, 1 flax factory, 1 foundry, 1 machine shop, 1 manufactory of reapers and fanning mills, 2 carriage and waggon factories, 1 scale manufactory, 1 woollen factory, and 1 candle and soap factory.

BEM, *P. O.*, in Greene county.

BENTON, *Creek*, rises in town 23, range 23 E., Kewaunee county, runs southerly, emptying into the west Twin River in Manitowoc county.

BERLIN, *Town*, in county of Marquette, being township 17 N., of range 13 E. It has 9 school districts.

BERRY, *Town*, in the county of Dane, being township 8 N., of range 7 E. It is 15 miles northwest from Madison.

BERRY, *P.O.*, in town of same name, Dane county, on section 29, town 8 N., range 7 E.

BIG BEND, *P. O.* in southern part of Waukesha county.

BIG, *Creek*, a small tributary from the southeast of Black River, in La Crosse county, into which it empties, in town 19 N., of range 5 W.

BIG PLOVER, *River*, is a tributary from the northeast of the Wisconsin, which it enters between Plover and Stevens' Point.

BIG, *Prairie*, Waushara county, is a crescent shaped prairie in the eastern part of the town of Oasis, town 20 N., of range 8 E. Its greatest length is six miles, and extreme width three miles. It contains about 15,000 acres of land.

BIG QUINNESEC, *Falls*, are rapids in the Menominee river, about one and a half miles in length, in which distance the fall is 134 feet. This distance is divided into four chutes, at the lowest of which the river dashes over a perpendicular fall of rocks forty feet in height.

BIG SUAMICO, *River*, rises in Oconto county, and runs east, through township 25, emptying into Green Bay from the west.

BILLING'S, *Creek*, in Bad Ax county, is a branch of the Kickapoo river.

BIRCH, *Lake*, on Red Cedar river, between Sketch and Pine lakes.

BIRD'S RUIN, see Hanchettville P. O.

Black, *Creek*, Sheboygan county, rises in the southwest part of town 13, range 23 E., and runs north easterly to the north-east corner of the town of Wilson, where it falls into Lake Michigan.

Black, *Creek*, is a small tributary, from the west of Fox River, which it enters near the line between towns 16 and 17, in Marquette county.

Black, *Creek*, rises near the N. E. corner of Outagamie county, and runs southwesterly, uniting with the outlet of White Lake, and falls into Wolf river, in the town of Ellington.

Black Earth, *Town*, (formerly Farmer'sville) in county of Dane, being township No. 8 N., range 6 E., located 20 miles from Madison. It has 3 school districts.

Black Earth, *P. V.*, Dane county, in town of same name, on section 26, town 8 N., range 6 E., 21 miles nearly west from Madison. Population 75; 15 dwellings, 1 store, 1 hotel and a good flouring mill. It is situated in the fertile valley of the Black Earth creek, 9 miles above its entrance into the Wisconsin. This village was laid out in 1850, and has a good water power.

Black Earth, *River*, rises in Middleton, in Dane county, and runs N. W., entering the Wisconsin at Arena, in Iowa county.

Black, *River*, (Sappah,) rises in Marathon county, and runs south west, entering the Mississippi, in La Crosse county, about half way between La Crosse and Trempeleau rivers. It is navigable to the Falls, to which place it maintains a width of 200 yards.

Black River, *Falls*, are about 50 miles from the mouth of the Black River, in Jackson county, at which place the stream is about 200 yards wide, and falls 22 feet in the distance of 100 yards.

Black River Falls, *P. V.*, on Black river, in Jackson county town 21 N., range 4 W.

Black River Pinery, is on Black river, and its tributaries mostly in La Crosse and Jackson counties. The amount of lumber manufactured in this section, aside from square timber, lath, and shingles, is shown by the following estimate:

Angle's Mills, on La Crosse river	500,000	Wm. Levice's Mills	1,800,000
La Crosse Mills	2,000,000	John Levice's „	800,000
Nichols „	800,000	Hall's „	800,000
Douglass „	1,000,000	Johnson's „	300,000
Polley's „	500,000	Blanchard's „	300,000
Robinson's „	500,000	Bailey's „	300,000
Valentine's „	800,000	Clarke's „	500,000
Shephard's „		Whipple's „	800,000
Patterson's „	500,000	O'Neall's „	500,000
Perry's „	800,000	Cowley's „	800,000
Spaulding's „	500,000	Eaton's „	500,000
		Total	14,500,000

Black Wolf, *P.O.*, in town of same name, Winnebago county.

Black Wolf, *Town*, in county of Winnebago, being township 17 N., of range 17 E.; located 18 miles northwest from Oshkosh, the county seat. It has 3 school districts.

Blake's, *Prairie*, is a large prairie, in range 5 W., in Grant county.

Block House, *Creek*, a branch from the east of Little Platte river, in Smeltzer, Grant county.

Bloomfield, *Town*, in the county of Walworth, being township 1 N., of range 18 E.; located 13 miles southeast from Elkhorn, the county seat. The population in 1850 was 879. It has 6 school districts.

Bloomfield, *P. V.*, in Walworth county, on section 35, of town of same name, (town 1 N., range 18 E.,) 18 miles southeast from Elkhorn and 80 miles southeast from Madison, on the Nippissing creek, with a good water fall.

Bloomingdale, *P. V.*, in town of Omro, Winnebago county, being in town 18 N., range 15 E.

BLOOMINGDALE, *Town*, see Omro.

BLOOMING GROVE, *Town*, in the county of Dane, being township 7 N., of range 10 E.; located 4 miles east from Madison, the county seat. Population in 1850 was 291. It has 6 school districts.

BLUE MOUNDS, *P. O.*, at the oldest settlement of Dane county, in town of same name, on section 5, town 6, range 6 E., 25 miles northeast from Mineral Point; and is the same distance west from Madison, on the great stage route and thoroughfare from the Mississippi to Milwaukee, via Madison. It was first settled in 1828, by Ebenezer Brigham, who made a valuable discovery of mineral at this place in that year.

BLUE MOUNDS, two conical shaped hills, the one in Iowa, the other in Dane county; 12 miles south from the Wisconsin river, and 25 miles west from Madison. The top of one of these mounds is 1001 feet above the level of the Wisconsin river at Helena, and is the highest point in the State.

BLUE MOUND, *Creek*, rises near the Blue Mounds in Dane county, and runs northwest, uniting with the Black Earth river in the town of Arena, Iowa county.

BLUE MOUNDS, *Town*, in county of Dane, being township 6 N., of range 6 E.; located 21 miles west from Madison. It has 5 school districts.

BLUE RIVER, *P. O.*, in Iowa county.

BLUE, *River*, rises in Highland, Iowa county, and runs northwest into the Wisconsin river, in the town of Fennimore, Grant county.

BLUE RIVER, *Diggings*, a mining point at section 24, town 6 N., of range 1 W., in Grant county.

BLUFF, *P. O.*, in town of Kingston, Sauk county, in town 10 N., of range 6 E.

BLUFFTON, *P. V.*, in Marquette county, being town 16 N., of range 13 E., on section 7. It is located 3 miles northwest from

5

Dartford, 54 miles north and 18 miles east from Madison. It is at the head of navigation on the Pukyaun river, the main east branch of the Upper Fox. The rapids afford a fine water power. It has 1 hotel, 1 mill, and a congregational and methodist denomination. The roads from Sheboygan to La Crosse, from Green Bay to Fort Winnebago, and from Oshkosh to the Upper Fox River, all cross the rapids at this place.

Boiling, *Creek*, is a small stream in the town of Black Earth, Dane county, emptying into the Wisconsin.

Bois Brule, *River*, (Burnt Wood,) a tributary of Lake Superior, into which it enters, about 20 miles east from Fond du Lac bay. It rises near the Upper St. Croix lake, and is nearly 100 miles in length.

Bois, *Creek*, a branch of Grant river, from the east, in the town of Potosi, Grant county.

Bois, *Prairie*, a long and narrow prairie, extending from Lancaster nearly to Potosi in Grant county.

Bonner's, *Creek*, rises near Belmont, Lafayette county, and runs east into the Pekatonica, in the town of Willow Springs.

Booth, *Lake*, is a small lake on the line between the towns of Troy and East Troy, Walworth county.

Bothelle, *P. V.*, in Fond du Lac county, on section 7, in the town of Eldorado, being town 16 N., of range 16 E., 15 miles northwest from the city of Fond du Lac, and 70 miles northeast from Madison.

Boyd's, *Creek*, a small stream entering the Wisconsin, in town 7 N., of range 4 W., in Crawford county.

Bradford, *Town*, in county of Rock, being township No. 2 N., of range 14 E., located 12 miles east from Janesville, the county seat. The population in 1850 was 703. It has 8 school districts.

BRIDGEPORT, *P. V.*, in Brown county, on section 2, town 21 N., of range 19 E.

BRIGHAM'S, *Branch*, a small tributary of the Fourth Lake, in Dane county.

BRIGHAM'S, *Prairie*, is a large prairie in the town of Blue Mounds, Dane county.

BRIGHTON, *P. V.*, in town of same name, Kenosha county.

BRIGHTON, *Town*, in county of Kenosha, being township 2 N., of range 23 E.; located 17 miles west from Kenosha, the county seat. The population in 1850 was 180. It has 7 school districts.

BRISTOL, *Town*, in county of Dane, being township 9 N., of range 11 E.; located 14 miles northeast from Madison, the county seat. It has 5 school districts.

BRISTOL, *Town*, in county of Kenosha, being township 1 N., of range 21 E.; located 10 miles southwest from Kenosha, the county seat. The population in 1850 was 1,125. It has 12 school districts.

BRISTOL, *P. V.*, Kenosha county, on section 4, town 1 N., of range 21 E., being in town of same name; located 11 miles west from Kenosha, and 95 miles southeast from Madison. The post office was established in 1839.

BROCK'S, *Crossing*, on L' eau Galle, in St. Croix county.

BROKEN GUN, *Channel*, the middle outlet of Black river.

BROOKFIELD, *P. O.*, in town of same name, Waukesha county.

BROOKFIELD, *Town*, in the county of Waukesha, being township 7 N., of range 20 E.; located 9 miles northeast from Waukesha, the county seat. The population in 1850 was 1,939. It has 13 school districts.

BROOKLYN, *Creek*, a small stream, entering the Wisconsin from the southwest, at Brooklyn, Grant county.

BROOKLYN, *Town*, in county of Green, being township 4 N., of range 9 E.; located 17 miles northeast from Monroe, the county seat. The population in 1850 was 531. It has 8 school districts.

BROOKLYN, *Town*, in county of Marquette, being township 16 N., of range 13 E. It has 9 school districts.

BROOKLYN, *Town*, in county of Sauk, having 7 school districts.

BROOKLYN, *Village*, in Grant county, on Wisconsin river, at the outlet of creek of the same name, in the town of Patch Grove.

BROWN, *County*, is bounded on the north by Oconto, on the east by Kewaunee, on the south by Manitowoc, and on the west by Outagamie, and a portion of Oconto. It derived its name from General Brown, commander-in-chief of the army, and was originally organized by an act of the legislative council of the territory of Michigan, approved 16th October, 1818, and then included all of the territory of the present state of Wisconsin, east of a line drawn due north from the northern boundary of Illinois, through the middle of the Portage between the Fox and Wisconsin rivers. Its limits have been decreased from time to time, until at present it contains only fourteen and a half townships, being 21 by 24 miles square, with an addition of 3 by 6 miles to its northwestern corner. The seat of justice is established by law at the village of Depere, on the Neenah, about eight miles from its mouth, although the courts are held, and most of the county business transacted at Green Bay. Its streams are: Fox, (Neenah), Manitoo, (or East), Ashwabena and Big Suamico rivers, and Duck creek. The soil is better adapted to grazing than the raising of grain, although it produces good crops of wheat, rye, oats, potatoes, &c. The surface is mostly level or slightly undulating, with but little swamp or waste land. It is mostly heavily timbered, with maple, beech, birch, &c., interspersed with pine and a good proportion of hemlock. Brown county is attached to the fourth judicial circuit, to the third congressional, and to the second senatorial district, and with Kewaunee and Door, forms an assembly district. The population in 1825 was 952; 1830, 964; 1836, 2,706; 1838, 3,084; 1840, 2,107; 1842, 2,146; 1846, 2,662; 1847, 2,914; 1850, 6,222. Farms, 267; manufactories, 23; and dwellings, 1,005. It must be borne in mind that new counties were established from the county of Brown, between nearly every taking of the census, and that the foregoing table, so far as showing the increase of population is concerned, is a very unsatisfactory one. The following are the county officers for 1853 and 1854: County Judge, David Agry; Sheriff, Orlo B. Graves; Clerk of Court, John Last; District Attorney, Baron S. Doty; Register of Deeds, E. Holmes Ellis; Clerk of Board of Supervisors, Wm. Field, Jr.; County Treasurer, Charles Henry; County Surveyor, Eli P. Royce; Coroner, David Cormier.

Brown, *Lake*, about one and a half miles east of the village of Burlington, in Racine county. It is nearly a mile in diameter, and discharges its waters into the Pishtaka.

Buena Vista, *P. V.*, Portage county, on section 20, town 22 N., of range 9 E.; 100 miles north from Madison, in a good farming country; with 100 inhabitants, 25 dwellings, 3 hotels, and 1 church.

Buena Vista, *Town*, in county of St. Croix.

Buck, *Creek*, empties into the Mississippi, in town 9, Crawford county.

Buffalo, *Town*, in county of Marquette, being township 14 N., of range 10 E. It has 4 school districts.

Buffalo, *Lake*, Marquette county, is an expansion of the Neenah river, about 12 miles in length. It is mostly in town 15 N., of ranges 9 and 10 E.

Buffalo, *River*, forms the boundary line for several miles between La Crosse and Chippewa counties, emptying into the Mississippi, in town 24 N., of range 6 E.

BUFFALO, *Slough*, the name given to the lower mouth of the Chippewa river.

BULLION, *P. O.*, in Waukesha county.

BURKE, *Town*, in the county of Dane, being township 8 N., of range 10 E.; located 6 miles from Madison, the county seat. It has 6 school districts.

BURLINGTON, *Town*, in the county of Racine, north ⅔ of town 2 N., and town 3 N., of range 19 E.; located 24 miles west of Racine, the county seat. The population in 1850 was 1,640. It has 8 school districts.

BURLINGTON, *P. V.*, on Fox river, in town of same name, in county of Racine, on section 32, in town 4 N., of range 19 E.

BURNETT CORNERS, *P. O.*, in town of Burnett, Dodge county.

BURNETT, *P. O.*, in town of same name, Dodge county.

BURNETTE, *Town*, in the county of Dodge, being town 12 N., of range 15 E.; located 6 miles north from Juneau, the county seat. The population in 1850 was 816. It has 6 school districts.

BURNT DISTRICT, *Falls*, two perpendicular falls in the Menominee river, near its source, about a mile apart, and 9 feet in height.

BURNT WOOD, *River*, see Bois Brule.

BUTLER, *P.O.*, Milwaukee county, on section 6 in town of Wauwatosa, (town 7 N., range 21 E.,) 8 miles northwest from Milwaukee, on the Lisbon plank road, being the route of the North Madison Territory road from Milwaukee, and 80 miles from Madison. It has 1 hotel and a steam saw mill.

BUTTE DES MORTS, *P. V.*, Winnebago county, on section 24 in town of Winneconne, (town 19 N., of range 15 E.), 10 miles northwest from Oshkosh, the county seat, and 85 miles northeast from Madison. It is beautifully situated on a high bluff on the left bank of the Fox river, near the head of lake Butte des Morts, from which it takes its name. It offers many inducements to the settler, being a very healthy location, and surrounded by a good farming country. Lumber is plenty, immense quantities being rafted on the river. Population, 100; with 15 dwellings, 5 stores, 3 hotels, 1 steam mill, 2 religious denominations, and various mechanical shops.

BYRON, *Town*, in county of Fond du Lac, being town 14 N., of range 17 E.; centrally located, 8 miles south from Fond du Lac, the county seat. The population in 1850 was 882. It has 9 school districts.

CADIZ, *P. V.*, in town of same name, Greene county; being on section 14, in town 1 N., of range 6 E.

CADIZ, *Town*, in the county of Green, being town 1 N., of range 6 E.; centrally located, 8 miles southwest from Monroe. The population in 1850 was 459. It has 5 school districts.

CADWELL, *P. O.*, in county of Racine.

CALAMUS, *Town*, in the county of Dodge, being town 11 N., of range 13 E.; centrally located, 12 miles west from Juneau, the county seat. It has 6 school districts.

CALEDONIA, *P. O.*, in town of same name, in county of Racine; being town 4 N., of range 22 E.

CALEDONIA, *Town*, in the county of Racine, being town 4 N., of range 22 E.; centrally located, 6 miles northwest from Racine. The population in 1850 was 1,065. It has 11 school districts.

CALEDONIA, *Town*, in the county of Columbia. It has 6 school districts.

CALEDONIA, *Town*, in the county of Portage.

CALUMET, *County*, is bounded on the north by Brown and Outagamie, on the east by Manitowoc, on the south by Sheboygan and Fond du Lac, and on the west by Winnebago. It was set off from Brown, December 7, 1836, and organized for county purposes, January 6, 1840. On the 13th of August, 1840, it was disorganized, and its territory attached to Brown.

It was again reorganized February 18, 1842, remaining in judicial connection with Brown until the organization of Fond du Lac, January 22, 1844, to which it was attached for judicial purposes. It was fully organized February 5, 1840. The seat of justice is at Chilton Centre, in the town of Charlestown, being in town 18 N., of range 20 E. It is well watered by tributaries of the Manitowoc river, and by small streams entering Lake Winnebago. The Brothertown and Stockbridge Indians have fine settlements, schools, and churches, in this county, and their farms and buildings compare favorably with others in the State. They are entitled to all the privileges of citizenship, and are frequently represented by some of their own number in the State legislature. This county contains much good land, which is for sale at low rates; the soil is good, and covered with a heavy growth of hard timber. It forms a portion of the fourth judicial circuit, of the third congressional, and of the first senate district, and sends one member to the assembly. The population in 1840 was 275; 1842, 407; 1846, 836; 1847, 1,060; 1850, 1,746. Farms, 243; manufactories, 5; dwellings, 381. The county officers for 1853 and 1854 are: County Judge, Moody Mann; Sheriff, J. S. Hammer; Clerk of Court, Charles Growing; Register, L. P. Fowler.

CALUMET, *P. V.*, in town of same name, Fond du Lac county.

CALUMET, *Town*, in the county of Fond du Lac, being the south fractional half of township 17 N., of range 18 and 19 E., and north fractional half of town 16 N., of range 19 E.; centrally located, 10 miles northeast from Fond du Lac. The population in 1850, as then organized, 1,704.

CALVIN'S, *Creek*, in Manitowoc county, a small stream, entering Lake Michigan about 5 miles southwest from the mouth of the Manitowoc river.

CAMBRIDGE, *P. V.*, in northern part of town of Christiana, Dane county, on stage route from Madison to Whitewater.

CAMP, *Creek*, rises in the north west corner of Richland county, and runs westerly into Otter creek, of Bad Ax connty.

CAMP, *Lake*, in Kenosha county, is a long and narrow lake near the centre of the town of Salem.

CARMA, *Island*, near the western shore of lake Michigan, in Door county.

CASCADE, *P. V.*, Sheboygan county, in town of same name, on section 29, town 14 N., of range 21 E.; 18 miles southwest from Sheboygan, and 110 miles northeast from Madison, on the most direct route between the same. It is situated on the east branch of the Milwaukee river, and has a good water-power; in the midst of a good, though new, farming country, mostly of timbered lands. It has 300 inhabitants, 25 families, 2 stores, 2 hotels, 1 saw, and 1 grist mill; 3 organized denominations, baptist, congregational, and methodist. It has a good charter for an academy.

CASSVILLE, *P. V.* in town of same name, Grant county, being in town 3 N., of range 5 W., on the Mississippi river, and was formerly a place of considerable importance.

CASSVILLE, *Town*, in county of Grant, being all of the same embraced in towns 3 and 4 N., of ranges 5 and 6 W.; centrally located, 15 miles southwest from Lancaster, the county seat. It has 7 school districts.

CASTLE ROCK, on the west bank of the Wisconsin river, in town 15 N., of range 5 E,, in Adams county.

CATFISH, *River*, rises in the Fourth Lake, and connecting the four lakes in Dane county, runs southeast, emptying into the Rock river in the town of Fulton, Rock county.

CEDARBURG, *P. V.*, in town of same name, Ozaukee county, being on section 34, town 10 N., of range 21 E.; located 10 miles southwest from Ozaukee.

CEDARBURG, *Town*, in county of Washington, being town 10 N., of range 21 E., excepting the easterly range of sections belonging to the town of Grafton; centrally located, 8 miles southwest from Ozaukee, the county seat. The population in 1850 was 1,134. It has 7 school districts.

Cedar Creek, *P. V.*, in town of Polk, Washington county, being on section 10, in town 10 N., of range 19 E.

Cedar Grove, *P. V.*, in Sheboygan county, in section 30, town 13 N., of range 23 E.; located 15 miles southerly from Sheboygan, and 75 miles east northeast from Madison. It has 6 dwellings, 1 hotel, and 2 stores.

Cedar, *Lake*, is a small lake on the line between the towns of Polk and West Bend, in Washington county.

Cedar, *Lake*, in the town of Rhine, Sheboygan county, on sections 31 and 32, town 16 N., of range 21 E.

Cedar, *Rapids*, of Fox river, about half way between Grand and Little Chute.

Cedar, *River*, rises in Cedar lake, and running southeasterly enters Milwaukee river in the southwest corner of the town of Grafton, Washington county.

Centre, *P. O.*, in town of same name, Rock county.

Centre, *Town*, in county of Rock, being town 3 N., range 9 E.; centrally located 10 miles west of Janesville. The population in 1850 was 625. It has 7 school districts.

Centre, *Lake*, a small lake in the centre of the town of Trenton, Washington county.

Centres, *River*, is a small tributary entering Manitowoc river about 10 miles from its mouth, having its source in Brown county.

Centreville, *P. O.*, in town of Randolph, Columbia county.

Centreville, *Town*, in county of Waupacca, being the northwest portion of the same.

Ceresco, *Town*, in county of Fond du Lac, being town 16 N., of range 14 E.; located 19 miles northwest from Fond du Lac city. It has 6 school districts.

CERESCO, *P. O.*, in town of same name, Fond du Lac county, on sections 16, 17, 20 and 21.

CHAGWAMIGON, or CHE-GOI-ME-GON, *Bay*, see Shagwamigon.

CHAGWAMIGON, *Point*, in La Pointe county, east of bay of same name.

CHAMBER'S, *Island*, near the eastern shore of Green Bay, in towns 32 and 33 N., of range 27 E., in Door county.

CHAMBER'S, *Lake*, is about a mile in length, on an island of same name in Green Bay.

CHAPPEAU, *Rapids*, of the Menomonee river, are above Menomonee Rapids.

CHARLESTON, *P. V.*, in town of same name, Calumet county, on section 6.

CHARLESTOWN, *Town*, in county of Calumet, being in the east part thereof. It has 6 school districts.

CHARLOTTE, *P. O.*, in town of Cassville, Grant county, being town 4 N., of range 5 W.

CHERRY HILL, *P. O.*, in Washington county.

CHESTER, *P. O.*, in town of same name, Dodge county, on section 28.

CHESTER, *Town*, in county of Dodge, being town 13 N., of range 15 E.; centrally located, 13 miles northwest from Juneau. Population in 1850 was 829. It has 4 school districts.

CHILTON CENTRE, *P. V.*, and *C. H.*, in town of Charleston, Calumet county, town 18 N., of range 20 E. The county seat was located at this place by a vote of the county, in 1852.

CHIPPEWA FALLS, *P. V.*, and *C. H.*, at falls of Chippewa river, in county of same name, at which place the river has a descent of 24 feet in half a mile. Population 250. Good hotel and several mills.

CHIPPEWA, *County*, is bounded on the N. by St. Croix and La Pointe, on the E. by Marathon, on the S. by La Crosse, on the S. W. by the Mississippi river, and on the W. by St. Croix. The southern boundary is rather indefinitely defined. It was established from Crawford, February 3, 1835, but has never been organized. Since the organization of La Crosse county, March 1, 1851, the county and judicial connection has been changed from Crawford to La Crosse. The boundaries were somewhat changed January 14, 1846. Population in 1850 was 615. The soil in the western portion is good, in the northeastern less valuable, and covered with forests of excellent pine timber. It is watered by Chippewa river and its branches, and tributaries of Buffalo and Mississippi rivers. The tributaries of the Chippewa river are numerous, and pass through large portions of the county, watering lands as valuable as any in the State. There are now in successful operation 11 saw mills, capable of cutting 30,000,000 feet of lumber annually. The largest of these mills is owned by Allen, at Chippewa Falls; Menomonee, owned by Knapp, Williams & Taintor; and Carson & Eaton, at the mouth of the Eau Galla, which average about 5,000,000 of feet each, per annum, and furnish employment for about 200 hands each. The county seat was established by an act of the legislature, at the January session 1853, at Chippewa Falls, on Chippewa river.

CHIPPEWA *Rapids*, in county of same name. This name has been given to two rapids in Chippewa river, one in town 29 N., of range 8 W., and the other in town 30 N., of range 7 W.

CHIPPEWA (Ojibwa), *River*, the largest tributary in Wisconsin of the Mississippi, into which it empties in town 22 N., of range 14 W. It rises near the head waters of Bad river of Lake Superior, and runs southerly, to its mouth, where it is 500 yards wide.

CHRISTIANA, *Town*, in county of Dane, being town 6 N., of range 12 E.; centrally located 17 miles southeast from Madison. The population in 1850 was 785. It has 10 school districts.

CHRISTIANA, *P. V.*, in town of same name, Dane county, on section 23, town 6 N., of range 12 E., being 23 miles southeast from Madison. It is situated on Koskonong creek—possesses good water power, with good lime stone and excellent quarries of sand stone. Population 200, dwellings 30, stores 2, hotels 1, mills 2, a stone school house, and 1 carding machine.

CHRYSTAL LAKE, *Town*, in county of Marquette, being town 17 N., of range 10.

CLAIRVILLE, *P. O.*, in Winnebago county.

CLARENCE, *P. O.*, in the county of Greene.

CLARNO, *Town*, in county of Green, being town 1 N., of range 7; centrally located, 7 miles south from Monroe. The population in 1850 was 714. It has 5 school districts.

CLAYTON, *Town*, in county of Winnebago, being town 20 N., range of 16 E.; centrally located, 13 miles from Oshkosh. The population in 1850 was 402. It has 4 school districts.

CLEARWATER, *P. V.*, in Chippewa county, in town 27 N., of range 9 W., at the mouth of L'eau Claire river. Population, 200; 2 mills, 1 store, and 1 hotel.

CLEARWATER, *River*, see L'eau Claire, Chippewa county.

CLIFTON, *Town*, in county of Grant, being town 5 N., of range 1 W.; centrally located, 12 miles west from Lancaster. It has 5 school districts.

CLIFTON, *Village*, in the town of Roxbury, Dane county, immediately opposite Prairie du Sac, on the Wisconsin river. The location is a beautiful one, possessing good shores and other facilities for unloading rafts and boats. As yet, but few improvements have been made. There is 1 store, 1 tannery, 2 lumber yards, and about 50 inhabitants. A large portion of the lumber used in Madison and the interior of Dane county, is brought from this place, to which it is floated from the immense pineries on the Upper Wisconsin river. Its prospects for being an important lumbering and trading point are, at present, very flattering.

CLINTON, *P. V.*, in town of same name, Rock county.

CLINTON, *Town*, in county of Rock, being town 1 N., of range 14 E.; centrally located, 14 miles southeast from Janesville. The population in 1850 was 1,176. It has 8 school districts.

CLYDE, *Town*, in county of Iowa, being part of townships 7 and 8 N., of ranges 2 and 3 E.; centrally located, 18 miles north of Mineral Point, the county seat. It has 3 school districts. It is on the Wisconsin river, on both sides of Otter creek. It is an agricultural town, well timbered and watered, and has one grist mill.

CLYMAN, *P. O.*, in town of same name, Dodge county.

CLYMAN, *Town*, in county of Dodge, being town 10 N., of range 15 E.; centrally located, 6 miles south from Juneau. The population in 1850 was 735. It has 9 school districts.

COLAMER, *P. O.*, in town of Kingston, Sauk county.

COLD SPRING, *Lake*, a small lake in the town of Fredonia, Washington county.

COLD SPRING, *P. V.*, in town of same name, in the county of Jefferson; 8 miles southeast from Jefferson.

COLD SPRING, *Race Course*, situated 2 miles west from Milwaukee, the property of E. B. Walcott, M. D., of Milwaukee.

COLD SPRING, *Town*, in county of Jefferson, being town 1 N., of range 15 E.; centrally located, 9 miles southeast from Jefferson. The population in 1850 was 568. It has 5 school districts.

COLUMBUS, *P. V.*, in town of same name, on section 12 Columbia county, on the Crawfish river. It is considerable of a village.

COLUMBUS, *Town*, in county of Columbia, being town 10 N., of range 12; centrally located, 24 miles southeast from Portage. The population in 1850 was 960. It has 7 school districts.

COLUMBIA, *County*, is bounded on the north by Adams and Marquette, on the east by Dodge, on the south by Dane, and on the west by Sauk; and is located mostly in the vicinity of the

Portage of the Fox and Wisconsin rivers. It was set off from Portage and organized February 3, 1846. The boundaries were somewhat changed March 6, 1849. The streams of this county are: the Fox, (Neenah), Wisconsin, and Crawfish rivers, and Rocky Run, Ockie, Spring, and Duck creeks. For fertility of soil and feasibility of lands, the most of which are openings and prairie, this county is unsurpassed by any other in the State. It is connected with the third judicial circuit, and with the third congressional district, and constitutes the twenty-fifth senate district; sends two members to the assembly, being divided into the north and south assembly districts, nearly of the same size. The towns of Winnebago, Port Hope, Marcellon, Scott, Randolph, Portage, Prairie, Spring Vale, and Wyocena, forming the first; and the towns of Columbus, Fountain Prairie, Hampden, Otsego, Leeds, Lowville, Lodi, Dekorra, Westpoint, and Caledonia, the second district. The vote of the electors at the annual town meeting in April, 1851, permanently located the seat of justice at Fort Winnebago, in accordance with an act approved March 15, 1851. The population in 1846 was 1,969; 1847, 3,791; 1850, 9,565. Farms, 998; manufactories, 25; dwellings, 1,855. County officers for 1853 and 1854: County Judge, Joshua J. Guppy; Sheriff, Perry Lee; Clerk of Court, James Delany, Register of Deeds, William Owen; Clerk of Board of Supervisors, Alvin Alden; County Treasurer, H. Hascall; County Surveyor, John Thomas; Coroner, Isaac Smith.

Como, *Lake*, in the south part of the town of Geneva, in Walworth county. It is about three miles long, and half a mile broad.

Concord, *P. O.*, in town of same name, Jefferson county, on section 15, known as "Kelloggs," formerly Union Centre.

Concord, *Town*, in county of Jefferson, being town 7 N., of range 16 E.; centrally located, 10 miles northeast from Jefferson. The population in 1850 was 725. It has 9 school districts.

COOKSVILLE, *P. V.*, (Waucoma village), in Rock county, being on section 6, town 4 N., of range 11 E. It is 16 miles northwest from Janesville, and 18 miles southeast from Madison, on the edge of a broad and gently sloping prairie of two miles in width. It is on the Badfish, with three good millsites within one and a half miles. Population, 250; dwellings, 35; stores, 3; hotels, 1; mills, 3. 1 Presbyterian church, 1 sash and door, 1 waggon, 1 harness, 1 shoe, 1 blacksmith, 1 cabinet, and 1 tailor shop.

COON, *Prairie*, in Bad Ax county, on section 5, town 13 N., of range 4 W.

COOPERSTOWN, *P. V.*, in Brown county, on section 1, town 21 N., of range 22 E.

COPPER, *Creek*, empties into the Mississippi, in town 6, Crawford county.

COPPER, *Creek*, is a small stream entering Baraboo river from the N., about 5 miles below Reedsburg.

COTTAGE GROVE, *P. O.*, in town of same name, Dane county, on section 23.

COTTAGE GROVE, *Town*, in county of Dane, being town 7, range 11 E.; centrally located, 10 miles east from Madison. The population in 1850 was 1,022. It has 12 school districts, and 3 hotels; the settlers are principally Irish and German.

COURT-EOREILLE, *Lake*, (Lac Court-eoreille, Agasowi Lake), a considerable lake in the southern part of La Pointe county, discharging its waters through a river of the same name, into the Chippewa river.

COURT-EOREILLE, *River*, rises in lake of same name, runs southeast into the Chippewa.

COURTLAND, *Town*, in county of Columbia.

CRANBERRY, *Creek*, in Adams county, is a northern branch of the Yellow river.

CRANBERRY, *Lakes*, several small lakes in the town of Concord, Jefferson county; have been so named on account of the great quantities of that fruit formerly found in their vicinity.

CRAWFISH, *River*, rises in the town of Hampden, Columbia county, and running southeasterly, uniting with Beaver Dam creek, in Dodge county, enters Rock river, at Jefferson. It is about the same size as Rock river.

CRAWFORD, *County*, is located at the junction between the Wisconsin and Mississippi rivers, and is bounded on the north by Bad Ax, on the east by Richland, on the southeast by Grant, and on the west by the Mississippi, which separates it from the State of Iowa. It was established October 16, 1818, when it embraced all of the territory between the Mississippi and "a line drawn due north from the northern line of the State of Illinois, through the centre of the Portage between the Fox and Wisconsin rivers to the Michilimacinac," and derived its name from Hon. Wm. H. Crawford, formerly Secretary of War, and afterwards Secretary of the Treasury. Its limits have now been so far reduced that it is one of the smallest counties in the State. The seat of justice is at Prairie du Chien, one of the oldest settlements in the State, on the Mississippi river, about three miles above the mouth of the Wisconsin, and is one of the most beautiful locations in the west. The surface of the country is broken by a ridge running between the two great rivers. The soil, for the most part, is good, producing wheat, oats, and most other grains, which find a ready home market, in supplying the lumber traders, military posts, and the great tide of emigration which is now turned to this and the neighboring counties of La Crosse and Bad Ax. It is watered by the Kickapoo river and its branches, and small streams emptying into the Mississippi and Wisconsin rivers. Between the Kickapoo river and Richland county, is one of the finest tracts of country in the State. It is well supplied with pure water; and good

6

timber is found along the banks of the small streams, and in groves, scattered at convenient distances, to be useful for the rapidly increasing population. A fine village has been regularly laid out midway between the mouth of the Kickapoo and the Richland county line, on the Wisconsin river, called Boyd's town. It has a good landing. There is much pine timber in this county, on and near the banks of the Kickapoo, from which large quantities of lumber are manufactured, finding an outlet to a market by said river, and the Wisconsin and Mississippi. Copper has been found in the northern part of the county, in such quantities and appearance as to indicate the near presence of a vast body of that mineral. Near the west bank of the Kickapoo, in town 8, has been found considerable quantities of lead, and there is no doubt that if a geological survey was made, that lead, rivalling in quantity and purity that raised in the counties of Iowa, Grant and Lafayette, would be discovered. It is connected with the sixth judicial circuit, and the nineteenth senate district, and with Bad Ax, is entitled to one member of the assembly. The estimated population of Crawford county in 1825, including most of the present State and a portion of Minnesota, was 492. The population in 1830 was 692; 1836, 854; 1838, 1,220; 1840, 1,502; 1842, 1,409; 1846, 1,444; 1847, 1,409; 1850, (including Bad Ax and La Crosse,) 2,399; 1850, within its present limits, 1,407. Farms, 81; manufactories, 14; dwellings, 665. The above will give but little information in regard to the increase of population, as new counties were set off between nearly every taking of the census. The present population of the county is upwards of 3,000. County Officers for 1853 and 1854: County Judge, Hiram A. Wright; Sheriff, Leander LeClerc; Clerk of Court, Ira B. Brunson; District Attorney, Samuel Cowden; Register of Deeds, Ira B. Brunson; Clerk of Board of Supervisors, Heman Baldwin; County Treasurer, I. P. Perrett Gentil; County Surveyor, Ira B. Brunson; Coroner, Henry H. Bailey.

CROCODILE, *River*, or Rice River, see Fond du Lac river.

CROOKED, *Lake*, a small body of water near the Wisconsin, in the town of Fennimore, Grant county.

CROOKED, *Lake*, an expansion of Bark river, in the south part of the town of Summit, Waukesha county, a short distance below the Nebahmin lakes.

CROOKED, *Lake*, near the centre of the town of Auburn, Fond du Lac county.

CROSS PLAINS, *P. O.*, in town of same name, Dane county.

CROSS PLAINS, *Town*, in the county of Dane, being town 7 N., of ranges 6 and 7 E.; centrally located, 17 miles W. from Madison. It has 7 school districts.

CRYSTAL, *Lake*, in Marquette county, in town 17 N., on a line between ranges 9 and 10 east, discharging its waters south-easterly, into the Neenah, near the line between towns 15 and 16 north.

CYAON, *Creek*, empties into the Kickapoo from the west, in town 9 north, in Crawford county.

DAKOTAH, *Town*, in county of Waushara, being town 18 N., of range 10; centrally located, 10 miles west from Sacramento.

DANE, *Town*, in county of Dane, being town 9 N., of range 8 E.; centrally located, 15 miles northwest from Madison.

DANE, *County*, is bounded on the northwest by the Wisconsin river, by which it is separated from Sauk; on the north by Columbia, on the east by Dodge and Jefferson, south by Rock and Green, and west by Iowa. It was established from Milwaukee and Iowa, and attached to Iowa for judicial purposes December 7, 1836, and fully organized March 11, 1839. The seat of justice is at Madison, near the geographical centre of the county, and the Court House is the best in the State. Dane county contains about 1,250 square miles, mostly of good tillable land, and a fertile soil, well apportioned between woodland, openings and prairie, and is well adapted to grazing, and the raising of grain, roots and fruit. There is, in the county, considerable non-resident land which can be bought on reasonable terms. One of the most attractive features of the county is its beautiful lakes of clear, pure cold water, originating in deep springs. The Catfish river forms the outlet of these lakes, and passes from the northwest to the southeast completely through the chain known as the Four Lakes. The county is connected with the second judicial circuit, the second congressional district, and constitutes the eleventh senate district. It is divided into assembly districts as follows: 1st. The towns of Dunkirk, Christiana, Pleasant Springs and Albion. 2d. The towns of Cottage Grove, Deerfield, Sun Prairie, Medina, York and Bristol. 3d. The towns of Verona, Montrose, Oregon, Greenfield, Dunn and Rutland. 4th. The towns of Perry, Primrose, Blue Mounds, Springdale, Cross Plains, Middleton, Springfield, Berry, Black Earth, Roxbury and Dane. 5th. The village and town of Madison, and the towns of Burk, Blooming Grove, Westport, Vienna and Windsor. The county is watered by the Catfish and Sugar rivers, and Black Earth, Badfish, Token, Waterloo and Koskonong creeks. The population in 1836 was Ebenezer Brigham; 1838, 172; 1840, 314; 1842, 8,289; 1847, 10,935; 1850, 16,654. Farms, 1,511; manufactories, 87; dwellings, 3,510. County Officers: County Judge, N. Bishop Eddy; Clerk of the Court, Charles Lumm; Sheriff, Willet S. Main; Register, John B. Sweat; Clerk of Board Supervisors, Gabriel Bjornsen; District Attorney, Samuel H. Roys; Treasurer, Philo Dunning; Surveyor, Russel Babbitt; Coroner, Andrew Bishop.

Darien, *P. V.*, in town of same name, Walworth county.

Darien, *Town*, in county of Walworth, being town 2 N., of range 15 E.; centrally located, 10 miles southwest from Elkhorn, the county seat. The population in 1850 was 1,013. It has 8 school districts.

DARTFORD, *P. V.*, in town of Brooklyn, the seat of justice of Marquette county, is located on the outlet of Green Lake, in the openings on section 21, town 16 N., of range 13 E.; 65 miles northeast from Madison. It contains about 400 temperate and industrious inhabitants. It is on the stage route from Milwaukee to Berlin and Plover, as also on the great western thoroughfare from Sheboygan and Fond du Lac. The climate of this vicinity is very healthy. It has 58 dwellings, 5 stores, 1 hotel, 4 mills, 5 mechanical shops, 1 church, and 3 organized religious denominations.

DAYTON, *Town*, (formerly Middletown), in county of Marquette.

DAYTON, *Town*, (formerly Embarrass), in northeast corner of the county of Waupacca. It was organized in the fall of 1852.

DAYTON, *Town*, in county of Waushara, being town 21, of range 11.

DEAD, *Lake*, in town 24 N., of range 14 W., in Chippewa county.

DEAD, *Lake*, near Madison, in Dane county.

DEATH'S, *Door*, the entrance from Lake Michigan to Green Bay, between Plum Island and the main land of Door county.

DECATUR, *P. V.*, in town of same name, in Green county.

DECATUR, *Town*, in the county of Green, being town 2 N., of range 9; centrally located, southeast from Monroe. The population in 1850 was 558. It has 7 school districts.

DEER, *Creek*, a tributary from the northwest, rises in Waushara county, entering Mechan river in town 17 N., of range 9.

DEER, *Creek*, a small stream, entering Rock river about 2 miles above Fort Atkinson.

DEERFIELD, *Town*, in conuty of Dane, being town 7 N., of range 12 E.; centrally located, 16 miles east from Madison.

DEERFIELD, *P. O.*, in Dane county, on section 9, town 7 N., of range 12 E.; 16 miles east from Madison, at Junction of Columbus and Janesville stage road with the great eastern mail route and thoroughfare from Galena to Milwaukee. It has 75 inhabitants, 13 dwellings, 2 stores, and 1 hotel; and is located in the vicinity of good timber, prairie and openings, and has excellent water. This place is well known as "Hyer's," in honor of D. R. Hyer, by whom it was settled in 1843, at which time he was the only settler within 6 miles.

DEER, *Lake*, is a small lake in the town of Harmony, Rock county.

DEKORRA, *Town*, in county of Columbia, being town 11 N., of ranges 9 and 10 E.; centrally located, 10 miles from Portage city. The population in 1850 was 661. It has 8 school districts.

DEKORRA, *P. V.*, in Columbia county, on section 6, town 11 N., of range 9 E.; 6 miles south from Portage city, and 30 miles northwest from Madison. Its location is on the east side of the Wisconsin river, at the mouth of Rocky Run creek, and has 150 inhabitants, 45 dwellings, 2 stores, 2 hotels, 1 mill, and 1 methodist church.

DEKORRA, *Mounds*, in La Crosse county, on sections 3 and 4, town 18 N., of range 7 W., near Black river.

DELAFIELD, *Town*, in county of Waukesha, being town 7 N., of range 18 E.; centrally located, 9 miles northwest from Waukesha. The population in 1850 was 1,134. It has 5 school districts.

DELAFIELD, *P. V.*, on Bark river, in town of same name in Waukesha county, on section 20. The former great western thoroughfare, from Milwaukee to Madison, passed through this place, but since the completion of the Watertown and Milwaukee plank road, which passes 2½ miles north, the village has lost, in a great degree, the activity and bustle that once characterized it. It has 2 good flouring mills, 1 machine shop, 4 stores, 3 hotels, 3 shoe shops, 3 blacksmiths, 2 cabinet and 2 waggon maker's shops.

DELAVAN, *P. V.*, in town of same name, Walworth county, being on section 18. It is the seat of the Wisconsin Deaf and Dumb Institution; has an excellent flour mill with good hydraulic power, and one of the best nurseries in the State. It is 60 miles southeast from Madison.

DELAVAN, *Town*, in Walworth county, being town 2 N., of range 16 E.; centrally located, 5 miles southeast from Elkhorn, the county seat. The population in 1850, was 1,260. It has 6 school districts.

DELAVAN, *Lake*, is in the southern part of the town of the same name. It is about three miles in length, and one in width, discharging its waters through its outlet into Turtle creek.

DELHI, *P. V.*, in Winnebago county, on section 20, town 18, of range 20. It is located on the south side of Fox river, 12 miles northwest from Oshkosh and 80 miles northeast from Madison. Population 150; 40 dwellings, 3 stores, 1 hotel, and 2 mills.

DELL, *Creek*, a considerable tributary from the west, entering the Wisconsin river in the town of New Buffalo, Sauk county.

DELL, *Creek, P. O.*, on creek of same name, in Sauk county.

DELL, *Prairie*, a large prairie near the Dells of Wisconsin.

DELLONA, *P. O.*, Sauk county, in town of the same name, near centre of town 13, of range 5 E.; 15 miles northerly from Baraboo, and 55 miles northwest from Madison. It is half-way between Reedsburg and Delton, being about 6 miles from each.

DELLONA, *Town*, in Sauk county, being town 13 N., of range 5 E., The population is about 400.

DELLS, in Chippewa river, in town 28, of range 9 W.

DELLS, in Wisconsin river, in town 15 N., of range 5 E. The river passes between rocks, 300 feet high, for 8 miles.

DELLTON, *P. V.*, in Sauk county, in town of Deltona, on section 21, town 13 N., of range 6 E.; 10 miles northerly from Baraboo, and 50 miles from Madison. It is well situated on Dell creek, one and a half miles from its mouth into the Wisconsin. It has a steamboat navigation with the Upper Mississippi, through the Wisconsin river, which is navigable to this point. It is also on the proposed route of the Milwaukee and

La Crosse railroad. It has 140 inhabitants, 34 dwellings, 2 stores, 2 hotels, 2 churches, and 7 mechanical shops.

Deltona, *Town*, in county of Sauk, being town 13 N., of range 6 E.; centrally located, northwest from Baraboo. It has 6 school districts.

Denoon, *P. V.*, Waukesha county, on the north line of Racine county, on section 32, town 5 N., of range 20 E. (Muskego), and section 5, town 4 N., of range 20 E. (Norway); 15 miles southeast from Waukesha, 25 miles northwest from Racine, and 80 miles southeast from Madison. It is located on the Milwaukee and Rochester plank road, 20 miles southwest from Milwaukee, on the east bank of Denoon lake. Population 100; 10 dwellings, 1 store, 1 hotel, several mechanical shops, and 1 Lutheran church.

Depere, *Rapids*, on the Fox river, 7 miles above Green Bay. They are improved by a dam at Depere.

Depere, *P. V.* and *C. H.*, in the county of Brown, in town 23 N., of range 21 E., 110 miles northeast from Madison. It was first settled A. D. 1672, and a small log church was built by the Jesuits. The first court house and jail in the State was erected here, also the first saw mill, which was built in 1824. It has a bridge and draw 2,500 feet long, across Fox river. It is the head of lake and foot of river navigation. It has a most beautiful and healthy location, being on both sides the river Neenah. Population 1,200; 400 dwellings, 10 stores, 4 hotels, 7 mills, 4 shingle factories, 2 extensive fisheries, yielding annually 1,500 barrels of fish; 2 churches, and 5 denominations.

Des Plaine, *River*, in Kenosha county. See O'Plaine river.

Detour, *River*, is a small stream, entering Lake Superior east of Herron river.

Detroit, *Island*, is at the connection of Green Bay and Lake Michigan, south from Pottawattame Island. It is 4 miles long and half a mile wide.

DEVIL'S, *Chimney*, so called, a natural curiosity, is situated near the village of Mount Vernon, in Dane county. It consists of a tall round arch about 20 feet in diameter and 125 feet high. The surrounding country being comparatively level.

DEVIL'S, *River*, see East river, Brown county.

DICKERMAN'S, *Creek*, rises in the south part of Nekimi, Winnebago county, and runs northeasterly into lake Winnebago.

DICKEY'SVILLE, *P.O.*, in Grant county, on section 22, town 2 N., of range 2 W., being in the town of Paris, 20 miles south from Lancaster, and 125 miles southwest from Madison, on the Galena and Mississippi stage route. Population 50, with 6 stores, 1 hotel, and 1 church.

DODGE, *County*, is bounded on the north by Marquette and Fond du Lac, on the east by Fond du Lac and Washington, on the south by Waukesha and Jefferson, and on the west by Dane and Columbia; and is 30 miles square. It was so named in honor of General Dodge, first Governor of the territory, and was set off from Brown, December 7, 1836, to which it remained attached for judicial purposes until January 13, 1840, when it was organized for county purposes, and its judicial connection changed to Jefferson. It was fully organized Jan. 20, 1844. The seat of justice is at the village of Juneau, formerly known as Dodge Centre. The surface of the country, west of Rock river, is diversified with openings, prairie, and good hay marsh; and the soil being good, it is well adapted to the raising of wheat and the summer grains, and to grazing. East of the river it is timbered with a heavy growth of maple and other hard woods, and the soil produces the grain crop with equal advantage with the other side, while it is more naturally adapted to the growth of the cultivated grasses. Near the banks of Rock river are beds of iron ore, which are successfully worked. Dodge county forms a part of the third judicial circuit, and of the third congressional district, and constitutes the twenty-second senate district. It is divided into six assembly districts, as follows: 1. Towns of Leroy, Lomyra, Williamstown and Theresa. 2. Towns of Hubbard, Hermon, Hustisford and Rubicon. 3. Towns of Emmet, Lebanon and Ashippun. 4. Towns of Elba, Lowell, Clyman, Portland and Shields. 5. Towns of Fox Lake, Trenton, Westford, Calamus and Beaver Dam. 6. Towns of Chester, Burnette and Oak Grove. It is watered by the Crawfish, Rock and Beaver Dam rivers, and their tributaries. The population in 1838 was 18; 1840, 67; 1842, 149; 1846, 7,787; 1847, 14,905; and 1850, 19,140. Dwellings, 3,561; farms, 2,338; manufactories, 30. County Officers: County Judge, S. L. Rose; Sheriff, Benj. Ferguson; Clerk of Court, J. B. Ribble; Register of Deeds, N. Juneau; Clerk of Board of Supervisors, E. Sweeney; County Treasurer, L. Merz.

DODGE CENTRE, see Juneau.

DODGE'S, *Branch*, of the Peckatonnica river, rises near Dodgeville, Iowa county, and runs southerly through the eastern portion of Iowa and Lafayette counties, entering the Peckatonnica in the southeast corner of Wyota, Lafayette county.

DODGEVILLE, *Town*, in the county of Iowa.

DODGEVILLE, *P. V.*, in town of same name, being on section 34. The village contains about 100 inhabitants, mostly miners, (English and Welsh.) There are 3 churches, 9 stores, and 1 smelting furnace. The country surrounding is well adapted to farming, and is well watered.

DOUGHERTY, *River*, rises in York, Green county, and runs southwest, entering the Peckatonnica, in the south part of the town of Argyle, Lafayette county.

DOUGLASS, *Creek*, a small branch from the north, in town 19 N., of range 5 W.

DOUGLASS, *Harbor*, on the western shore of Lake Michigan, in town 30, Door county.

DOOR, *County*, is located between Green Bay and Lake Michigan, and is bounded on the north and east by the State line of Michigan, on the south by Kewaunee, and on the west by Oconto. It was set off from Brown, February 11, 1851. It then included the present county of Kewaunee, and was attached to Manitowoc for judicial government. The county seat was established at Gibralter, on Gibralter Bay, heretofore known as Bailey's Harbor, on the west shore of Lake Michigan, in town 30 N., of range 28 E. Door county is for legislative and county purposes, in connection with Brown county. It has several small streams emptying into the Bay and into Lake Superior.

DOOR, *Creek*, Dane county, rises in Sun Prairie, and runs south, emptying into First Lake.

DOOR CREEK, *P. O.*, is on Liberty Prairie, in town of Cottage Grove, county of Dane, on section 33, town 7 N., of range 11 E. It is 11 miles east of south from Madison, and contains 1 store, 1 hotel, and methodist and presbyterian congregations.

DOTY'S, *Island*, is between the villages of Menasha and Neenah, in lake Winnebago, at its outlet. It contains about 750 acres of land, the residence of Governor Doty.

DOTY'S, *River*, a small tributary of Rock river, which it enters, in the north part of Dodge county.

DOTYVILLE, *P. V.*, in town of Forest, Fond du Lac county, on sections 13 and 14.

DOVER, *Town*, in county of Racine, being town 3 N., of range 20 E.; centrally located, 16 miles west of Racine. The population in 1850 was 840. It has 5 school districts.

DOVER, *P. V.*, on section 24, town of same name, in Iowa county, 33 miles northeast from Mineral Point, and 27 northwest from Madison. The location is near the junction of the Blue Mound and Black Earth rivers, 2 miles above the Wisconsin, at the crossing of the western thoroughfare to the pinery, and the eastern thoroughfare from Richland county. Population 100; with 20 dwellings, 2 stores, 1 hotel, 1 flouring mill, a school house, mechanics of nearly all kinds, and several religious denominations.

DUCK, *Creek*, Columbia county, rises in the northeast corner of the county, and running southwest, enters the Wisconsin about 3 miles below the Portage.

DUCK CREEK, is the outlet of Golden Lake, on the line between Waukesha and Jefferson counties, and empties into Bark river about half way between Palmyra and Fort Atkinson.

DUCK, *Lake*, Walworth county, see Como Lake.

DUCK, *River*, (or Duck Creek of Green Bay), rises in the northwest corner of the town of Kaukauna, and runs northeast parallel to the Neenah, through the Oneida Reservation, entering Green Bay a few miles below the mouth of the Neenah.

DUNDAS, *P. O.*, in Calumet county.

DUNKIRK, *Town*, in couny of Dane, being town 5 N., of range 11 E.; centrally located, 16 miles southeast from Madison. It has 7 school districts.

DUNKIRK FALLS, *Rapids*, in the Catfish river, in which the descent is 6 feet, in a distance of little over a mile.

DUNN, *Town*, in county of Dane, being town 6 N., of range 10 E.; centrally located, 8 miles southeast from Madison. The population in 1850 was 288. It has 6 school districts.

EAGLE, *Town*, in the county of Waukesha, being town 15 N., of range 17 E.; centrally located, 18 miles southwest from Waukesha. The population in 1850 was 816. It has 6 school districts.

EAGLE, *Bay*, a bay of Green Bay, about 16 miles northeast from Sturgeon Bay, extending easterly into Door county.

EAGLE, *Creek*, rises in the northwest corner of Richland county, and running southeast enters the Wisconsin, near the fourth principal meridian.

EAGLE, *Creek*, a small tributary of the Mississippi, near range line between ranges 11 and 12 east.

EAGLE, *Harbor*, western part of Eagle Bay of Green Bay, Door county.

EAGLE, *Lake*, is about a mile and a half long, near the centre of the town of Dover, in Racine county.

EAGLE, *Mills*, on Eagle creek, about two miles above its mouth.

EAGLE POINT, *Town*, in county of Portage, being all of same, west of range 5.

EAGLE, *Prairie*, a large prairie in the southwest part of town of same name, in Waukesha county, on which is located a depot of the Milwaukee and Mississippi railroad.

EAGLEVILLE, *P. O.*, in the southeast corner of the town of Eagle, on section 25, in Waukesha county.

EAST *Branch*, of the Peckatonica river. See Dodge's branch.

EAST *Branch*, of the Menomonee river of Milwaukee, which it enters from the west, in the town of Granville.

EAST FORK, *Creek*, the northeastern branch of Grant river, rises in Wingville, Grant county, and runs southwesterly, through Lancaster, into that river in Beetown.

EAST *River* (Manitoo or Devil's), Brown county, rises in the south part of the county, running parallel, on the east, to Fox river, into which it empties about two miles below the village of Green Bay.

EAST TROY, *P. V.*, Walworth county, on sections 19, 20, 29 and 30, in town of same name, 12 miles northeast from Elkhorn, and 73 miles southeast from Madison. It is a beautiful inland village, in a good farming district, 35 miles southwest from Milwaukee, and 33 miles northwest from Racine.

Population 400, with 75 dwellings, 5 stores, 2 hotels, 2 mills, several mechanical shops, a Baptist, Presbyterian and Methodist denomination.

East Troy, *Town*, in county of Walworth, being town 4 N., of range 13 E.; centrally located, 13 miles southeast from Elkhorn. The population in 1850 was 1,318. It has 7 school districts.

Eau Plaine, *P. V.*, on Wisconsin river, at Dubay's trading post at the mouth of Little O'Plaine, in northern part of Portage county.

Eden, *Town*, in the county of Fond du Lac, being town 14 N., of range 18 E.; centrally located, 10 miles southeast from Fond du Lac. The population in 1850 was 840. It has 8 school districts.

Eden, *P. O.*, in same town, Fond du Lac county.

Eight Mile, *Creek*, rises in the town of Nekimi, Winnebago county, and runs westerly into the outlet of Rush lake.

Elba, *P. O.*, in town of same name, Dodge county.

Elba, *Town*, in the county of Dodge, being town 10 N., of range 13 E.; centrally located, 12 miles southwest from Juneau. The population in 1850 was 1,548. It has 7 school districts.

El Dorado, *Town*, in the county of Fond du Lac, being town 16 N., of range 16 E.; centrally located, 7 miles northwest from Fond du Lac. The population in 1850 was 504.

El Dorado, *P. O.*, in town of same name, Fond du Lac county.

Elk, *P. O.*, in Bad Ax county.

Elk, *River*, a branch from the north, of Chippewa river, rises in town 26 N., of range 11 W.

Elkhart, *Lake* (Big), in the town of Rhine, Sheboygan county, on sections 29 and 30 of town 16 N., of range 21 E.

Elkhart, *Lake* (Little), on sections 33 and 34, of town 16, of range 21 E.

Elkhart, *P. V.*, Sheboygan county, on section 31, in the town of Rhine, town 16 N., of range 21 east, 20 miles northwest from Sheboygan.

Elkhorn, *P. V.*, and *C. H.*, Walworth county, on section 36, town 3 N., of range 13 E., at the geographical centre of the county. It is in town of same name, 65 miles southeast from Madison. Population 250, with 60 dwellings, 4 stores, 2 hotels, steam mill, various mechanical shops, and 4 religious denominations.

Elkhorn, *Town*, in county of Walworth, comprising section 1, town 2 N., of section 36 of town 3, range 16 E., and section 6, of town 2, and section 31 of town 3 N., of range 17 E. It is the county seat. The population is 600.

Ellenboro', *P. V.*, Grant county, on section 28, in the town of Highland, town 4 N., of range 2 W.; 7 miles southeast from Lancaster, and 95 miles southwest from Madison. It is located on Platte river, about half way between Platteville and Lancaster, on the mail route from Galena to the Upper Mississippi, and is in a good farming district, with excellent water power, with considerable vacant land, and unimproved hydraulic power. Population 51, 7 dwellings, 1 store, 1 hotel, 2 mills, and a blacksmith and carpenter's shop.

Ellenboro', *Town*, (recently south half of Highland), in county of Grant, being town 4 N., of range 2 W.; centrally located 8 miles southeast from Lancaster.

Ellington, *P. V.*, in county of Outagamie, on section 20, of town 22 N., of range 16 E.; 13 miles northwest from Grand Chute, 130 miles northeast from Madison. It is located on the road from Green Bay (36 miles) to Plover Portage (70 miles). It is 28 miles from Oshkosh, and 35 miles from Lake Shawanaw. Population 150, with 35 dwellings, 2 mills, 2 hotels and several religious denominations.

Ellington, *Town*, in county of Outagamie, being towns 23 and 24 N., of range 16 E.; centrally located, 20 miles northwest from Grand Chute. It has 3 school districts.

EMBARRASS, *Town*, in county of Waupacca, being towns 23, 24 and 25 N., of range 14 E.; centrally located, north from Mukwa.

EMBARRASS, *River*, see Bad or Mannaise river of La Pointe county.

EMERALD GROVE, *P. V.*, in town of Bradford, Rock county.

EMMET, *P. O.*, in town of same name, Dodge county.

EMMET, *Town*, in county of Dodge, being town 9 N., of range 15 E.; centrally located, 12 miles south from Juneau. The population in 1850 was 1,207. It has 7 school districts.

EMPIRE, *Town*, in county of Fond du Lac, being town 15 N., range 18 E.; centrally located, 6 miles southeast from Fond du Lac.

ENGLISH, *Lake*, a small lake in the northwest corner of town 18 N., of range 23 E.

ERIN, *Town*, in county of Washington, being town 9 N, of range 18 E.; centrally located, 26 miles southwest from Ozaukee. The population in 1850 was 849. It has 5 school districts.

ERVANDIGO, *River*, a tributary, from the north, of St. Croix river, in La Pointe county.

EUREKA, *P. V.*, in Winnebago county, on section 28, town 18 N., range 14 E., in town of Rushford, 16 miles west from Oshkosh, and 70 miles northeast from Madison. It is beautifully situated on the southern shore of Fox river, surrounded by a rich farming country, and possesses plenty of lime stone, sand, clay and timber, for building purposes. The settlement was first commenced in 1850. Population 70, with 14 dwellings, 2 stores, 1 hotel, 1 mill, and various mechanical shops.

EVANSVILLE, *P. V.*, on Allen's creek, section 27, town 4 N., range 10 E., in Rock county, 18 miles northwest from Janesville, and 23 miles southeast from Madison. It has a population of about 200 temperate and industrious people, with 25 dwellings, 2 stores, 1 hotel, 2 mills, 1 machine, 1 waggon, 1 shoe, and 1 blacksmith's shop; 1 meeting house, and two religious denominations, and a large and commodious school house. The Madison and Beloit railroad is located through this place.

EVERFLOWING, *River*, a tributary from the north of the St. Croix river, in the western part of La Pointe county.

EXETER, *P. V.*, Green county, on section 33 of town of same name, being town 4 N., of range 8 E., 16 miles northeast from Monroe, and 24 miles southwest from Madison. Population 105, with 22 dwellings, 2 stores, 2 hotels, and 6 religious denominations. The principal occupation of the inhabitants is mining.

EXETER, *Town*, in the county of Green, being town 4 N., of range 8; centrally located, 15 miles northeast from Monroe. The population in 1850 was 450. It has 6 school districts.

FAIRFIELD, *P. O.*, (Maxson's Mill), in town of Bradford, county of Rock, on section 13, town 2 N., of range 15 E. It is 14 miles southeast from connty seat, and 50 miles east of south from Madison. Population 100, 12 dwellings, 2 stores, 1 grist mill, and Presbyterian and Baptist denominations. It is on Turtle creek, 16 miles from Beloit, and on the county line between Rock and Walworth, 9 miles from the state line. The first settler was Joseph Maxson.

FAIRPLAY, *P. V.*, in Grant county, on section 25, in the town of Jamestown, town 1 N., of range 2 W., in a good mineral and farming district; 30 miles southeast from Lancaster, 12 miles northwest from Galena, 6 miles northeast from Dubuque, and 85 miles southwest from Madison. Population 800, with 110 dwellings, 2 stores, 2 hotels, 1 church and 3 religious denominations. A Roman Catholic college is located at this place.

FAIR PLAY, *Diggings*, on section 25, town 1 N., of range 1 W., in Grant county.

FAIRWATER, *P. V.*, Fond du Lac county, on section 31, town 15 N., of range 14 E.; being in the town of Metomon, 22 miles west from Fond du Lac, and 65 miles northeast from Madison. It is situated on the road from Watertown to Ceresco and Berlin, in a fine and healthy section, of good farming land, on the north branch of Grand river. It has two good water powers, one of which is improved by a fine flouring mill; the other is unimproved, with 28 feet head, and sufficient water for three run of stone. Population 40, 5 dwellings, 1 store, and 1 hotel.

FALLEN *Rocks*, on the Wisconsin, a few miles below Helena, in Iowa county, where the river has undermined the rocks about 200 feet long.

FALL RIVER, *P. V.*, Columbia county, in the town of Fountain Prairie, on section 26, town 11 N., of range 12; 25 miles east of southeast from Portage City, and the same distance northeast from Madison. It has an excellent water power, with a fall of 16 feet, on which is a good saw and flouring mill, being the best hydraulic power in the vicinity. Population 175, with 35 dwellings, 3 stores, 1 hotel, 2 mills, 3 religious denominations, and a good school house.

FALLS OF ST. CROIX, *P. V.*, and *C. H.*, on St. Croix river, in town 34, Polk county.

FALLS OF ST. CROIX, *Town*, in county of Polk, comprising the same.

FARMER'S GROVE, *P. O.*, in town of York, Green county, being town 4 N., of range 6 E.

FARMERSVILLE, *P. O.*, in Dodge county.

FARMINGTON, *Town*, in county of Washington, being township 12 N., of range 20 E.; centrally located, 15 miles northwest from Ozaukee. Population in 1850 was 504. It has 9 school districts.

FARMINGTON, *Town*, in county of Jefferson, being town 7 N., of range 15 E.; centrally located, 8 miles northeast from Jefferson. The population is 900. It has 6 school districts. The surface is rolling, with heavy timber and good springs, and small streams of water. The soil on the high land is mostly a clay loam, in the vallies a black, vegetable and sandy loam, with subsoil of clay. The timber is mostly maple, basswood, oak, elm, walnut, and ash.

FARMINGTON, *P. O.*, Jefferson county, on section 14 of town of same name, being town 7 N., of range 15 E.; 11 miles northeast from Jefferson, 38 miles east from Madison, midway between Milwaukee and Madison, via Aztalan and Concord.

FARWELL'S *Addition* TO MADISON, is on the northeast side of the Catfish, and is laid out into lots of an acre each, conspicuous to the business portion of the village.

FARWELL'S *Mill*, a small settlement on the Catfish river, near Madison. At this place is the best flouring mill in the State, with 8 run of stone; also a good saw mill, woollen factory, brewery, and several mechanical shops.

FAYETTE, *P. V.*, La Fayette county, on section 8, town 3 N., of range 4 E.; 18 miles northeast from Shullsburg, and 50 miles southwest from Madison, in a good mineral region. Population 100, 30 dwellings, 2 stores, 2 mills, 1 hotel, and 1 Methodist and 1 F. W. Baptist denomination.

FENNIMORE, *P. V.*, in town of same name, town 6 N., of range 2 W., Grant county.

FENNIMORE, *Town*, in county of Grant, being all south of the Wisconsin river of towns 6 and 7 N., of ranges 2, 3 and 4, and fractional town 8 N., of range 3 W. It is centrally located, 12 miles north from Lancaster. It has 9 school districts.

FENNIMORE FORK, *River*, a branch from the south of Blue river, Grant county.

FEVRE, *River*, rises near Belmont, Lafayette county, and running southerly, through Galena, into the Mississippi, 7 miles below that place.

FILLMORE, *P. V.*, in town of Farmington, Washington county, being in 12 N., of range 20 E.

FIRST, *Lake*, the lowest of the chain of Four lakes, in the towns of Dunn and Pleasant Springs, Dane county, 12 miles southeast from Madison. It has an area of five square miles.

FISH, *Lake*, a small lake in the northeast corner of Deerfield, Dane county.

FISK'S, *Corners, P. V.*, Winnebago county, on section 11, town 17 N., of range 15; it is 8 miles from Oshkosh, and 90 miles from Madison. Population 600, 100 dwellings, and 2 hotels.

FITCHBURG, *P. V.*, in town of same name, formerly Greenfield, on section 33, town 6 N., of range 9 E. It is an excellent region of farming land, 10 miles south from Madison, on stage route to Janesville. It has 1 hotel, 2 stores, a school-house, meeting-house, 3 religious denominations, 15 dwellings, and 80 inhabitants.

FITCHBURG, *Town*, Dane county, town 6, range 9 E., late Greenfield.

FLAMBEAU, *Lake*, in latitude nearly 46°, the outlet running north to nearly the state line, thence southwest into the Chippewa.

FLEMING, *Creek*, a small tributary of Black river, from the south-east, into which it empties in town 18 N., of range 6 W.

FLORA, *Town*, in county of Sauk; centrally located, north-east from Baraboo. It has 3 school districts.

FOND DU LAC, *County*, is bounded on the north by Winnebago and Calumet, on the east by Calumet and Sheboygan, on the south by Washington and Dodge, and on the west by Marquette and portions of Dodge and Winnebago. Its name is derived from its locality, being at the "end of the lake." It was established December 7, 1836, and set off from Brown, to which it remained attached until March 11, 1839, when it was organized for county purposes. The seat of justice is at the city of Fond du Lac, at the head of Lake Winnebago. This county is generally well watered with springs, brooks, and small streams of pure water. The largest streams in the western part of the county are the two branches of the Rock river; one flowing eastwardly through the towns of Alto and Waupun, and the other rising in Metomon, and flowing southwardly through Springvale and the eastern part of Waupun. There are also the two branches of Fond du Lac river (the east and west); the one rising in the town of Rosendale, and passing through a portion of Eldorado and

Lamartine, and the other (the east) rising from small streams and springs in the towns of Lamartine, Oakfield, and Byron, and passing through the town of Fond du Lac, unites with its west branch within the city, about a mile from lake Winnebago. There is also another beautiful stream, known as the Chrystal Creek, (or the Green lake inlet), passing westwardly through the town of Ceresco into Marquette county, affording, at the villages of Ripon and Ceresco, some of the best water power in the county; and also Grand river, which rises and runs southwesterly through Metomon, affording excellent water power at the village of Fairwater. In the eastern and southern portions of the county are several small lakes and numerous streams, also affording good water power. The most northerly branch of the Milwaukee river rises in a small lake in the town of Eden, within about eight miles of Winnebago lake, and flows southerly through the town of Auburn, where there are numerous water powers. Another fine stream rises in Dodge county, and flows eastwardly through the town of Ashford, and unites with the last mentioned stream near the south line of Auburn. The east branch of the Milwaukee river rises by separate branches in the towns of Empire and Forest, and flows through the town of Osceola, passing through Long Lake, and affording excellent water power at its outlet. It is worthy of remark that the lake in Eden, which gives origin to the Milwaukee river, is also the source of a small stream running northwardly into lake Winnebago, and is within a mile or so of the source of the Sheboygan river, which runs north and eastwardly through the towns of Forest and Kossuth; affording, also, more or less water power to those towns. In the northeast part of the county, in the town of Taycheedah, and within 3 miles of lake Winnebago, arises the southerly branch of Manitowoc river, which runs northeasterly through the town of Calumet into the county of that name. In addition to these, there are numerous small streams and branches of the above mentioned rivers, watering almost every portion of the county. Water powers are already improved in the city and town of Fond du Lac, in Ceresco, the village of Ripon, Metomon, Eldorado, Oakfield, Alto, Waupun, Ashford, Auburn, Osceola, Empire, and Forest. The soil of the county is somewhat diversified. The eastern and southeastern portions being mostly heavy timbered land, having a dark, rich soil in the bottoms, and fine gravelly ridges upon the swells. In the western portion, which is composed of small prairies and openings, and indeed in the whole open portion of the country, which comprises more than two-thirds of the whole area, the soil is an argillaceous loam, moderately mixed with sand and lime, resting on a thin layer of limestone much broken, and occasionally interspersed with knobs of drift gravel. Underlaying a considerable portion of the whole is a red sandstone, which occasionally outcrops in ravines. On many of the highest points of the prairies and openings, in the towns of Ceresco, Metomon, Waupun, Lamartine, Oakfield, Byron, Empire, Taycheedah, and Calumet, the limestone comes to the surface, affording the best of material for building and fencing; and in many places furnishing the most beautiful flagging stones of any thickness, from one inch to ten, of a texture nearly as fine and compact as marble. The face of the country is gently rolling, and from the quality of the soil, the county is well adapted to all the more northern productions of agriculture. The peculiar geographical position of this country, embracing nearly the southern half of Winnebago lake, which is connected with the great lakes by Fox river and Green Bay, and being within some thirty-five miles of lake Michigan, at Sheboygan, as well as the character of its soil, renders it one of the most important inland counties. Fond du Lac county forms a part of the fourth judicial circuit, and of the the third congressional district. It constitutes the twentieth senatorial district, and is divided into four assembly districts, as follows: 1st. Ceresco, Metomon, Alto, Waupun, Springvale, and Rosendale. 2d. Byron, Eden, Osceola, Ashford, and Auburn. 3d. Eldorado, Lamartine, Oakfield, Friendship, Fond du Lac, and the city of Fond du Lac. 4th. Calumet, Forest, Taycheedah, Kossuth, and Empire. The population in 1840 was 139; 1842, 295; 1846, 3,544; 1847, 7,459. Dwellings, 2,722; farms, 1,073; manufactories, 16. County Officers for 1853 and 1854: County Judge, C. M. Tompkins; Sheriff, Robert Jenkinson; Clerk of Court, John J. Driggs; Register of Deeds, Randolph Ebert; Clerk of Board of Supervisors, A. W. Paine; County Treasurer, O. S. Wright.

FOND DU LAC, *Town*, in county of same name, being town 15 N., of range 17 E. It is the seat of justice of the county. Population in 1850 was 2,016. It has 6 school districts.

FOND DU LAC, *City*, see Appendix.

FOND DU LAC, *River*, rises in Oakfield, Fond du Lac county, and runs northeast, emptying into lake Winnebago, at Fond du Lac city.

FORT ATKINSON, *P. V.*, on section 3, town 5 N., of range 14 E., Jefferson county, being in the town of Koskonong, at the junction of Bark with Rock river. It is 6 miles south of Jefferson, and 32 miles southeast from Madison. It derives its name from General Atkinson, who built a temporary fort at this place during the Black Hawk war—hence its name. Population 350, with 70 dwellings, 8 stores, 3 hotels, 1 steam saw mill, 3 tailors, 2 shoe, 3 blacksmith, 2 cooper, and 1 cabinet shops. 1 Presbyterian and 1 Methodist church.

FORT CRAWFORD, formerly a military station near Prairie du Chien, in Crawford county, about 540 miles above St. Louis.

FORT HOWARD, formerly a military station at mouth of Fox river, see Fort Howard village.

FORT HOWARD, *Village*, is situated on the west side of the Fox river, near its mouth, opposite to the old town of Green Bay. The site of the village of Fort Howard was purchased and surveyed into village lots by Joel S. Fisk and the Hon. Urial H. Peak, in the spring of 1850, since which there has been a rapid growth and settlement of the place, and it bids fair to become one of considerable commercial importance. It derived its name from being situated immediately in the vicinity of Old Fort Howard, a military post of considerable notoriety. The village contains some four or five hundred inhabitants; it has several stores, three public houses, a large foundry and machine shop which gives employment to some thirty or forty workmen; there is also in the course of erection two steam saw mills, together with shops for various mechanical purposes. The soil on which the village is located is alluvial, on a clay subsoil, and is well adapted to gardening and the growth of fruit trees and shrubs; it possesses a back country of very considerable extent, which is rapidly filling up with an intelligent, industrious and *go-a-head* population; and although the pioneer settler is under the necessity of undergoing the fatigue and labor incident to the settlement and clearing up of a heavy timbered country, yet when it is brought under a state of proper cultivation it will not be surpassed by any section of the state in fertility of soil, and all the other appendages which make a country desirable for farming purposes.

Fort Winnebago, *P. O.*, at the old military station of same name, at the Portage of Fox and Wisconsin rivers, near Portage city.

Fort Winnebago, *Town*, in county of Columbia, being town 13 N., of range 9 E. Population in 1850 was 1,642. It has 11 school districts.

Forrest, *Town*, in county of Fond du Lac, being town 15 N., of range 19 E.; centrally located, 12 miles east from Fond du Lac. The population in 1850, as then organized, was 1,218. It has 8 school districts.

Fountain, *Prairie*, is the name of a large prairie south and west of Columbus, in Columbia county.

FOUNTAIN PRAIRIE, *Town*, in county of Columbia, being 11 N., of range 12 E.; centrally located, 23 miles from Portage city. The population in 1850 was 546. It has 5 school districts. This is an excellent farming town, and has a good water power at Fall river, with a mill capable of making 500 barrels of flour per week.

FOURTH, *Lake*, adjoining and north and northwest of Madison, is the uppermost and largest of the Four Lakes. It has an area of nearly 16 square miles. Its diameter is 6 miles, and its periphery 19¾. It is also called Mendota.

FOWL, *River*, (Sand Creek), a tributary from the north of St. Croix river, in the west part of La Pointe county.

FOX, *Lake*, (Waushara), in town of same name, in northwest corner of Dodge county, is three miles long and two wide. It is of an oval form, and discharges its waters into the Crawfish river, through Beaver Dam creek.

FOX LAKE, *P. V.*, see Waushara.

FOX LAKE, *Town*, (formerly Waushara), in county of Dodge, being north half of town 12, and town 13 N., range of 13 E.; centrally located, 14 miles northwest from Juneau. The population in 1850 was 856. It has 6 school districts.

FOX, *River*, of Illinois, (Pishtaka), rises in the north part of Waukesha county, and running south through the counties of Waukesha, Racine, and Kenosha, into the State of Illinois, discharges its waters into the Illinois river at Ottawa, Lasalle county.

FOX, *River*, of Green Bay, (Neenah), rises near the middle of the town of Randolph, being in the northeast corner township of Columbia county, runs southwesterly to the Portage, where its course is turned to the northeast, passing through extensive marshes, covered with wild rice. It enters on the west side of Lake Winnebago, at Oshkosh, and forms the outlet of the same lake, which it leaves on either side of Doty's island,

Menasha on the north, and Neenah on the south. Below the lake it has a succession of rapids as far down as Depere, 7 miles above its outlet, into Green Bay.

FRANKLIN, *Town*, in county of Milwaukee, being town 5 N., of range 21 E.; centrally located, 12 miles southwest from Milwaukee. The population in 1850 was 1,246. It has nine school districts.

FRANKLIN, *P. V.*, Milwaukee county, in town of same name, on section 7, town 5 N., of range 21 E., 12 miles southwest from Milwaukee, and 80 miles east from Madison. It is beautifully located, 2 miles south of the Milwaukee and Janesville plank road, and three miles northeast from Muskego lake. Population 60; with 17 dwellings, 2 stores, and 2 hotels.

FREDONIA, *Town*, in county of Washington, being town 12 N., of range 21 E.; centrally located, 9 miles northwest from Ozaukee. The population in 1850 was 672. It has 9 school districts.

FREDONIA, *P. O.*, in county of Washington, being town 12 N., of range 21 E.; centrally located, 9 miles northwest from Ozaukee.

FREEDOM, *Town*, in county of Outagamie, being all of said county, not included in the Oneida Reservation, in towns 22 and 23 N., of range 18 and 19 E; centrally located, 15 miles northeast from Grand Chute. It has two school districts.

FREEDOM, *Town*, in county of Sauk, located west from Baraboo. It has 5 school districts.

FREMONT, *P. V.*, in Waupacca county, being on section 25, town 21 N., of range 13 E.; it is 11 miles southwest from Mukwa. Population 50; 12 dwellings, 2 stores, and 1 hotel. It is situated on the left bank of the Wolf river; is a steam boat landing, and the only feasible crossing on the river in the route from Menasha to Plover Portage.

FRENCH, *Creek*, in Columbia county, a small tributary of the Fox or Neenah river, from the east, in Port Hope.

FRENCH, *Creek*, a branch from the east of Little Platte river, in the towns of Paris and Smeltzer.

FRIENDSHIP, *Town*, in county of Fond du Lac, being town 16 N., of range 17 E. The population is 415. It has 5 school districts.

FRIENDSHIP, *Town*, in county of Fond du Lac, being town 16 N., of range 17 E; centrally located, 6 miles north from Fond du Lac city.

FULTON, *P. V.*, in town of same name, Rock county, on section 7, town 4 N., of range 12 E.

FULTON, *Town*, in county of Rock, being town 4 N., of range 12 E.; centrally located, 10 miles north from Janesville. The population in 1850 was 1828. It has 7 school districts.

GARLICK, *Island*, in Lake Winnebago, near its west shore.

GAUCHE, *River*, enters Fond du Lac Bay, (Lake Superior,) near St. Louis river, in La Pointe county.

GENESEE, *Town*, in county of Waukesha, being town 6 N., of range 18 E.; centrally located, 8 miles from Waukesha, the county seat. The population in 1850 was 1,290. It has 9 school districts.

GENESEE, *P. V.*, Waukesha county, in town of same name, being town 6 N., of range 18 E., 8 miles west southwest from Waukesha, and 66 miles east from Madison. It is one mile south of the depot on the M. & M. R. R. It has 160 inhabitants, 30 dwellings, 1 store, 1 hotel, 1 new congregational church, 1 flouring mill, 1 saw mill, 1 woollen factory. It is beautifully situated on White creek, which falls 76 feet in one mile, and is used for three separate powers of 20, 22 and 22 feet each.

GENESEE, *Farm*, residence of the Hon. E. W. Edgerton, in town of Summit, Waukesha.

GENESEE, *Lake*, forms the head waters of Battle creek, and is located one mile south of the centre of the town of Summit, Waukesha county.

GENEVA, *Town*, in county of Walworth, being town 2 N., of range 17 E.; centrally located, 5 miles southeast from Elkhorn. The population in 1850 was 1533. It has 8 school districts.

GENEVA, *P. V.*, in town of same name, in Walworth county, being on sectian 36, at the northeast extremity of Lake Geneva.

GENEVA BAY, *P. O.*, in town of Geneva, Walworth county.

GENEVA, *Creek*, has its source in Geneva Lake, Walworth county, and running northeasterly enters Peckatonnica at Burlington, Racine county.

GENEVA, *Lake*, is in the southern part of Walworth county, 8 miles long, with a mean breadth of 1 mile. It is supplied mostly from springs, and discharges its waters into the Pishtaka river, through Geneva creek.

GENOA, *P. V.*, in town of Geneva, Walworth county, being town 2 N., of range 17 E.

GENTHER'S, *Creek*, a branch from the north of Chippewa river, Chippewa county.

GERMANTOWN, *Town*, in county of Washington, being town 9 N.; of range 20 E.; centrally located, 18 miles south west from Ozaukee, the county seat. The population in 1850 was 1,722. It has 10 school districts.

GIBBSVILLE, *P. O.*, in Sheboygan county, on section 26, town 14 N., of range 22 E.; 9 miles southwest from Sheboygan, and 100 miles northeast from Madison. It is on the road from Milwaukee, 50 miles; to Green Bay, 65 miles. It was first settled by three brothers, whose name it bears, in 1836.

GIBRALTER, *Creek*, a small stream entering Green Bay, in the northeast corner of Brown county.

GIBSON, *Creek*, is a small tributary from the north of Baraboo river, which it enters three miles above Baraboo village.

GILBERT'S MILLS, on Red Cedar river, in Chippewa county, town 28 N., of range 13 W.

GOLDEN, *Lake*, is on the line between Jefferson and Waukesha counties, 3 miles in circumference, and discharges its waters through Duck creek into Bark river.

GOOD HOPE, *P. V.*, in county of Milwaukee, on section 8, town 8 N., of range 22 E.

GRAFTON, *P. V.*, in town of same name, county of Washington.

GRAFTON, *Town*, in county of Washington, being town 10 N., of range 22 E., and east tier of sections of town 10 N., range 21 E.; centrally located, 6 miles southwest from Ozaukee. The population in 1850 was 626. It has 6 school districts.

GRAND ROCHE-A-GRIS, *Creek*, empties into the Wisconsin in range 5 N., Crawford county.

GRAND CHUTE, *Town*, in county of Outagamie, being town 21 N., of range 17 E.; centrally located, 3 miles northwest from Grand Chute, the county seat. It has 6 school districts.

GRAND CHUTE, *Rapids*, of the Neenah river, 7 miles below Winnebago Rapids, with a fall of 30 in 8525 feet.

GRAND KAKALIN, *Rapids*, of Neenah river, with a fall of 44 feet in a distance less than 9,000 feet. These rapids are 9 miles below Grand Chute.

GRAND MARSH, *P. O.*, in Columbia county.

GRAND PRAIRIE, *P. O.*, in town of Middleton, Marquette county, being on section 35, in town 15 N., of range 12 E.

GRAND, *Rapids*, are shoals of the Menominee river, about 2 miles in length, below White Rapids.

GRAND, *Rapids*, town in county of Portage.

GRAND RAPIDS, *P. V.*, in county of Portage, being on section 17, town 22 N., of range 6, in town of same name. It is 16 miles southwest from Plover, county seat, and 115 miles northwest from Madison. Population 400; 30 dwellings, 3 stores, 3 hotels, 4 saw mills, 1 Catholic church. It possesses the best water power in the State, abounding with springs of pure soft water. Lumber and shingles have been the chief products, although some attention has been paid to farming. There is plenty of government land in the vicinity, and timber enough to last for years. Iron ore is found. Most of the buildings have been erected within two years.

Grand, *River*, rises in the western portion of Fond du Lac county, and running near the line between towns 14 and 15 N., enters the Neenah about a mile above the head of Apuckaway lake.

Grand Springs, name given to large springs in Montrose, Dane county, emptying into Sugar river.

Grand Springs, *P. V.*, in Dane county, on section 25, town 5 N., of range 8 E.; 16 miles southwest from Madison. Its general location and advantages are good, being on the outlet of large springs emptying into Sugar river, and in a good farming region. It has 109 inhabitants, 25 dwellings, 1 store, 1 hotel, 1 mill, 1 manufactory, and 1 religious denomination.

Grant, *County*, is bounded on the northwest and north by the Wisconsin river, which separates it from Crawford and Richland, on the east by Iowa and Lafayette, on the south by the northern line of the State of Illinois, and on the southwest by the State of Iowa, from which it is separated by the Mississippi river. It was set off from Iowa, and fully organized by an act approved Dec. 7, 1836. The eastern boundary extends north, on the 4th principal meridian, about 50 miles. The southern boundary on Illinois river is only about 10 miles, and its river coast is about 100 miles in length. The seat of justice is at Lancaster, near the centre of the county. Its principal streams are Grant, Big and Little Platte, Greene and Blue rivers. The surface of the country consists of a series of ridges, high rolling prairie and timbered lands. The ridges are filled with fissures, which are abundantly supplied with ores of zinc, lead, and occasionally copper. It is one of the best mineral counties in the State, and there is no other in which the soil is better adapted to the raising of wheat and corn. The county is well supplied with timber, and has many fine streams abounding in springs of pure water. It is said that there is neither lake, swamp, nor stagnant pool of water in the county. It is attached to the fifth judicial circuit, and to the second congressional district, and constitutes the 16th senate district, and sends five members to the assembly, as follows: 1. Towns of Hazel Green, Jamestown and Smeltzer. 2. Towns of Paris, Ptosi and Harrington. 3. Towns of Platteville, Lima, Clifton, Muscoda and Wingville. 4. Towns of Fennimore, Ellenboro', Liberty and Lancaster. 5. Towns of Waterloo, Beetown, Patchgrove and Cassville. The population in 1838 was 2,763; 1840, 3,926; 1842, 5,937; 1846, 12,034; 1847, 14,016; 1850, 16,169; 2861 dwellings, 707 farms, 78 manufactories. County Officers for 1853 and 1854: Judge, Cyrus K. Lord; Clerk of Court, A. W. Kendall; District Attorney, J. Allen Barber; Register, George H. Cox; Clerk of Board of Supervisors, Wood A. Beach.

GRANT, *Diggings*, a mining settlement, on section 15, town 4 N., of range 4 W., in county of Grant.

GRANT, *River*, waters the central portion of Grant county, and enters the Mississippi in the southwest corner of the town of Potosi.

GRANVILLE, *P. O.*, in town of same name, Milwaukee county.

GRANVILLE, *Town*, in county of Milwaukee, being town 8 N., of range 21 E.; centrally located, 12 miles northwest from Milwaukee. The population in 1850 was 1,739. It has 9 school districts.

GRASS, *Lake*, in Columbia county, a small lake in town 12 N., of range 8 E.; between Baraboo and Wisconsin rivers, 5 miles west from Portage.

GRATIOT, *Town*, in county of Lafayette. Over 7,000 acres of land were sold in this town during the year 1852. No discoveries of mineral have been made in this town, except *float*. The inhabitants are mostly farmers.

GRATIOT, *P. V.*, in Lafayette county, in town of the same name, on section 9, town 1 N., of range 4 E.; 12 miles east from Shullsburg, 28 from Galena, 28 from Mineral Point, and 65 southwest from Madison. Population 50; 10 dwellings, 1 store, 1 hotel, and 1 schoolhouse.

GREAT BUTTE DES MORTS, *Lake*, is an expansion of the Neenah river, just below the mouth of the Wolf, and 5 miles west of Oshkosh. It is four miles long and two wide.

GREEN, *Bay*, is an arm of Lake Michigan, from its northwest extremity, extending southwest 120 miles, having a coast of 320 miles in length, and being from 6 to 30 miles wide. Its mean length is 100 miles, breadth 20 miles, and depth 50 feet, with an area of 2,000 square miles, at an elevation of 518 feet above the Atlantic Ocean. Green Bay was so called from the fact that voyagers, upon leaving Mackinaw in the early spring before the trees put forth their buds, found the borders of this Bay covered with the finest verdure and vegetation. It was called the Bay of Puans, by the early French, and has also been called Menominee Bay.

GREEN BAY, *P. V.* The village of Green Bay is an incorporated borough, comprising the town plats of both Navarino and Astor, the former being designated in the act of incorporation as the north, and the latter as the south wards. The town stands in the junction of the Fox and East rivers, on the east bank of the former, and about one mile above the mouth or entrance into Green Bay. The site of the town, although partly low and flat, is handsome and pleasant; the soil is alluvial, with large proportion of sand, which forms dry streets and walks, and proves most excellent for garden and cultivation. The present population of Green Bay proper is about 2,000, and is constantly increasing. The town is laid out with streets and alleys running at right angles. The corporation embraces a tract about one and a half miles in length on Fox river, and about one mile in width from east to west. The buildings are of wood, mostly frame, and many of them very neat and commodious as dwellings, stores, warehouses, offices, &c. The streets are generally of good width, and the lots larger than usually laid out in villages. Directly opposite, on the west shore of Fox river, stands Old Fort Howard, and the new and flourishing town of that name, lately laid out, and now containing a large number of houses, stores and inhabitants. The scenery around Green Bay and on the Fox river, is beautiful; the climate unsurpassed by any in the West for salubrity and healthfulness. It is even, and not subject to sudden change, as in many parts of the United States; and all kinds of fruits and vegetables capable of culture in the eastern, or northern or western States, are easily raised here, and most of them in great perfection and abundance. The bay and river abound with a vast variety of the finny tribe, of delicious and palatable flavor, and wild duck and other game are abundant. The winter season may be said to commence about the first of December, and continues with but slight change or variation, until about the middle or latter part of March. The Fox river is navigable, for six miles from its mouth, to Depere, for the largest class of steamers and vessels navigating the lakes. Its medium width between the two points mentioned is about 1,400 feet. The harbor at Green Bay is one of the most spacious and secure on the whole chain of lakes, and, as a *natural* one, it is next to Detroit. The geographical position of this place, situated as it is at the head of steamboat navigation on the lakes and upon the Fox river, connecting with the Wisconsin and Mississippi by canal, must necessarily be a commanding one—and it only requires the completion of the public work for the improvement of the Fox and Wisconsin river, to insure its permanent prosperity and future importance as a commercial and manufacturing depot. The principal articles of export from Green Bay and the surrounding country at the present time, are fish, lumber, shingles, and furs and peltries. An estimate of the amount of each of these articles is made below. The water power on the Fox river is equal to, if it does not surpass, any other in the West. It is a natural one, of great magnitude; but when the improvement, or public works, are completed, it will be unlimited in power and extent.

GREEN BAY, *Pinery*, under this name is given the amount of lumber manufactured at the several mills on Green Bay and its tributaries, which is shown by the following estimate: Depere, 2,500,000; Green Bay, 2,500,000; Duck Creek, 1,500,000; Hill Creek, 500,000; Little Suamico, 500,000; Pensankee, 2,000,000; Oconto, 4,500,000; Oconto Falls, 6,000,000; Pishtego, 3,000,000; Menominee, 5,000,000; making a total of 28,000,000. This statement is exclusive of shingles, &c. There was computed to be in store, at Green Bay alone, on the 15th of March, 1853, 14,000,000 feet of lumber logs and timber.

GREEN BUSH, *P. V.*, in county of Sheboygan, being on section 11, in town of same name 15 N., of range 20 E.

GREEN BUSH, *Town*, in county of Sheboygan, being towns 15 and 16, of range 20 E.; centrally located, northwest from Sheboygan. It has 8 school districts.

GREEN, *County*, is bounded on the north by Dane, on the east by Rock, on the south by the State line, and on the west by Iowa and Lafayette, and is 4 townships, or 24 miles square. It wat set off from Iowa, Dec. 7, 1836, to which it remained attached until Jan. 15, 1838, when it was fully organized. The seat of justice is at Monroe, about 7 miles south from the centre of the county. The soil in the northern part is generally a sandy loam, and in the south mostly prairie, with a subsoil of clay, and is very productive, being adapted to all the purposes of tillage and grazing. It is well watered by the Peckatonnica and Sugar rivers and their branches, and is well apportioned between meadow, prairie and timbered lands. This county comprises the twenty-fourth senate district, and sends one member to the assembly. It is connected with the first judicial circuit and to the second congressional district. The mineral region extends east nearly through this county, and several valuable lodes are being worked. The population in 1840 was 933; 1842, 1,594; 1846, 4,758; 1847, 6,487; 1850, 8,583. Dwellings, 1,487; farms, 805; manufactories, 46. County Officers for 1853 and 1854: County Judge, John A. Brigham; Sheriff, John Moore; Clerk of Court, Noah Phelps; District Attorney, E. T. Gardiner; Register of Deeds, James L. Powell; Clerk of Board of Supervisors, Horace B. Poyer; County Treasurer, Francis Emmerson.

GREENFIELD, *P. V.*, in town of same name, Milwaukee county, town 6 N., of range 21 E.

GREENFIELD, *Town*, in county of Milwaukee, being town 6 N., of range 21 E.; centrally located, 7 miles southwest from Milwaukee. The population in 1850 was 1,894. It has 15 school districts.

GREENFIELD, *Town*, in county of Dane, (name changed to Fitchburg,) being town 6 N., of range 9 E.; centrally located, 10 miles southwest from Madison. The population in 1850 was was 598. It has 8 school districts.

GREEN, *Island*, near the middle of Green Bay, opposite the mouth of Menominee river.

GREEN LAKE, *P. O.*, in town of same name, Marquette county, being on section 4, in town 15 N., of range 13 E., 18 miles east from Montello.

GREEN LAKE, *Town*, in county of Marquette. It has 8 school districts.

GREEN, *Lake*, Marquette county, is east of Lake Apuckawa. It is eight miles long and two broad, and discharges its waters into the Fox River. It is very deep, and its waters remarkably pure and clear.

GREEN, *River*, rises in town 6, of range 3 W., and runs northeast, emptying into the Wisconsin.

GREENVILLE, *P. V.*, in town of same name, Outagamie county.

GREENVILLE, *Town*, in county of Outagamie. It has 2 school districts.

GREEN WOOD, *P. O.*, in Marquette county.

GRIGNON'S *Mills*, on the Wisconsin river, in the west part of town 22, of range 6 E., in Portage county.

GROVE, *P. O.*, in town of Lafayette, Walworth county.

GROVELAND, *P. V.*, in Winnebago county, on section 1, town 19 N., of range 16 E. It is 10 miles northwest from Oshkosh, on the town line road, and 5 miles from Neenah, with roads leading from Hortonville, Ball Prairie, Winneconna, and Appleton. It has 5 dwellings, and 1 hotel.

HALFWAY, *Creek*, a small stream in La Crosse county, entering the old channel of Black river, about half way between Black river and the present outlet.

HALFWAY, *Creek*, a small branch of Black Earth creek, from the northeast rising in Berry, Dane county.

HALL'S *Creek*, empties into the Kickapoo from the west, in town 9, Crawford county.

HAMPDEN, *Town*, in county of Columbia, being town 10 N., of range 11; centrally located, 20 miles southeast from Portage. The population in 1850 was 489. It has 4 school districts.

HANCHETVILLE, *P. V.*, in town of Medina, Dane county, town 8 N., of range 12 E.

HARDEN, *Town*, (formerly Albany,) in county of Marquette. It has 6 school districts.

HARDSCRABBLE, *Diggings*, a mining settlement on the line between Grant and Lafayette counties.

HARMONY, *Town*, in county of Rock, being town 3 N., of range 13 E.; centrally located, 5 miles southeast from Janesville. The population in 1850 was 840. It has 5 school districts.

HARRISON, *Town*, in county of Grant, being town 3 N., of range 2 W.; centrally located, 10 miles southeast from Lancaster. It has 8 school districts.

HARRISVILLE, *P. O.*, Marquette county, on section 14, town 16 N., of range 9 E., 20 miles west from Dartford, on the Montello river, and 50 miles north from Madison. It has a good mill power and is well located for a village, in a good farming country of land.

HARTFORD, *Town*, in county of Washington, being town 10 N., of range 18 E.; centrally located, 24 miles southwest from Ozaukee. The population in 1850 was 1,078. It has 9 school districts.

HARTLAND, *P. V.*, Waukesha county, on section 3, town 7 N., of range 18 E., being in the town of Delafield, 10 miles northwest from Waukesha, and 60 miles east from Madison. Population 175, with 30 dwellings, 3 stores, 3 hotels, 1 flouring mill, a large and commodious school house. This place is situated on the Milwaukee, Watertown and Madison plank road, at the crossing of Bark river.

HAT, *Island*, about 4 miles southeast from Chamber's Island, in Green Bay, near the eastern shore, in town 30 N., of range 26 E.

HAY, *River*, a large tributary of Chippewa river from the northwest, empties in town 20 N., of range 12.

HAY, *Creek*, is a small tributary from the north of the Baraboo, which it enters at Reedsburgh, Sauk county.

HAZLE GREEN, *Town*, in county of Grant, being town 1 N., of range 1 W.; centrally located, 18 miles southeast from Lancaster. It has 5 school districts.

HAZLE GREEN, *P. V.*, Grant county, on sections 24 and 25, town 1 N., of range 1 W., 32 miles east of south from Lancaster, and 80 miles southwest from Madison, on the mail route to Galena, from which place it is 10 miles north. It has 750 inhabitants, 100 dwellings, 7 stores, 3 hotels, 1 mill, 5 blacksmith, 3 waggon, 2 cooper, 3 tailor, 2 shoemaker, and 2 butcher shops; 2 drug stores and 2 physicians; 3 carpenters, and 1 cabinet maker; 1 Presbyterian, 1 Catholic, 1 Baptist, and 1 Methodist church.

HEART, *Lake*, is at the head of a small stream entering the east end of Lake Apuckawa, in town of Middleton, Marquette county.

HEART PRAIRIE, *P. V.*, in town of Lagrange, Walworth county, being on section 27, in town 4 N., of range 16 E.

HEBRON, *Town*, in county of Jefferson, being town 6 N., of range 15 E.; centrally located, 6 miles east from Jefferson. The population in 1850 was 640. It has 6 school districts.

HELENA, *Village*, in town of Arena, Iowa county, town 8 N., of range 4 E.

HELLENVILLE, *P. O.*, on section 23, in town of Hebron, town 6 N., of range 15 E., Jefferson county. It is 6 miles east from Jefferson C. H., and 41 miles southeast from Madison. It has 1 store, 1 hotel, 1 Lutheran church, and 2 saw mills.

HERMAN, *Town*, in county of Sheboygan, being town 16 N., of range 22 E.; centrally located, northwest from Sheboygan. It has 5 school districts.

HERMAN, *Town*, in county of Dodge, being town 11 N., range 17 E.; centrally located, 12 miles northeast from Juneau. It has 5 school districts.

HERMON, *P. O.*, in town of same name, Dodge county.

HERRON, *River*, enters Lake Superior, at Bark Pointe.

HIGHLAND, *Town*, in county of Iowa, being parts of townships 6 and 7 N., of ranges 1 and 2 E.; centrally located, 15 miles northwest from Mineral Point. It has 7 school districts.

HIGHLAND (recently) *Town*, in county of Grant, being townships 4 and 5 N., of ranges 2 W.; divided by Board of Supervisors in 1852, by the erection of the towns of Liberty and Ellenboro'.

HIGHLAND, *P. V.*, in town of same name, in Iowa county, containing 400 inhabitants, 6 stores, 2 smelting furnaces, 3 hotels, and 1 church. Blue river runs through the southern part of the town.

HINGHAM, *P. V.*, in county of Sheboygan, being on section 26, in town of Lima, 14 N., of range 22 E.

HOADLEY, *P. O.*, in the county of Racine.

HOLLAND, *Town*, in county of Sheboygan, being town 13 N., of range 22 E.; centrally located, 15 miles southwest from Sheboygan. It has 7 school districts.

HOLMES' *Landing*, near the mouth of Eagle creek, in La Crosse county.

HONEY CREEK, *P. V.*, in town of Spring Prairie, Walworth county, being in town 3 N., of range 18 E.

HONEY CREEK, *Town*, in county of Sauk, being parts of towns 9 and 10 N., of ranges 3, 4 and 5; centrally located, southwest from Baraboo.

HONEY, *Creek*, rises near Monroe, Green county, and runs southwest into the Peckatonnica, Green county.

HONEY, *Creek*, has its source in several small lakes in the town of Lagrange, Walworth county, and running southeast, unites with Sugar Creek at Vienna, in the town of Sugar Prairie.

HONEY, *Creek*, rises in town 10 N., in the western part of Sauk county, and running eastwardly unites with Otter creek, and enters the Wisconsin about 6 miles below Prairie du Sac.

HOOSICK, *P. O.*, Green county, in southeast corner of the town of Albany, town 3 N., range 9 E., on section 36. It is 14 miles northeast from Madison, and 30 miles south from Madison.

HOOZIER GROVE, *P. O.*, in Green county.

HOPE, *Lake*, is a small lake about half a mile in diameter, on the town line between Lake Mills and Oakland. Its waters are discharged with those of Ripley lake, into lake Koskonong.

HORICON, *Lake*, is a lake in Dodge and Fond du Lac counties, in ranges 15 and 16 E., formed by a dam across Rock river, at Horicon, at the lower point of Winnebago marsh. It is 16 miles long, and about 6 miles wide.

HORICON, *P. O.*, in town of Hubbard, Dodge county, on section 6, town 11 N., of range 16 E., at outlet of lake of same name, on Rock river, possessing good water power.

HORSE-SHOE, *Island*, in Eagle harbor, Green Bay.

HORTONIA, *Town*, in county of Outagamie, being 22 N., of ranges 15 and 16 E., 16 miles northwest from Grand Chute. It has 3 school districts.

HOWARD'S GROVE, *P. V.*, in county of Sheboygan, being on section 24, in town of Hermann, 16 N., of range 22 E.

HOWARD, *P. O.*, in town of Pewaukie, Waukesha, 6 miles northwest from Waukesha, on the mail route to Delafield from Milwaukee.

HUBBARD, *Town*, in county of Dodge, being town 11 N., of range 16 E.; centrally located, 6 miles east from Juneau. It has 7 school districts.

HUBBLETON, *P. V.*, in town of Milford, Jefferson county, on the Crawfish river, at the crossing of the M. W. & M. plank road.

HUDSON, *Town*, in county of Walworth, being town 2 N., of range 18 E.; centrally located, east from Elkhorn. The population in 1850 was 1,273. It has 7 school districts.

HUDSON, *P. V. & C. H.*, (formerly Willow River,) in county of St. Croix, on section 24 and 25, town 29 N., of range 20 W., of the fourth principal meridian. It is 200 miles northwest from Madison. Population 500; 94 dwellings, 6 stores, 4 hotels, 2 churches, 4 denominations; 2 shoe, 1 harness, 3 blacksmith, 11 carpenter, 2 cabinet maker, 2 turner, and 2 tailor shops. It is beautifully located on an eminence gradually rising from the eastern bank of Lake St. Croix, surrounded by a farming country second to none in the Northwest, and is eligibly situated to command the lumbering interests of the St. Croix. In the winter season it is the only thoroughfare and mail route between Galena and Minnesota. It is rapidly increasing in population and wealth. It has in its vicinity 4 saw mills and 2 grist mills. The U. S. Land Office for the Chippewa district is located at this place.

HUDSON, *Town*, in St. Croix county, see Willow River, its former name.

HUGHLANS' *Creek*, a branch from the east of Little Platte river, in Smeltzer, Grant county.

HUMES' *Rapids*, on Rock river, 16 miles north of State line of Illinois; is about one and a half miles in length, with a descent of 7 feet.

HURD'S *Mills*, a small stream entering Red Cedar river, in Chippewa county, in town 28 N., of range 13.

HURD'S *Mills*, (see Okauchee.)

HURRICANE GROVE, *P. O.*, in town of Lancaster, on section 36, Grant county, town 4 N., of range 3 W.

HURRICANE, *Neighborhood*, embraced in parts of Lancaster, Beetown and Waterloo, contains the heaviest growth of timber in the State. The timber region took its name from a tornado or hurricane of wind that once swept over and prostrated most of the timber, perhaps 75 or 100 years ago. As we have only tradition and decayed logs for testimony, nothing very particular is known of the extent or time of the storm. The present size of the trees, and quantity standing upon the ground indicate, however, that the hurricane took place before the generation of timber now occupying the country had more than fairly germinated. There are large quantities of walnut, basswood, red and white oak, and maple trees of large size. The soil of this timber region differs from most any in Wisconsin. It resembles most the black limestone soil of Pennsylvania and New York; but in many places is of lighter quality, and is always deeper before coming to the clay. Its productiveness is absolutely astonishing—yielding under good cultivation an hundred bushels corn to the acre. The only complaint is the work required in clearing the ground of the wood, which many prefer to do rather than settle on prairie land. The Hurricane will be a rich settlement in a few years.

HUSTISFORD, *Town*, in county of Dodge, being in town 10 N., of range 16 E.; centrally located, 8 miles southeast of Juneau. It has 8 school districts.

HUSTISFORD, *P. V.*, in Dodge county, on section 9, town 10 N., of range 16 E. It is 8 miles southeast from Juneau, and 60 miles northeast from Madison. It is situated on Rock river, on the route of the Milwaukee and La Crosse railroad. Population 75; 12 dwellings, 2 stores, 1 hotel, 2 mills, and 1 Methodist denomination.

HUSTIS' *Rapids*, on Rock river, in Dodge county, three-fourths of a mile in length, in which distance is a descent of about 7 feet.

HYLAND'S *Prairie*, is in the town of Burnette, Dodge county.

INDIA, *P. O.*, in county of Green, being on section 2, town 1 N., of range 8 E.

INMANSVILLE, *P. V.*, in town of Newark, Rock county, a Norwegian village, on town 1 N., of range 11 E. The only Norwewegian paper in the State is printed in this village.

IOWA, *County*, is bounded on the north by Richland and Sauk, on the east by Dane and a portion of Green, on the south by Lafayette, and on the west by Grant. It was formed from Crawford by an act of the legislative assembly of Michigan October 9, 1829, at which time it included all of the present State of Wisconsin, south of the Wisconsin river, and west of "a line drawn due north from the northern boundary of Illinois, through the middle of the Portage between the Fox and

Wisconsin rivers." On the 6th September, 1834, the southern boundary of Iowa county was changed to the line between the Green Bay and Wisconsin land districts, which was a north and south line from the northern boundary of Illinois along the range of township line next west of Fort Winnebago, to the Wisconsin river, on the range line between ranges 8 and 9. The seat of justice is at Mineral Point. It is watered by branches of the Peckatonnica river, Blue river, and Mineral and Pipe creeks. The county contains about 750 square miles, and is eminently a mining county, but is also equally valuable for its agricultural resources. The soil is not surpassed in fertility by any in the State. Prairie and timber land in about equal proportions. The wheat or corn crop along the Wisconsin river never fails. The population is composed of Americans, Germans, English, Welsh, and Irish. The whole northern portion of the county, to a distance of eight or ten miles from the Wisconsin river, is peculiarly an agricultural country, and unsurpassed for stock raising. South from this, the mineral region extends in every direction, over prairie and woodland. The central and southern portion of the county is a mining country, but none the less adapted to farming—for its rich soil and abundant water render any part of it attractive. Prairie and timber alternately predominate. Streams of water meander through every ravine, furnishing not only irrigation for the land but a large quantity of water power. The ague and fevers of the West are unknown here. The advantages of this county are briefly, health, mineral wealth, agricultural resources, and abundant water power. The railroad to State line and connection with Chicago will give the settlers here a constant market. This county is connected with the fifth judicial circuit, the second congressional district, and, with Richland, forms the fifteenth senate district. It is divided into two assembly districts: 1. Towns of Highland, Dodgeville, Ridgway, Arena, Wyoming, Pulaski, and Clyde. 2. Towns of Mineral Point,

Mifflin, Lyndon and Waldwick. The population in 1830 was 1,589; 1836, 3,218; 1838, 5,234; 1840, 3,978; 1842, 5,029; including Richland—1846, 14,905; 1847, 7,963; 1850, 10,479. County Officers for 1853 and 1854: County Judge, Parley Eaton; Sheriff, H. N. Mumford; Clerk of Court, James Hutchinson; Clerk of Board of Supervisors, James B. Gray; Register of Deeds, N. B. Boyden; County Treasurer, John B. Uren; District Attorney, Amasa Cobb; County Surveyor, Henry Madden.

Iron Ridge, *P. V.*, in town of Hubbard, on section 13, town 11 N., of range 16 E., of Dodge county, 8 miles east from Juneau, and 50 miles northeast from Madison. It was first settled in 1849, and is on the Milwaukee and Mayville plank road, in a good farming region of land, with abundance of water, and an inexhaustible bed of the best quality of iron, occupying about 80 acres of surface, and from 10 to 50 feet deep. Population 60; with 15 dwellings, 1 store, 1 hotel, 1 mill, 2 asheries, 1 pearl-house and saleratus manufactory.

Iron, *River*, a tributary of Lake Superior, in La Pointe county, east of Bois Brule river.

Island, *Lake*, in town of Dunn, Dane county, on section 27, town 6 N., of range 10 E.

Ives' Grove, *P. O.*, in Racine county.

Ixonia, *P. O.*, in town of same name, Jefferson county, on section 30, town 8 N., of range 16 E., known as Piperville, on Rock river, 6 miles above Watertown.

Ixonia, *Town*, in county of Jefferson, being town 8 N., of range 16 E.; centrally located, 14 miles northeast from Jefferson. The population in 1850 was 1,113. It has 11 school districts.

Jackson, *Town*, in county of Washington, being town 10 N., of range 20 E.; centrally located, 15 miles southwest from Ozaukee. The population in 1850 was 1,038. It has 10 school districts.

JAMESTOWN, *Town*, in county of Grant, being fractional town 1 N., of range 2 W.; centrally located, 20 miles southwest from Lancaster. It has 3 school districts.

JAMESTOWN, *P. V.*, Grant county, on section 1 of town of same name, 26 miles south from Lancaster, and 85 miles southwest from Madison, is in a healthy location, on the head waters of the Menominee creek. It has a population of 100; with 25 dwellings, 1 store, 1 hotel, 1 good public school, 2 religious denominations, a lodge of I. O. O. F., and a division of Sons of Temperance.

JANESVILLE, *City*, see Appendix.

JANESVILLE, *Town*, in county of Rock, being town 3 N., of range 12 E.; located in the southeast corner of which is Janesville, the county seat. The population in 1850 was 3,419. It has 12 school districts.

JEFFERSON, *County*, is bounded on the north by Dodge, east by Waukesha, south by Walworth and Rock, and west by Dane, and is four townships square, containing 576 sections. It was set off December 7, 1836, and established from Milwaukee, to which it remained attached until 29th February, 1839, when it was completely organized. The county seat is at the village of Jefferson, opposite the forks of the Crawfish with Rock river, and near the centre of the county. Its streams are, Rock, Crawfish, and Bark river, and Johnson's, Scupernong, Whitewater, Waterloo, Duck, and Battle creek. The northeastern portion of the county is covered by the best growth of hard timber in the State, the southeast by prairie, and the remainder by openings. The surface of the western portion of the county is level or gently undulating. The excellent farming land, being well watered and timbered, together with its location and enterprizing inhabitants, entitle it to a position among the best counties in the State. The county of Jefferson constitutes the fifteenth senate district, and is divided into three assembly districts, viz.: 1. The town of Watertown. 2. The town of Waterloo, Milford, Lake Mills, and Oakland. 3. Jefferson and Koskonong. 4. Ixonia, Concord, Farmington and Aztalan. 5. Hebron, Sullivan, Coldspring and Palmyra. It is connected with the second judicial circuit, and the third congressional district. The population in 1838 was 468; 1840, 914; 1842, 1,638; 1846, 8,680; 1847, 11,464; 1850, 15,339. Dwellings, 2,933; manufactories, 25; farms, 1,042.

JEFFERSON, *Town*, in county of Green, being town 1 N., of range 8; centrally located, 6 miles southeast from Monroe. The population in 1850 was 692. It has 7 school districts.

JEFFERSON, *Town*, in county of Jefferson, being town 6 N., of range 14 E. The county seat is in this town. The population in 1850 was 1,610. It has 11 school districts.

JEFFERSON, *P. V.* and *C. H.*, in town and county of same name, on sect. 11, is located at the junction of Crawfish and Rock rivers, near the centre of the county, and 32 miles east from Madison, on the line of R. R. V. U. R. R. This place is between the timber and openings, and has not been properly developed on account of the poor roads from the east; they, however, have recently been much improved. The surrounding country is thickly settled, having a family upon nearly every 40 acre tract of land. These farms are just beginning to pay well, and this vicinity is destined to be one of the best farming districts of the West. There is a good water power on Rock river, and another on the Crawfish. It has 950 inhabitants, 150 dwellings, 10 stores, 2 hotels, 4 mills, 1 chair factory, 3 shoe shops, 2 churches, a courthouse and jail.

JEFFERSON, *Prairie*, is the name of a large prairie in Clinton, Rock county.

JOHNSON'S *Creek*, rises in the town of Watertown, runs south into Farmington, and thence west into Rock river, in the town of Aztalan, Jefferson county.

JOHNSON'S *Rapids*, this was the former name of the excellent hydraulic power of Rock river, at the present village of Watertown, Jefferson county. The descent of the river in two miles is about 25 feet.

JOHNSTOWN, *Town*, in county of Rock, being town 3 N., range 14 E.; centrally located, ten miles east from Janesville. Population in 1850 was 1,271. It has 9 school districts.

JOHNSTOWN, *P. V.*, on section 23 of town of same name, 13 miles east from Janesville, and fifty miles southeast from Madison. It has about 40 dwellings, 2 stores, 2 hotels, 1 Baptist and 1 Congregational church. It has a pleasant and healthy location on Rock Prairie, and in a vicinity of farms of good soil and well cultivated. Much attention has been paid to the raising of sheep, with satisfactory results.

JOHNSTOWN CENTRE, *P. V.*, on section 24 of town of same name, 10 miles east from Janesville, and 42 miles southeast from Madison. It has 200 inhabitants, 40 dwellings, 2 stores, and 1 hotel. It is located at the junction of the Chicago and Madison with the Janesville and Milwaukee stage roads, on the north edge of Rock Prairie.

JORDAN, *Town*, in the county of Greene, being town 2 N., of range 6. The population in 1850 was 389. It has 4 school districts.

JUNEAU, *P. V.* (formerly Dodge Centre,) and county seat of Dodge county, is situated on section 21 of town 11 N., of range 15 E., being the town of Oak Grove, formerly Fairfield. It has a beautiful location, on the surveyed route of the R. R. V. U. R. R. Population 300; with 50 dwellings, 3 stores, 2 hotels, and 3 religious denominations.

KAGINE, *Lake*, La Pointe county, forms the head waters of the principal branch of the Mashkeg river.

KANGAROO, *Lake*, in town 30 N., of range 20, Door county, near shore of Lake Superior.

KAMANOSA, *River*, of Lake Superior, see Poplar river.

KAUKAUNA, *Town*, in Outagamie county, being town 21 N., of range 18, and W. half of 19; centrally located, 6 miles from Grand Chute. It has 5 school districts.

KAUKAUNA, *P. V.*, Outagamie county, on section 24 of town of same name. It is eight miles northeast from Appleton, and 115 northeast from Madison. It is situated at the present head of navigation on the Lower Fox, 20 miles above Green Bay. At Kaukauna (formerly Grand Kaukaulin) there is a descent in the river of 44 feet, which is being improved by a canal one mile in length, which is to be passed by four locks, and will probably be completed during the present season. This place has an abundance of water power, and is surrounded by good farming lands, both timbered and openings. Population 200; with 30 dwellings, 3 stores, 4 hotels, 1 saw mill, and a Baptist and Catholic church.

KAUKAULIN, *Creek*, a small tributary from the south of the Neenah river, which it enters at Grand Kaukalin.

KAYISIKING, (or Shell,) *River*, is the outlet of Shell Lake, in south part of La Pointe county.

KAYONGWA-SOGOKA, *River*, a tributary from the east of Bad river, in La Pointe county.

KENDALL, *Town*, in Lafayette county, 12 miles north from Shullsburg.

KENINGAMORE, *Lake*, a small lake in the northeastern part of the town of Rochester, Racine county.

KENOSHA, *County*, is bounded on the north by Racine, east by Lake Michigan, south by the State of Illinois, and west by Walworth and a portion of Racine. The county seat is at Kenosha, formerly known as Southport, on the lake shore, about midway between the northern and southern extremity of the county. It was set off from Racine and fully organized, 30th January, 1850. The eastern portion of the county is mostly prairie, with occasional groves of timber. In the northeast part is a large tract of heavy timber. The western portion is mostly openings. The soil is productive in the highest degree, and well adapted to the growing of all the crops of the climate, and the raising of stock. It has the best of market facilities—Kenosha close at hand, and Milwaukee and Chicago easy of access. It has a healthy climate, and is settled by an intelligent and enterprizing class of farmers. The principal streams are the Fox, (Pishtaka,) the Aux Raines and Pike creeks. Population 10,734; 927 farms, and 1,812 dwellings. This county belongs to the first congressional district, the first judicial circuit, and forms the eighth senate district, sending two members to the assembly as follows: 1. City of Kenosha and towns of Southport, Somers, and Pleasant Prairie; 2. Towns of Paris, Bristol, Brighton, Salem and Wheatland. County Officers for 1853 and 1854: County Judge, Hon. Isaac N. Stoddard; 2. Sheriff, Patrick Cosgrave; Clerk of Court, Oscar F. Dana; Register of Deeds, Samuel Y. Brande; County Treasurer, Michael Frank; District Attorney, Isaac W. Webster; County Surveyor, M. Howland; Clerk of Board of Supervisors, R. H. Deming; Coroner, Philip Carey.

KENOSHA, *City*, is situated upon Lake Michigan, 55 miles north from Chicago, and 35 miles south from Milwaukee, and is distant from Madison 104 miles. It is the most southern port on Lake Michigan in the State. When the resources of the county are fully developed—when capital finds its account in making necessary improvements, this place is destined to be a city of wealth, business and importance. The country which surrounds it is eminently productive, and its surface is agreeably diversified and beautiful. The city itself presents a great diversity of soil and surface, and is generally estimated on this account to occupy a more favorable position than those places which have a uniform level surface, and a perfect uniformity of soil. There is no considerable stream emptying itself into the lake at this place; but the harbor is mainly formed by a small bay, which extends in a circular form for about one mile, where it again intersects the lake, forming an island, and making two outlets from the bay into the lake, thus creating, in the opinion of many, when it shall have been properly improved, one of the most convenient and picturesque harbors upon the whole chain of lakes. In the spring of 1835, a company was formed in western New York, whose object was to effect a settlement at some favorable point in the West, and Hon. John Bullen, now resident here, was selected as the agent of the company, to proceed to the West and select a location. He arrived at this place, then uninhabited, and also far distant from any settlement, on 12th June, 1835, and from that time became a permanent resident of the place. The first building, a log one, was erected in the month of July following. The company which he represented having, in part, soon after arrived, the place immediately assumed an appearance of activity. The growth of the place has been greatly retarded for want of sufficient appropriation from Congress for the construction of a harbor and piers. The harbor still remains in an unfinished state, though its improvement is slowly, but steadily advancing. The first bridge pier ever erected on Lake Michigan was built here by Benjamin P. Cahoon, since which time two others have been built out into the lake by private enterprize. These, in absence of better facilities, answer in a manner, though, it must be acknowledged, not in an entirely satisfactory manner, the wants of business and the demands of commerce. In addition to private schools and academies, there are two large public schools. The building in the first ward accommodates 700 scholars, and the one in the second ward about 300, and both have a corps of well accomplished instructors. There are three public papers printed—whig, democrat and free soil. What are termed Artesian wells have been sunk with manifest success and advantage, by boring from 135 to 180 feet, a vein of water is struck, which overflows the surface, furnishing an unfailing supply of the purest of water. A plank road has been built to Fox river, distance 20 miles, and will ultimately be constructed to Beloit. There is a charter for a railroad to terminate at the same point. City Officers: Mayor, Charles C. Sholes; Clerk, J. Murray; Treasurer, Daniel M. Clarkson; Marshal, Richard B. Winsor; Justices, J. Mansfield, O. Colwell, F. J. Whitlock.

KORO, *P. O.*, in Winnebago county.

KESHAYNIC, *River*, see Grand river.

KEWASKUM, *Town*, (formerly North Bend,) in county of Washington, being the north two-thirds of town 9, range 19 E.; centrally located, 20 miles northwest from Ozaukee. The population in 1850 was 672. It has 6 school districts.

KEWAUNEE, *County*, is bounded on the north by Door county, on the east by the state line in Lake Michigan, on the south by Manitowoc, and on the west by Brown, and contains about thirteen townships of land. It was set off from Door, April 16, 1852, and is attached to Manitowoc for judicial purposes. The streams are Kewaunee and Red rivers, Benton's, Martin's, Ashnepee and Thorn-apple creeks. It is attached to the second senatorial and third congressional districts and with Brown and Door, sends one member to the assembly. The county having been so recently established, has not as yet reached to much dignity as a county.

KEWAUNEE, *Town*, in county of Kewaunee, embracing the whole county.

KEWAUNEE, *River*, in county of same name, rises in the eastern portion of Brown county, and running southeast, enters Lake Michigan, in town 23 N., of range 25 W. It is about 25 miles long, and is navigable for 5 or 6 miles from the lake.

KEWAWIYE, *Lake*, on the line between Chippewa and La Pointe county.

KEYES' *Lake*, see Rock Lake.

KEYES' *Creek*, is the outlet of Rock lake, in the towns of Lake Mills, Aztalan and Milford, in Jefferson county.

KICKAPOO, *River*, rises in Bad Ax county, and runs south, nearly parallel with the Mississippi, in town 7 N., of range 4 E., in Crawford county.

KILBER, *River*, a small stream entering the Mississippi, in the western part of Cassville, Grant county.

KILBOURN, *Diggings*, mining point in town 1, range 1 W.

KILBOURNTOWN, see Milwaukee city.

KILLDARE, *Town*, in county of Sauk.

KILLMAKE, *Creek*, a small tributary of the north branch of Manitowoc river, in town 19 N., of range 20, Calumet county.

KINEDO, *Lake*, see Tomahawk lake.

KINGSTON, *P. V.*, in town of Kingston, Marquette county, being on section 13, in town 14 N., of range 11, 14 miles from Montello.

KINGSTON, *Town*, in county of Marquette. It has 5 school districts.

KINNIKINNICK, *Town*, in county of St. Croix, being towns 27 and 28 N., of south half of town 17; southeast from Willow river. It has 1 school district.

KINNIKINNICK, *River*, rises in the centre of St. Croix county, and runs southwest, entering St. Croix river about six miles from its mouth.

KINO, *Lake*, a crescent shaped lake, in Red Cedar river, below Lake Mukwa.

KINONJE, *Lake*, on outlet of Lake Meminis, on the head waters of St. Croix.

KNAPP'S, *Creek*, rises in town 11, meridian, and running south, near the line between Richland and Crawford counties, falls into the Wisconsin river.

KNAPP & BLACK'S *Mills*, on Red Cedar river, in Chippewa county.

KOSHKONONG, *Town*, in county of Jefferson, being town 5 N., of range 13 and 14 E.; centrally located, 10 miles southwest from Jefferson. The population in 1850 was 1,512. It has 9 school districts.

KOSHKONONG, *Lake*, is an enlargement of Rock river, in southwest corner of Jefferson county. It is about 8 miles long, and nearly three miles wide.

KOSHKONONG, *Prairie*, is in south part of Deerfield, Dane county.

KOSSUTH, *Town*, in county of Fond du Lac, being town 16 N., of range 19 E.; centrally located, 10 miles northeast from Fond du Lac city. It forms a part of the old town of Calumet.

KOSSUTH, *P. O.*, in the county of Racine.

KOSSUTH, *Town*, in county of Winnebago.

LA BELLE, *Lake*, is the largest and lowermost lake of the Oconomowoc creek, on the east bank of which, is the village of Oconomowoc. It is nearly 3 miles long, and a mile and a half wide. It has a beautiful island near its centre.

LABICHE, *Lake*, in the eastern part of Chippewa county, discharges its waters through a river of the same name into the Manidowish.

LABICHE, *River*, rises in Flambeau-dore lake and Labiche lake, and running southwest discharges its waters through Manidowish river, into the Chippewa.

LABRAUGH, *Lake*, (Oconomowoc Group), see Beaver lake.

LAC BRULE, is the source of the Wiscatota or Brule river of the Menominee.

LA CROSSE, *County*, is bounded on the north by Chippewa, on the east by Portage, Adams, and a portion of Sauk, and on the west by the Mississippi, by which it is separated from the territory of Minnesota. This county was set off from

Crawford, and organized March 1, 1851, the seat of justice being established at La Crosse, on a beautiful prairie of the same name, on the eastern bank of the Mississippi, 90 miles above the junction of the Wisconsin, and on the line between townships 15 and 16 north. It is watered by Black and La Crosse rivers, and Mormon, Eagle and Billings' creeks, and the headwaters of the Lemonwier. Many of the streams are of pure water, with abundance of hydraulic power, abounding with speckled trout. The soil may be considered as first rate, and is mostly of vegetable mould, mixed with a sufficient quantity of sand to give it warmth. In the northeastern portion of the county is a heavy growth of pine timber, which is manufactured into lumber and shingles, the export of which amounts to $175,000 per annum. Near the head of some of the large streams are cranberry marshes, yielding in good seasons several hundred bushels per acre. The population in 1850, all of which was confined to Black river, was 460. In 1851, about 46,000 acres of school lands, known as a part of the 500,000 acre grant, was brought into market upon very reasonable terms, and many of the enterprizing and industrious inhabitants of the older counties have changed their residence to one in this. The increase of population has probably been greater during the last two years than in any other locality in the State. This county is connected with the nineteenth senate district, and forms a portion of the sixth judicial circuit, and of the second congressional district, and, with Chippewa, sends one member to the assembly. County Officers for 1853: County Judge, George Gale; Sheriff, A. Eldred; Clerk of Court, Robert Looney; District Attorney, Edward Flint; Register, Chase A. Stevens; Treasurer, F. M. Rublee; Surveyor, William Hood.

La Crosse, *P. V.* and *C. H.*, in town and county of same name, on section 31, town 16 N., of range 7 W., 130 miles northwest from Madison. It is situated on a prairie 5 miles long and 3 wide, on the Mississippi river, immediately below the mouth of the Black and La Crosse rivers, and about equidistant between Galena and St. Paul. The prairie is high enough from the river to be free from all danger of innundation, and as a site for a village or city, is unsurpassed by beauty and natural advantages by any spot on the river. The first claim was made by H. J. B. Miller and Nathan Myrick, who took up their residence in 1842. The Government survey was not made until 1847; John M. Levy opened a store in 1846, and the next year erected the first hotel. Nothing was done towards laying out the town until after the advent of Timothy Burns, now Lieutenant Governor of the State, to whom it is largely indebted for its present progress. A post office was established in 1844. The plat was surveyed in May 1851. In the second year of its organization, the town paid into the State treasury over $900. The population in March, 1853, in the village, was 543. It contains 4 stores of general assortment, 1 drug, 1 hardware, 1 furniture, 1 stove and tin, 3 groceries, 1 bakery, 1 livery stable, 1 harness, 4 tailor, 3 shoemaker shops, and mechanics of every description; 6 physicians, 6 lawyers, 4 clergymen, 3 religious societies, a division of the Sons of Temperance, a Free Masons' lodge, 1 church edifice, court house, steam saw mill and grist mill, and 5 hotels. La Crosse, from the advantages of its position, cannot fail to become one of the largest and most important places in the Northwest. The large extent of excellent farming land in the river vallies, and the extensive pine country bordering on the Black river, will always furnish a large amount of business which will concentrate at this point, in addition to which, it is the natural depot through which the immense business of the Upper Mississippi must naturally pass. It has been selected as the terminus of a rail road from Milwaukee, and the route selected is the most feasible one from Lake Michigan to the Mississippi, north of Dubuque. Minnesota already contains a population of many thousands, and is settling rapidly. The large tract of lands recently acquired by treaty from the Sioux Indians, is situated directly opposite La Crosse, on the Minnesota side of the river, and possesses advantages for emigrants unsurpassed by any section of the country now open for settlement.

La Crosse, *Town*, in county of La Crosse, was, until recently, all of said county, south of town 17. It has 15 school districts.

La Crosse, *River*, (Mazwini or Ball river,) rises in the eastern part of county of the same name, and running southwest, empties into the Mississippi at the village of La Crosse, on the beautiful prairie of the same name.

Lac Vieux Desert, (Kattakittekon), is the name of a lake, the middle of which is the boundary line between this State and Michigan, between the northern corner of Marathon and Oconto counties. It is the source of the Wisconsin, and occupies a high level above the lakes. Upon this elevation are the sources of several large streams, the Ontonagon and Montreal of Lake Superior, the Menominee of Lake Michigan, and the Wisconsin and Chippewa of the Mississippi. This lake is about 4 miles long from north to south, and of very irregular shape. In the middle of it is an island which is made a point in the boundary between Michigan and Wisconsin.

Lafayette, *County*, is bounded on the north by Iowa, on the east by Green, on the south by the State line, and west by Grant, and is 21 miles north and south, by 30 miles east and west. The country embracing the present county was set off by a division of Iowa county, and the formation of the counties of Lafayette and Montgomery, January 31, 1846, subject to the approval of the voters of said county, at the general election in September of the same year, at which election a majority voted against the "County Division Law." At the next session of the legislature, an act passed establishing the county of Lafayette, and it was organized February 4, 1847. The county seat has been a vexed question since the organization, but it has finally become established at the village of Shullsburg, a few miles southwest of the geographical centre. This county is more celebrated for its mining operations than for its agricultural products; simply, however, because the former has been prosecuted to the neglect of the latter. It is in connexion with the fifth judicial circuit, and the second congressional district, and forms the thirteenth senate district, and sends 3 members to the assembly, viz: 1. Towns of White Oak Springs, Benton and New Diggings. 2. Towns of Shullsburg, Monticello, Gratiot, Wayne and Wyota. 3. Elk Grove, Belmont, Kendall, Center, Willow Springs, Fayette and Argyle. The Peckatonnica and Fevre rivers are the principal streams. The population in 1847 was 9,335; 1850, 11,556. Dwellings, 2,079; farms, 399; manufactories, 21. County Officers for 1853 and 1854: County Judge, Jas. H. Knowlton; Sheriff, Peter C. Meloy; Clerk of Court, D. W. Kyle; District Attorney, Hamilton H. Gray; Register, Elias Slothower; Clerk of Board of Supervisors, Thomas McMannus; Treasurer, Ephraim Ogden; Surveyor, Thomas Bowen.

LAFAYETTE, *P. O.*, in town of same name, Walworth county, being in town 3 N., of range 17 E.

LAFAYETTE, *Town*, in county of Walworth, being town 3, of range 17; centrally located, 5 miles northeast from Elkhorn. The population in 1850 was 1,008. It has 9 school districts.

LAGRANGE, *P. V.*, in town of same name, Walworth county.

LAGRANGE, *Town*, in county of Walworth, being town 4 N., of range 16 E.; centrally located, 8 miles northwest from Elkhorn. The population in 1850 was 961. It has 9 school districts.

LAKE, *Town*, in county of Milwaukee, being town 6 N., of range 22 E.; centrally located, 4 miles south from Milwaukee. Population in 1850 was 1,474. It has 8 school districts.

LAKE ELLEN, is adjoining the village of Cascade, Sheboygan county. It abounds in fish, and covers an area of 320 acres.

Lake Emily, in the northeast part of town of Fox Lake, Dodge county.

Lake Huron, is a small lake near the centre of town 20 N., of range 9 E., in Washington county. It covers about 200 acres.

Lake Kattakittekon, see Lac Vieux desert.

Lake Maria, a small lake in southwest corner of Mackford, Marquette county, and has its outlet into Grand river.

Lake Maria, *P. V.*, on section 25, town 14 N., of range 12, Marquette county, 20 miles south from Dartford, 65 miles east of north from Madison, on the road from Watertown to the Pinery, 4 from Granville, 5 from Mackford, 8 from Kingston, and 10 from Marquette. Population 60; 10 dwellings, with Methodist, Baptist, and Presbyterian denominations.

Lake Mason, in the southwest corner of Marquette county, discharges its waters into the Neenah river.

Lake Mills, *Town*, in county of Jefferson, being town 7 N., of range 13 E.; centrally located, 8 miles northwest from Jefferson. Population in 1850 was 884. It has 7 school districts.

Lake Mills, *P. V.*, on section 13, in town of same name, Jefferson county, 8 miles northwest from Jefferson, 26 miles east from Madison, at the outlet of Rock lake, on the mail route from Madison to Watertown. Population 400; with 50 dwellings, 3 stores, 1 hotel, 1 church and several religious denominations, 1 iron foundry, 1 grist mill, 1 saleratus factory, 2 cabinet and 3 blacksmith shops.

Lake Nine, in north part of Richmond, Walworth county.

Lake of the Hillocks, in Marathon county, near the 45° north latitude, discharging its waters easterly into the Wisconsin, about half way between Big and Little Bull Falls.

Lake of the Hills, located in town 11 N., of range 8 E. It is nearly two miles long, and three-fourths of a mile in width.

LAKE SARAH, forms the head waters of the Neenah, in the northeast corner of Columbia county.

LAKE VIEW, *P. O.*, in town of Fitchburg, Dane county, on section 13, town 6 N., of range 9 E.

LAKE VIEUX DESERT, or Kattakittekon Lake, see Lac Vieux Desert.

LAKE WAUCOUSTA, two small lakes in Osceola, Fond du Lac county.

LAKE WINGRA, or Dead Lake, mostly on section 27, in Madison, Dane county, a mile long, and three-quarters of a mile wide.

LAMARTINE, *Town*, in county of Fond du Lac, being town 15 N., of range 16 E.; centrally located, 8 miles west from Fond du Lac. Population in 1850 was 588. It has 9 school districts.

LAMARTINE, *P. V.*, Fond du Lac county, on section 34 of town of same name. It has 2 stores, 1 hotel, and a Baptist church. It is 7 miles southwest from Fond du Lac city, and 67 miles northeast from Madison.

LANCASTER, *Town*, in county of Grant, being towns 4 and 5 N., of range 3 W., and is the county seat. It has 9 school districts. There is 1 grist mill and 2 saw mills in the town, from three to four miles from the village; some of the most productive lead mines are in this town. There are large quantities of land yet unentered in the town, and the great fertility of the soil, convenience of building materials and fuel, of springs and brooks, offer inducement to settlers. Population about 1,500.

LANCASTER, *P. V.* and *C. H.*, in town of same name, on section 3, town 4, near the geographical centre of the county, upon the edge of Boyce prairie, and in the most beautiful and healthy portion of the mining region. The business and trade of the township, as also of the town of Fennimore, are concentrated at the village. Population 400; 75 dwellings, 1 drug, 4 dry goods and grocery, 1 tin and sheet iron, and 1 stove stores, 1 waggon, 3 smith, and 2 cabinet shops, 4 hotels, 1 Baptist church of brick, 1 Methodist and 1 Presbyterian church of wood, and an Episcopal church in progress of erection. Court house of brick, 40 by 56, with fire-proof offices for county purposes.

LANSING, *P. V.*, in town of Freedom, Outagamie county.

LANSING, *Town*, in county of Outagamie, being towns 22 and 23 N., of range 17; centrally located, 10 miles north from Grand Chute. It has 1 school district.

LA POINTE, *County*, is bounded on the northwest and north by the State line, in Lake Superior, on the east by Marathon, on the the south by Chippewa and St. Croix, and west by Minnesota. It was set off from St. Croix Feb. 19, 1845. It was, and remained attached to Crawford for judicial purposes, until the complete organization of St. Croix, Feb. 26, 1849. The boundaries were changed 6th March 1849, and it was fully organized 9th Feb. 1850. The county seat is established at La Pointe, on the southeast end of Madeline Island, in Lake Superior, the oldest settlement in the State. The county is watered by Bois Brule, (Burnt Wood,) Mauvais, (Bad,) or Maskau rivers, and other small streams entering the lake from three to ten miles apart, and by lakes. The country, for a short distance along the margin of the lake, is low and wet; further south it is generally rolling. The western portion of the country is prairie land; and the soil being good and winters mild, offers great inducements to agriculturists. In the more eastern parts, the timber in most places is very thick, comprising white and yellow Norway pine, and the different species of oak, maple, birch, and the soft woods. The county is in connexion with the nineteenth senate district, the sixth judicial circuit, and the second congressional district, and with St. Croix sends one member to the assembly. French missionaries visited this country as early as 1661. In 1850 the population was 489; 5 farms and 74 dwellings. R. D. Boyd is Register of Deeds, and Clerk of the Circuit Court and of the Board of Supervisors.

La Pointe, *P. V.* and *C. H.*, is situate on Madeline Island, in Lake Superior, La Pointe county, at about town 50 N., of range 4 W. It has a bay nearly three miles across, capable of containing at anchor, secure from all winds, a numerous fleet of the largest class vessels, and is the favorite harbor of the lake. La Pointe was originally settled by the North Western Fur Company as the most eligible point for a depot and trading port on the lake. As a site for a town, and as a resort for health and pleasure, La Pointe offers advantages equal to any other place in Wisconsin. It has the best fishing-grounds on the whole lake for trout, siscowet and white fish, or lake shad, more than one thousand barrels of which are packed annually at La Pointe. Tempered, as well in summer as in winter, by the vast expanse of water which surrounds it, and which, except at the immediate surface, is almost always at 40° Farnheit, its climate is milder and more equable than any part of Wisconsin, whether it be on the mainland of Lake Superior, or further south on the Mississippi. Chiefly for this reason, but also on account of the bracing winds that sweep across the lake, Madeline Island is probably not surpassed, in point of health, by any locality throughout the entire western country.*

La Pointe, *Town*, in county of La Pointe, comprising the same. Population in 1850 was 598.

La Prairie, *Town*, in county of Rock, being town 2 N. of range 13 E.; centrally located, 6 miles southeast from Janesville. The population in 1850 was 378. It has 6 school districts.

Lawrence, is the name of a town in the county of Brown.

Leach *Creek*, a small tributary from the west of Baraboo river, which it enters near its mouth.

L'Eau Claire, *Lake* and *Mills*, on river of same name, in town 26 N., of range 13 W., in Chippewa county, also called Clearwater and O'Claire.

* See Owen's Geological Survey of Wisconsin.

L'Eau Galla, *River*, in St. Croix county, runs southeast, and empties into Chippewa river, in Chippewa county.

L'Eau Clare, or O'Clare *River*, in Chippewa county, a branch of Chippewa river from the west, in town 27 N.. of range 9 W.

Lebanon, *Town*, in county of Dodge, being town 9, of range 16 W.; centrally located, 12 miles southeast from Juneau. The population in 1850 was 1,031. It has 7 school districts.

Leland's Mill, *P. O.*, in town of Honey Creek, Sauk county.

Lemonwier,. *Town*, in county of Sauk; centrally located, northwest from Baraboo. It has 3 school districts.

Lemonwier, *River*, rises in La Crosse county, and runs southeast through Adams, emptying into the Wisconsin in town 15 N., range 5 E.

Leon, is the name of a new town in county of La Crosse.

Leroy, *Town*, in county of Dodge, being town 13 N., of range 16 E.; centrally located, 12 miles northeast from Juneau. The population in 1850 was 397. It has 4 school districts.

Leroys, *Town*, in county of St. Croix.

Lewiston, *Town*, in county of Columbia. It was set off by the County Board in November 1852.

Lewiston, *V.*, (Beaver Creek P. O.) in Columbia county, on section 24, town 13 N., of range 8 E. It is 45 miles northwest from Madison, and 7 miles northwest from Fort Winnebago. Population 350; 50 dwellings, 1 hotel, 5 stores, 1 Lutheran congregation. It is situated on the road from Portage city to Stevens' Point, in a good farming country, and well supplied with water and timber.

Leyden, *P. V.*, in town of Janesville, Rock county.

Liberty, (recently the north half of Highland), *Town*, in county of Grant, being town 5 N., of range 2 W.; centrally located, 8 miles northeast from Lancaster.

LIBERTY, *P. V.*, on section 25, Kenosha county, in town of Salem, 16 miles southwest from Kenosha, and 110 southeast from Madison, on the Racine and Wilmot plank road. It has 60 inhabitants, 10 dwellings, 2 hotels, 2 religious denominations, and several mechanics.

LIBERTY *Prairie*, Dane county, 2 miles south from Deerfield P. O.

LIMA, *Town*, in county of Sheboygan, being town 14 N., of range 22 E.; centrally located, 6 miles southwest from Sheboygan. It has 9 school districts. The soil is composed of sand and clay, and when properly tilled is very productive.

LIMA, *Town*, in county of Grant, being town 4 N., of range 1 W.; centrally located, 12 miles east from Lancaster. It has 8 school districts.

LIMA, *P. O.*, in town of same name, Rock county, on town 4 N., of range 14 E.

LIMA, *Town*, in county of Rock, being town 4 N., of range 14 E.; centrally located, 13 miles northeast from Janesville. Population in 1850 was 839. It has 9 school districts.

LIND, *Town*, in county of Waupacca, being town 21 N., of range 12 E.; centrally located, 15 miles from Mukwa. It abounds in prairie, timber and water, and is fast being settled by an agricultural population.

LIND, *P. V.*, in county of Waupacca, town of same name, on section 22, town 21 N., of range 12 E., 15 miles from Mukwa, and 100 miles north from Madison. Population 500; 100 dwellings.

LINDEN, *Town*, in county of Iowa.

LINDEN, *P. V.*, in town of same name, Iowa county, 6 miles from Mineral Point. It contains 200 inhabitants, mostly miners. The country is well adapted to agriculture.

LINN, *Town*, in county of Walworth, being town 1 N., of range 17 E.; centrally located, 8 miles southeast from Elkhorn. Population in 1850 was 805. It has 7 school districts.

LISBON, *Town*, in county of Waukesha, being town 8 N., of range 19 E.; centrally located, 10 miles north from Waukesha. The population in 1850 was 1,010. It has 8 school districts.

LITTLE BARABOO, *Creek*, rises in Richland, and runs southeast into the Baraboo river, near the centre of town 13 N., of range 3 E.

LITTLE BUTTE DES MORTS, *Lake*, an expansion of the Lower Fox just below the outlet of Lake Winnebago, it is nearly 5 miles long, and 1 mile broad.

LITTLLE CHUTE, *P. V.*, Outagamie county, 5 miles below Appleton, on Fox river.

LITTLE CHUTE, *Rapids*, of the Neenah river, 4 miles above Grand Kaukalin, with a fall of 31 feet in a distance of about 9,000 feet.

LITTLE ENINANDIGO, *River*, a tributary from the north of St. Croix river.

LITTLE GREEN, *Lake*, Marquette county, in southwest corner of Green Lake. It is two miles long and nearly one in width, and forms a tributary to Grand River. It is 4 miles south of Green Lake, and is noted for the purity of its water.

LITTLE KAUKAULIN, *Rapids*, is on the Neenah river, 5 miles above Depere, at which place the navigation has been improved by a dam.

LITTLE OTTER, *Creek*, a small tributary from the west of Peckatonnica, into which it empties in the town of Centre, Lafayette county.

LITTLE PRAIRIE, *P. O.*, in town of Troy, Walworth county.

LITTLE PLATTE, *River*, rises in Clifton, Grant county, and runs southwest, emptying into Platte river, in Paris.

LITTLE PLOVER, *River*, a tributary from the northeast, entering the Wisconsin at Plover.

LITTLE QUINNESEC, *Falls*, of the Menominee river, at which place is a fall of 35 feet in an extent of 250 feet. At these Falls the river is contracted to 85 feet in width.

LITTLE ROCHE-A-GRIS, *River*, in east part of Adams county, runs west into the Wisconsin, in town 17 N.

LITTLE, *River*, is a considerable tributary from the north of Oconto river.

LITTLE STURGEON, *Bay*, on east shore of Green Bay, in Door county, near line between towns 27 and 28 N.

LITTLE SUAMICO, *River*, rises in range 18, and runs east, in town 26, entering Lake Michigan.

LITTLE SUGAR, *Creek*, rises in the northwest corner of Green county, and running southeast into Sugar River at Albany.

LITTLE TAIL, *Pointe*, name given to a point of land extending into Green Bay from the west, near the line between Brown and Oconto counties.

LITTLE WISCONSIN, *River*, a tributary from the northeast of the Wisconsin, in Marathon county.

LITTLE WOLF, *River*, a tributary of Wolf river, from the west, which it enters near the line between Outagamie and Waupacca counties.

LODI, *Town*, in county of Columbia, being town 10 N., of ranges 8 and 9; centrally located, 12 miles south from Portage city. It has 3 school districts. The soil is well adapted to farming and raising of stock; the surface is rolling.

LODI, *P. V.*, on section 27, town 10 N., of range 8 E., in town of same name, Columbia county. It is 16 miles south from Fort Winnebago, 20 miles northwest from Madison, and 4 miles from the head of Spring Creek. Population 150; 20 dwellings, 4 stores, 2 hotels, 2 flouring mills, 1 saw mill, 1 shoe, blacksmith, waggon, chair, cooper and harness shops; and Presbyterian, Baptist, and Methodist organizations.

LOMIRA LAKE, *P. O.*, in town of Lomira, Dodge county, being town 13 N., of range 17 E.

LONG, *Lake*, a small Lake in the east part of Osceola, Fond du Lac county, is two and one half miles long, and is the source of the Milwaukee river.

LONG TAIL, *Pointe*, name given to a point of land extending into Green Bay from the west, in town 25 N., of range 20 E., in Brown county.

LOST, *Lake*, a small lake in the north part of Calamus, Dodge county.

LOUISA, *Town*, in the county of Dodge, being town 13 N., of range 17; centrally located, 14 miles northeast from Juneau, The population in 1850 was 653. It has 8 school districts.

LOWELL, *Town*, in county of Dodge, being town 10 N., of range 14 E.; centrally located, 12 miles southwest from Juneau. The population in 1850 was 835. It has 8 school districts.

LOWELL, *P. V.*, Dodge county, on section 15 of town of same name, located 8 miles southwest from Juneau, and 38 miles northeast from Madison. It is on Beaver Dam river, 10 miles south from Beaver Dam. Population 200; 35 dwellings, 2 stores, 2 hotels, 1 saw, 1 grist mill; and Baptist and Methodist denominations.

LOWVILLE, *Town*, in county of Columbia, being town 11 N., of range 10 E. Population in 1850 was 297. It has 4 school districts.

LOWVILLE, *P. V.*, on section 32 of town of same name, 14 miles south east from Portage city, and 22 miles north from Madison, on the stage route from Madison to Fort Winnebago; also on the nearest and best road from Madison to Stevens' Point and the Wisconsin Pinery. It is in a region of first rate improved farms. Population 40; 7 dwellings, 1 hotel, 1 school house; and Baptist, Methodist, and Presbyterian congregations.

LYNDON, *Town*, in county of Sheboygan, being town 14 N., of range 21 E.; centrally located, 14 miles southwest from Sheboygan. It has 11 school districts.

LYONS, *P. V.*, on section 10, town 2 N., of range 18 E., in town of Hudson, Walworth county, is pleasantly situated on White river, the outlet of Geneva Lake, at the point where it is crossed by the main road from Geneva to Racine *via* Burlington. It is 9 miles southeast from Elkhorn, and 75 miles from Madison. Immediately adjacent to the village, above and below, are extensive water powers, one of which has been improved by the erection of a flouring mill of three run of stones, and a saw mill, both doing a flourishing business. The other power remains unimproved, and offers great inducements, as it is unsurpassed in capacity by any privilege in this part of the State. Population 130; dwellings 30, 2 stores, 1 hotel, and 1 religious denomination.

MACKFORD, *Town*, in county of Marquette. It has 8 school districts.

MADISON, *Town*, in county of Dane, being town 7 N., of range 9 E. The population in 1850 was 1,871. It has 4 school districts.

MADISON, *Village*, the capital of Wisconsin, and seat of justice of the county of Dane, is situated on sections 13, 14, 23 and 24, in town of same name, at the geographical centre of the county, and midway between Lake Michigan and the Mississippi river, being about 80 miles from each. It is widely noted for the beauty, health and pleasantness of its location, which is on an isthmus about one mile in width, lying between the Third and Fourth Lakes. The surface is somewhat uneven, but in no place too abrupt for building purposes. From either lake it rises to an altitude of about fifty feet, and is then depressed and elevated alternately, making the site of the village a series of gently undulating swells. The State house, a substantial edifice of lime-stone, is built, at the corners of the sections, in the centre of a square park, containing fourteen acres, covered with a luxuriant growth of native oaks, and upon the highest point between the lakes, overlooking each and the surrounding village. It has a large hall through the centre, and contains all of the State offices—the state library, the legislative chambers, and several committee rooms. The corners of the Capitol square are to the cardinal points of the compass, and from each of them a street extends, terminating, excepting the western, in the water. The streets are all straight, sixty-six feet wide, and, with the exception of those just described, are parallel to the sides of the Capitol square, and, consequently, diagonal with the meridian. From the centre of each side of the park, and at right angles with it and the principal streets, broad avenues, eight rods wide, extend completely across the town plat. At the termination of the street leading from the western corner of the park, and one mile directly west from the Capitol, on College Hill, near the shore of Fourth Lake, and in the middle of a park of fifty-five acres, commanding an extensive view of the town, lakes, and surrounding country, the buildings of the University of Wisconsin are located. Near the southern corner of the Capitol square, the Court House of Dane county, a large structure of lime-stone, containing commodious rooms for courts and county officers, is built. About a mile from the northern corner of the Capitol park, on the shore of Fourth Lake, at its outlet, is the best flouring mill in the State, and other machinery, owned by L. J. Farwell, present Governor of Wisconsin. Near the eastern corner of the square, the Post Office, Bank, Hotels, Stores, and other business stands, are located. The site of the town was located as early as 1833 by James Duane Doty, afterwards Governor of the Territory, and more recently Member of Congress; and the village plat was made out by his direction in 1836. A large addition to this plat was laid out in 1850, near the University, known as the " University Addition." Another addition has just been surveyed, on the northeast, by Governor Farwell, by whom it is owned. Several causes operated to retard the prosperity of Madison until 1847, since whieh time it has gradually and healthfully increased in growth, wealth, and population. Several rail roads are in progress of construction to this place, one at least of which will be completed during the present year, and the others soon after. From its location in the centre of a large agricultural district, having no important rival within a circle of forty miles, and being the permanent Capital of the State, and the seat of the richly endowed University, Madison has special advantages that cannot fail to make it a commanding business point, and a large and flourishing town. To the man of business, the merchant and manufacturer, there are offered great inducements to settle in this thriving and rapidly increasing community. The retired merchant—the student—the lover of the picturesque seeking a healthy and pleasant location for a home, is presented the refreshing breezes and pure air of the lakes—the beautiful scenery, unrivalled in any country—the quiet of a country residence, united with the social advantages and the excitements of a city, while the great abundance of game in the prairies and openings, and the variety of fish in the lakes and streams, afford a relaxation to all in pursuit of health or pleasure. As the Capital of the State, the shire town of the county, it becomes the great centre of public business, calling together, at frequent intervals, people from all parts of the State and county, at the annual meetings of the legislature, at the session of the courts, the convocations of political conventions, and the sessions of the different benevolent societies of the day. The present population of Madison is about 3,500, with 700 dwellings, 26 stores, 15 groceries, 11 taverns, 2 large printing offices, and a book bindery; a grist mill, with eight run of stone, 3 saw mills, an iron foundery, a woollen factory, an oil mill, 2 steam planing mills, a hominy mill propelled by steam; a bank, the first organized in the State; three churches, with three others to be built during the present season; and mechanical shops of all kinds.

MADORA, *V.*, on section 11, town 10 N., of range 7 E., being in town of Lodi, county of Columbia. It lies on the Wisconsin river, at the mouth of Spring Creek; contains 1 hotel, 1 warehouse, 2 saw mills, and 2 flouring mills in contemplation. The water power is a superior one.

MAGNOLIA, *Town*, in county of Rock, being town 3 N., of range 10 E.; centrally located, 15 miles west from Janesville. It is settled by New-Yorkers. The population in 1850 was 1,871. It has 7 school districts, and 7 well-finished frame and stone school houses, a good water power, 6 feet head, with 1 grist and 1 saw mill. The face of the country is generally undulating, with burr oak openings and prairie advantageously mixed. It is well watered by springs of the best and purest quality. The soil is a sandy loam, on a subsoil of yellow clay, and is excellent grass land. Large quantities of grass seed, of a superior quality, is annually produced and shipped East. The town boasts of having some of the best improved stock farms in the State.

MAGNOLIA, *P. V.*, in town of same name, Rock county, being on sections 22 and 23, town 3 N., of range 10 E. It has 15 dwellings, 1 tavern, 1 store, 4 mechanics' shops, 1 church, and 1 stone school house.

MAIDEN'S *Rock*, on east bank of Lake Pepin, in Chippewa county, on section 2, town 23 N., of range 16 W.

MAKWA, *Lake*, the most northern lake on Red Cedar river.

MANCHESTER, *Town*, in county of Calumet. It has 4 school districts.

MANIDOWISH, *Lakes*, are a chain of lakes in north part of Marathon county, tributary to the Chippewa river, through river of same name.

MANIDOWISH, (MANITOISH or DEVIL'S), *River*, rises in lake of same name, running southwest, empties into Chippewa river, of which it is the largest tributary.

MANITOU, *River*, see East River, Brown county.

MANITOWOC, *County*, is bounded on the north by Brown and Kewaunee, on the east and southeast by the State line in Lake Michigan, on the south by Sheboygan, and on the west by Calumet and a portion of Outagamie. It was set off from Brown, December 7, 1836; organized and attached thereto for judicial purposes, December 17, 1836; fully organized, March 2, 1848. The northern boundaries were somewhat changed February 9, 1850. The seat of justice is established at Manitowoc Rapids, on Manitowoc river, 3 miles from its mouth, and a few miles east of the geographical centre of the county. The general formation of the surface is moderately undulating, and in some parts very agreeably diversified with hills and valleys. The soil is good and well watered, with springs and creeks, and is well adapted to tillage and grazing. The county is densely timbered with maple, oak, elm, birch, ash, pine, and hemlock. The county forms a part of the fourth judicial circuit, of the thirtieth congressional district, and of the first senate district. It sends one member to the assembly. The population in 1840 was 235; 1842, 263; 1846, 629; 1847, 1,285; 1850, 3,713; at present estimated, 7,000. Dwellings, 716; farms, 37; and manufactories, 22. County Officers for 1853 and 1854: County Judge, Ezekiel Ricker; Sheriff, D. H. Van Valkenburg; Clerk of Court, Frederick Salomon; District Attorney, J. H. W. Colby; Register of Deeds, Fred. Salomon; Clerk of Board of Supervisors, Charles A. Reuter; Treasurer, Wm. Bach; Surveyor, Fayette Arnsby; Coroner, Lyman Emmerson.

MANITOWOC, *River*, has its origin in two branches; the one heading at near the southern extremity of Lake Winnebago, and the other near the north western part of the same, in Calumet county; unite near the southeast corner of town 19 N., of range 20 E., draining about 400 square miles of lands. It runs nearly east, entering Lake Michigan at the village of Manitowoc, and is navigable to the village of Manitowoc Rapids, 5 miles from its mouth.

MANITOWOC, *P. V.*, see Appendix.

MANITOWOC RAPIDS, *P. V.* and *C.H.*, see Appendix.

MANLY, *Lake*, a small lake in the south part of Farmington, Washington county.

MAPLETON, *P. O.*, in town of Oconomowoc, Waukesha county, 22 miles northwest from Waukesha, on the Ashippun river, at which place are good mills.

MARATHON, *County*, is bounded on the north and northeast by the State line, east by Waupacca and Oconto, south by Portage, and on the west by Chippewa and La Pointe. It was established from Portage, and fully organized February 9, 1850. Wausau, at Big Bull Falls on the Wisconsin river, about 20 miles north from the south line of the county, is the seat of justice. It is celebrated for its extensive regions of pine timber, and the production of pine lumber, rather than for agricultural pursuits. The mills in Adams, Portage, and Marathon, cut nearly sixty millions feet per annum. The county forms a part of the first senate and of the second congressional districts, and of the third judicial circuit, and, with Portage, sends one member to the assembly. County Officers for 1853 and 1854: Judge, Wm. H. Kennedy; Sheriff, Thos. Minton; Clerk of Court, Asa Lawrence.

MARATHON, *Town*, in county of Marathon, comprising the whole of the same. The population in 1850 was 466.

MARCELLON, *P. V.*, in town of same name, Columbia county.

MARCELLON, *Town*, in county of Columbia, being town 13 N., of range 10; centrally located, 8 miles from Portage city. The population in 1850 was 405. It has 4 school districts.

MARINE MILLS, *P. O.*, in Polk county, 9 miles below the Falls of St. Croix.

MARION, *Town*, in county of Waushara, being town 18 N., of range 11.

MARION, *P. V.*, in town of Paris, Kenosha county.

MARKESAN, *P. O.*, in Marquette county, 16 miles from Montello.

MARQUETTE, *County*, is bounded on the north by Waushara, east by Winnebago and Fond du Lac, on the south by Dodge and Columbia, and on the west by Adams, and is 24 by 30 miles square. It was set off from Brown, December 7, 1836, and was organized and attached to Brown, for judicial purposes, January 22, 1844. It was fully organized July 31, 1848. The bounds of the county were extended March 6, 1849. Of late the subject of the county seat has created considerable excitement, and the question is now being litigated between the villages of Dartford, on the north side of Green Lake, in the eastern portion of the county, and Marquette, on the south side of Puckawa Lake, in the southern portion of the county. The county is celebrated for its good lands, deep lakes, fine water powers, and its industrious and thrifty inhabitants. It is watered by Fox river (Neenah) and its branches. The county is attached to the twenty-third senate, to the third congressional districts, and to the third judicial circuit, and, with Waushara, constitutes two assembly districts, as follows: 1. Towns of Berlin, Brooklyn, Pleasant Valley, Middleton, Mackford, Albany and Green Lake, in the county of Marquette, and the county of Waushara; 2. All that portion of Marquette county, being west of the range line between ranges 10 and 11 E., and the town of Marquette and Kingston, in the county of Marquette. The population in 1840 was 18; 1842, 59; 1846, 986; 1847, 2,264; including Waushara, 1850, 8,642; 237 farms, 9 manufactories, 1,747 dwellings. County Officers for 1853 and 1854: Judge, John S. Horner; Sheriff, James C. Potter; Clerk of Court, Dominic Devenna; Register of Deeds, J. Edmund Millard.

MARQUETTE, *Town*, in county of same name. It has 5 school districts.

MARQUETTE, *P. V.* and *C. H.*, (?) on south side of Puckawa Lake, Marquette county.

MARSTON, is the name of a new town in county of Sauk.

MARTIN'S *Creek*, rises in town 22 N., of range 23 E., Kewaunee county, is about 7 miles in length, emptying into East Twin river.

MASKAU, *River*, see Mauvaise River, of La Pointe county.

MASHKEG, *River*, see Mauvaise River, of Lake Superior.

MAUVAISE, *Creek*, a small stream, about 9 miles in length, entering East Twin river, between Benton and Martin's creek.

MAUVAISE, (BAD or MASHKEG), *River*, La Pointe county, a considerable stream tributary to Lake Superior, rises in Kagine Lake, near the head waters of the St. Croix, and enters Lake Superior about 15 miles west from Montreal river.

MAYVILLE, *P. V.*, Dodge county, on section 23, town 12 N., of range 13 E., in town of Williamstown, 12 miles northeast from Juneau, and 65 miles northeast from Madison. It is situated on the principal branch of Rock river, and possesses the superior advantages of good water power, iron ore, timber, and a good soil.

McCARTNEY'S *Creek*, a small stream in Waterloo, Grant county, entering the Mississippi.

MECHAN, *River*, rises in the northern portion of Waushara county, and runs southeast into Fox river, which it enters near the line between towns 15 and 16 N.

MEDINA, *Town*, in county of Dane, being town 8 N., of range 12 E.; centrally located, 16 miles northeast from Madison. It has 7 school districts.

MEEKER, *P. O.*, in town of Germantown, Washington county

MEGIDCHEQUE, or Namebin Lake, La Pointe county.

MEMEE, *Creek*, rises in Manitowoc county, runs south between and nearly parallel to the lake shore and Sheboygan river, enters the lake a few miles northeast of the mouth of the latter.

MEMEE, *P. O.*, in Manitowoc county, on section 14, town 17 N., of range 22 E., being in the town of Memee, 15 miles south from Manitowoc, and 130 miles from Madison.

MENASHA, *P. V.*, see Appendix.

MENIMI, *Lake*, one of the sources of the St. Croix, in La Pointe county.

MENOM, *Lake*, an expansion of Neenah river immediately above Buffalo Lake, in Marquette county.

MENOMONEE, *Town*, in county of Waukesha, being town 8 N., of range 20 E.; centrally located, 12 miles northeast from Waukesha. The population in 1850 was 1,340. It has 7 school districts.

MENOMONEE, *River*, (of Milwaukee,) rises in the southern part of Washington county, and runs southeast through a town of same name in Waukesha county, and the towns of Granville, Wauwatosa and Milwaukee, enters Milwaukee river, in the city of Milwaukee.

MENOMONEE, *River*, rises near the head waters of the Wisconsin, and running southeast, forming the line between the States of Michigan and Wisconsin, enters Green Bay, at about the middle of the western shore. This river passes a large quantity of water into Green Bay, but owing to its rapidity and falls is not navigable except for canoes. The banks of the Menomonee are covered with a heavy growth of excellent and fine timber. Its valley contains much good land.

MENOMONEE, *Creek*, rises near the northeast corner of Jamestown, Grant county, and runs southwest into the State of Illinois.

MENOMONEE, *Diggings*, a mining point at the corners of town 1 and 2, N., of ranges 1 and 2 W.

MENOMONEE, *Falls*, on river of same name, 15 miles from Milwaukee, at which place is a descent of 40 feet in half a mile.

MENOMONEE MILLS, *P. O.*, in Chippewa county.

MENOMONEE, *Rapids*, are rapids in the river of same name.

MEQUON, *Town*, in county of Washington, being towns 9 N., of range 21 and fraction 22 N.; centrally located, 12 miles southwest from Ozaukee. The population of 1850 was 2,148. It has 14 school districts.

MEQUON, *River*, rises in the northwest corner of town of same name, and runs east, uniting with the Milwaukee river, at the village of Mequon.

MEQUON RIVER, *P. V.*, in county of Washington, on section 23, of the town of Mequon, town 9 N., of range 21 E., on the Milwaukee and Fond du Lac plank road, 15 miles southwest from Ozaukee, and 90 miles easterly from Madison. Population 160 ; with 20 dwellings, a good school house, and various mechanics.

MERRIT'S *Mill*, on the Wisconsin river, near the southwest corner of town 22 N., of range 5 E., in Portage county.

MERTON, *Town*, in county of Waukesha, being town 8 N., of range 18 E.; centrally located, 15 miles northwest from Waukesha. The population in 1850 was 1,763. It has 8 school districts.

METOMEN, *P. V.*, is on section 10, in town of same name, being town 15 N., of range 14 E. It is in Fond du Lac county, 20 miles west from the county seat, with which it is connected by a plank road, and is 65 miles northeast from Madison. It has 250 inhabitants; with 2 stores, 3 hotels, and 2 mills; 2 churches, and 5 religious denominations. It is a good location for a woollen factory, as much attention is paid to the raising of sheep in the vicinity.

METOMEN, *Town*, in county of Fond du Lac, being town 15 N., of range 14 E.; centrally located, 18 miles west from Fond du Lac. The population in 1850 was 756. It has 9 school districts.

MICHICONI, *Lake*, forms a portion of the head waters of the Manidowish branch of the Chippewa river.

MICHIGAN, *Lake*, the eastern bounds of the State, is the only one of the great chain of inland seas that lies wholly within the United States. It is estimated to have a length of about 320 miles, and a mean or average breadth of 70 miles—having, therefore, an area of 22,400 square miles, exclusive of Green Bay. The surface of Lake Michigan is 578 feet above the level of the Ocean, and its mean depth is estimated at 1,000 feet. The bottom is, therefore, about 400 feet below the Ocean level. Its greatest width is opposite Milwaukee, where it is nearly 100 miles. The length of coast of this lake, in Wisconsin, from the State of Illinois to the north point of Rock Island, at the entrance of Green Bay, is 257 miles.*

MIDDLE MILLS, *P. O.*, in Chippewa county, town 28 N., of range 13 W. Population, 300; with 1 mill, 2 stores, and 1 hotel.

MIDDLETON, *P.O.*, in town of same name, Dane county.

MIDDLETON, *Town*, in the county of Dane, being town 7 N., of range 8 E.; centrally located, 8 miles west from Madison. It has 6 school districts.

MIDDLETON, *Town*, Marquette county, see Dayton.

MIFFLIN, *P. V.*, in town of same name, Iowa county, formerly called Black Jack, consists of two small villages, from a half to three-fourths of a mile apart, containing about 200 inhabitants, principally miners. It has 4 stores, 1 grist mill, and 1 smelting furnace. A large branch of the West Peckatonnica flows through both villages. The country around is mostly prairie. It is 11 miles west from Mineral Point.

MIFFLIN, *Town*, in the county of Iowa.

MILLARD, *P. V.*, on section 9, town 3 N., of range 16 E., in the town of Sugar Creek, Walworth county. It is 7 miles northwest from Elkhorn, 60 miles southeast from Madison, on the east side of Sugar Creek prairie. Population 100, with 15 dwellings, 1 store, and Baptist church.

* Lapham.

MILL CREEK, a small stream entering the Neenah, in the town of Grand Chute, Outagamie county.

MILFORD, *Town*, in county of Jefferson, being town 8 N., of range 15 E.; centrally located, 12 miles north from Jefferson. Population in 1850 was 728. It has 6 school districts.

MILLVILLE, *P. V.*, in town of Patch Grove, Grant county, on the Wisconsin river, in town 6 N., of range 6 W.

MILTON, *Town*, in county of Rock, being town 4 N., of range 13 E.; centrally located, 14 miles northeast from Janesville. Population in 1850 was 1,032. It has 8 school districts.

MILTON, *P. V.*, in town of same name, in Rock county, on section 27. It is 8 miles northeast from Janesville, and 36 miles southeast from Madison. Population 400, with 40 dwellings, 5 stores, 3 hotels, 2 churches, 3 societies, and 1 academy of about 70 scholars. It is 60 miles southwest from Milwaukee, on the line of the M. & M. R. R., with a branch to Janesville.

MILWAUKEE, *City*, the county seat of Milwaukee county, and the largest town in the State, is situated in town 7, of range 22, E., and near the mouth of the river of the same name, and on the shores of a bay, or indentation of Lake Michigan, some six miles between the outer points, and two and one half to three miles in width, affording deep water at all times, and good holding ground for vessels at anchor. The river comes from the north in a direction parallel with the lake shore, the land rising from the lake in almost perpendicular bluffs, and descending gradually to the bed of the river. On the west, the land rises again to a considerable height. Within the limits of the corporation, the Menominee river comes in from the west, and joins the Milwaukee, about a mile from its present mouth. Piers were erected some years since by the United States Government, at the mouth of the river; but the citizens have long felt the necessity of dispensing with the circuitous route which the river takes through the low grounds near its mouth, and have projected a cut through an isthmus of some 200 feet in width between the river and lake, and the erection of piers at that point, thus forming a new harbor or opening into the river. There is always water enough in the river for the largest class of lake craft, as far up as the mills, some two miles from its mouth. Recently, (May, 1853,) the citizens have voted a loan of $50,000, to be expended in connection with a Government appropriation of $15,000, in the improvement of the harbor. Milwaukee was laid out as a village in 1835. Its rapidity of growth may be seen from the following, giving the population for the years mentioned: In 1838, 700; 1840, 1,751; 1842, 2,700; 1846, 9,655; 1847, 14,061; 1849, 18,000; 1850, 20,061. The above presents a rate of increase unparalleled in the history even of the rapidly growing West. At present, the population is estimated at over 25,000 souls. A dam is thrown across the Milwaukee river, near the north limits of the city, and a canal is conducted from it parallel with the stream, affording an abundant water power; the present capacity of which may be increased at comparatively small expense. Five large flouring mills, one woollen factory, oil mill, pail factory, and numerous machine shops, are situated upon this water power, and are accessible to vessels of the largest class. The town of Milwaukee was incorporated as a city by the territorial Legislature, January 31, 1846, with five wards; and the first election under the charter was held on the first Tuesday of April succeeding. Solomon Juneau, who, as an Indian trader, had first built his cabin on the site of the city, and remained for many years the only white settler, was chosen the first mayor. The number of buildings erected in 1850 was 325, at a cost of $369,000. Since that time the city has greatly enlarged its borders, and increased in the number and quality of its buildings. The color of the brick used being a light cream, with their excellent quality, add very much to the appearance of the city. Great taste is exhibited in the architecture of many of the dwellings and blocks of stores; some of the latter rivalling any buildings of the kind west of New York. Seven daily newspapers, four in English and three in German, are published in the city. All of these publish weekly editions, and most of them tri-weeklies. There are, besides, two other weeklies, and two monthly publications issued. The public schools of this city are under the charge of a board of three commissioners from each ward. A commodious brick edifice has been erected in each ward for the purpose, at an average cost of about $5,000. A large portion of the children of the city receive gratuitous instruction in these schools. Besides these, there are numerous private academies and schools, among which may be mentioned the Milwaukee University Institute, which is incorporated with a University charter—the Milwaukee Female College, for which a very tasteful and extensive brick building has been erected—the Spring street Female Seminary—the Milwaukee Commercial and English School—the Milwaukee Academy, &c. For the last mentioned, a commodious brick building is erected and in use. There are in Milwaukee 35 church organizations, and nearly 30 church edifices. In 1852 there were 29 organizations, of the following denominations: 2 Baptist, 2 Congregational, 4 Roman Catholic, 3 Protestant Episcopal, 1 Norwegian Lutheran, 6 German Protestant, 3 Methodist Episcopal, 5 Presbyterian, 1 Universalist, and 2 Wesleyan Methodist. Among the associations for various objects and purposes, there were last year in operation a City Bible Society, Tract Society, 2 Musical Societies, 3 Orphan Asylums, 2 Benevolent Societies, several Literary Associations, 5 Odd Fellows' Lodges, 3 Masonic Lodges, 2 Temperance Divisions, besides numerous Insurance and other Companies, belonging more appropriately to business matters. Eight Fire Companies constitute that department, well supplied with the necessary machines, and it is conducted with efficiency and harmony. The city is lighted with gas, supplied from extensive works erected in 1852. The United States District Court holds its sessions in this city. The Circuit and County Courts also hold several terms during the year; and a Municipal Court will probably be soon established. Several consulships for German States are located in Milwaukee, for the benefit of the very large number of Germans who arrive at Milwaukee and other Wisconsin ports, and settle within the State. During the past three years, much has been done to increase the facilities of intercourse between Milwaukee and the interior of the State. Several plank roads stretch out in various directions, there being now near 200 miles constructed and in operation. The Milwaukee and Mississippi rail road is completed as far as Janesville, 71 miles, and is under contract from Milton, 8 miles northeast from Janesville to Madison, to be completed by the 1st January, 1854, whence it is to run westward to Prairie du Chien, on the Mississippi, at the mouth of the Wisconsin. Other roads are chartered, and portions of them contracted, or ready for contract, as follows: Green Bay, Milwaukee and Chicago, running north and south. The portion of this road, south of Milwaukee, is expected to be complete within 18 months.—Milwaukee and Beloit, (chartered;) about 70 miles in length, but the connexion can be made through other roads in half that distance.—Milwaukee and Watertown, under contract to Watertown, 46 miles north of west, to be extended to Portage city immediately, and thence to La Crosse on the Upper Mississippi.—La Crosse and Milwaukee, nearly in the same direction as the last named, passing through Dodge county. A large amount of stock subscribed, and the enterprize in energetic hands.—Milwaukee, Fond du Lac and Green Bay, fully organized by the subscription of stock, and with a prospect of early completion. These several lines of railway, once completed, will make Milwaukee the business centre of a very rich and rapidly growing region of country. Measures are now prosecuted with energy for the building of a railroad across the State of Michigan, which, in connexion with the Canadian system of roads, will place Milwaukee on almost an air line route from the northwest to the great Eastern cities. The value of articles manufactured in the city in the year 1852, was over $2,000,000. Tonnage of vessels owned in the city, 8,548. Number of arrivals at the port in 1852, about 1600; and departures the same. Of principal articles, the following quantities were exported during the year 1852, viz: flour, 88,597 bbls.; wheat, 394,386 bushels; barley, 345,620 bushels; oats, 428,800 bushels; rye, 67,759 bushels; hogs, live and dressed, 1,771,314 lbs.; pork, 19,603 bbls.; bacon, 188,286 lbs.; beef, 7,773 bbls.; eggs, 54,000 doz.; butter, 80,000 lbs.; saleratus, 150,000 lbs.; mill feed, 300 tons; hops, 11,625 lbs.; brick, 700,000; wool, 321,121 lbs.; hides, 12,990 lbs.; flax, 4,211 lbs.; broom corn, 270 tons; ashes, pot and pearl, 3,291 casks; grass seed, 5,852 bbls.; furs, 139 bales; lead and shot, about 1,000,000 lbs.; staves, dressed, 189,000, &c. &c.

MILWAUKEE, *County*, is bounded on the north by Washington, east by the State line, south by Racine, and west by Waukesha. It was established and set off from Brown, Sept. 6, 1834, and fully organized. Its original limits extended from the south and east lines of the present State of Wisconsin north to the north line of township 12, and west to the line between the Green Bay and Wisconsin land districts, which was established June 26, 1834, and was "a north and south line drawn from the northern boundary of Illinois, along the range line next west of Fort Winnebago to the Wisconsin river," or the range line between ranges 8 and 9 E. The seat of justice is established at the city of Milwaukee. This county was originally covered with a heavy growth of hard timber. The soil is good and well adapted to the raising of grain and to gardening. The streams are the Milwaukee, Menomonee, and Root rivers and Oak creek. This county is in the second judicial circuit and the first congressional district. Its legislative representation is as follows: The first and second wards of the city of Milwaukee, and towns of Wauwatosa, Milwaukee and Granville, constitute the fifth senate district. The third, fourth, and fifth wards in the city of Milwaukee, and the towns of Greenfield, Lake, Oak Creek and Franklin, constitute the sixth senate district. The first ward in the city of Milwaukee constitutes an assembly district. The second ward in the city of Milwaukee constitutes an assembly district. The third ward in the city of Milwaukee constitutes an assembly district. The fourth ward in the city of Milwaukee constitutes an assembly district. The fifth ward in the city of Milwaukee constitutes an assembly district. The towns of Franklin and Oak Creek constitute an assembly district. The towns of Greenfield and Lake constitute an assembly district. The town of Wauwatosa constitutes an assembly district. The towns of Milwaukee and Granville constitute an assembly district. County Officers for the years 1853 and 1854: Judge, Horatio N. Wells; Sheriff, Herman L. Page; Clerk of Court, Matthew Keenan; District Attorney, A. R. R. Butler; Register of Deeds, Charles J. Kern.

MILWAUKEE, *Town*, in county of same name, being fractional towns 7 and 8 N., of range 22 E.; in which is located the city of Milwaukee. The population in 1850 was 1,364.

MILWAUKEE, *Falls*, on the Milwaukee river, near the mouth of Cedar river, in Washington county.

MILWAUKEE, *River*, has its source in the towns of Eden and Osceola, Fond du Lac county, and running southerly, through Washington county, unites with the Menomonee, at Milwaukee city, and enters Lake Michigan.

MINERAL, *Creek*, is a tributary from the Wisconsin, from the south, in Iowa county. It rises near Dodgeville.

MINERAL POINT, *P. V.*, county seat of Iowa county, contains about 2,500 inhabitants and is rapidly increasing. It has 5 churches, 4 smelting furnaces in operation, and the value of mineral raised in crude state is $500,000 per annum; 11 dry good stores, 5 groceries, 3 drug stores, and 1 book store. Inhabitants are mostly miners. It is surrounded by a rich farming country; is the terminus of the Mineral Point railroad from the Illinois state line to Mineral Point, a distance of 31½ miles, where it intersects the central railroad. A branch of the Peckatonnica runs near the village, affording water power.

MISSISSIPPI, *River*, "The Father of Waters," is the most important stream in the United States. Its entire length, according to Nicollett's Report to Congress, is 2,986 miles; about 275 miles of this distance forms the western boundary of Wisconsin. The principal tributaries of the Mississippi in this State are the St. Croix, Chippewa, Trempeleau, Black, and Wisconsin.

MITCHELL, *P. V.*, in county of Sheboygan.

MITCHELL, *Town*, in county of Sheboygan, being on section 12, town 14 N., of range 20 E.; centrally located, 20 miles southwest from Sheboygan. It has 4 school districts.

MOMINIKAN, *Lake*, on Red Cedar river.

MONCHES, *P. O.*, in Waukesha county.

MONTFORT, *P. O.*, (Village of Wingville,) on section 24, town 6 N., of range 1 W., 18 miles northeast from Lancaster, and 50 miles west from Madison, on a high and beautiful prairie on the thoroughfare from Madison to the Mississippi, and is surrounded by a rich and fertile farming country, which is becoming rapidly improved. Population 100, with 30 dwellings, 2 hotels, 2 stores, a melting furnace, and a Methodist church.

MONISH, *Lake*, in Waukesha county. See Denoon Lake.

MONROE, *C. H.* and *P. V.*, in town of same name, Green county, on section 35, town 2 N., of range 7 E. It is 40 miles south from Madison. Population 900, with 200 dwellings, 7 stores,

3 hotels, 2 mills, 4 waggon, 5 blacksmith, 4 cabinet, 4 shoe and 4 carpenter shops, 1 broom and 1 chair factory, 2 lath saws, and several turning lathes connected with machinery at the mills, 1 Methodist and 1 Christian church. Monroe is situated on the direct route from Janesville to Dubuque and Galena, 35 miles from the former, and 50 miles from the latter place. It is surrounded by a rich farming country and large tracts of the best quality of timber. The location is very healthy. The flouring mill runs 4 run of stone, and, with the saw mill, is driven by steam.

MONROE, *Town*, in county of Green, being town 2 N., of range 7 E., in which is located the county seat. Population in 1850 was 1,146. It has 7 school districts.

MONTELLO, *P. V.*, in Marquette county, on section 16, of town 15 N., of range 10 E., 19 miles west from Dartford, and 47 miles north from Madison, at the mouth of Montello river, and the outlet of Buffalo Lake. It possesses an excellent water power, having a fall of 14 feet, with sufficient water at all seasons of the year to carry five run of stone. It has all the advantages of the navigation of Neenah river. Population 200, with 50 dwellings, 7 stores, 2 hotels, 1 mill, 1 church, and several mechanical and manufacturing shops.

MONTELLO, *Town*, in county of Marquette, being town 15 N., of range 10. It has 3 school districts.

MONTELLO, *River*, rises in the northwest corner of Marquette county, and running southeasterly, empties into the Neenah river at the foot of Buffalo Lake.

MONTEREY, *P. O.*, in Oconomowoc, Waukesha county, on Ashippun creek.

MONTEVILLE, *Town*, in county of La Crosse.

MONTEZUMA, *P. V.*, in town of Jefferson, Green county, being in town 1 N., of range 8 E.

MONTICELLO, *P. V.*, on section 7, town 3 N., of range 8 E., in Green county. It is situated on the Madison and Monroe, and Beloit and Mineral Point stage routes, near the centre of the county, with a fine farming country surrounding it, and possesses a fine water power. It is 10 miles north of Monroe, and 30 miles south from Madison. Population 100, with 18 dwellings, 1 store, 1 hotel, 1 saw mill, 1 tin and sheet iron, 1 waggon and 1 cabinet shop; 1 Methodist Episcopal denomination.

MONTREAL, *Bay*, in La Pointe county, on the southern shore of Lake Superior, at the mouth of Montreal river.

MONTREAL, *River*, rises near the head of the Wisconsin and Ontonagon rivers, west of Lake Vieux Desert, and running quite rapidly northwesterly, enters Lake Superior at Montreal Bay, forming a portion of the boundary line between Michigan and Wisconsin, (La Pointe county.)

MONTROSE, *Town*, in county of Dane, being town 5 N., of range 8 E.; centrally located, 15 miles southwest from Madison. It has 7 school districts.

MORMAN, *Creek*, rises in range 5 W., La Crosse county, and runs westerly in township 15 N., entering the Mississippi.

MORRISON'S *Creek*, a small branch of Platte river, in Highland, Grant county.

MOUNDVILLE, *Settlement*, in Iowa county, one mile west of Blue Mounds *P. O.*

MOUNDVILLE, *P. O.*, in Marquette county, 12 miles from Montello.

MOUNDVILLE, *Town*, in county of Marquette.

MOUNTAIN ISLAND, *River*, see Tempeleau river.

MOUSE, *Lake*, is between Okauchee and Pine lakes, on the Oconomowoc river, in Waukesha county.

MOUNT HOPE, residence of R. M. Meigs, on section 1, in Ottawa, Waukesha county, adjoining village of Waterville.

MOUNT MORIAH, this name has been given to an elevation of land near Grand River, in the town of Kingsboro', Marquette county.

MOUNT MORRIS, Waushara county, an elevation in the south part of the town of Ontario.

MOUNT MORRIS, *Town*, in county of Waushara, being town 19 N., of range 11.

MOUNT PLEASANT, *Town*, in county of Racine, being town 3 N., of range 22 E.; centrally located, 6 miles west from Racine.

MOUNT PLEASANT, *Town*, in county of Green, being town 3 N., of range 8; centrally located, 8 miles northeast from Monroe. Population in 1850 was 579. It has 7 school districts.

MOUNT PLEASANT, *P. O.*, in town of same name, Green county, being in town 3 N., of range 8 E.

MOUNT STERLING, *P. V.*, in Crawford county, on section 26, town 10 N., of range 5 W.

MOUNT TREMPELEAU, a bluff about 500 feet high, at the mouth of the river of the same name, in Jackson county, having a beautiful and extensive view of the surrounding country.

MOUNT TOM, in Marquette county, in the town of Pleasant Valley.

MOUNT VERNON, *P. V.*, on the town line between Primrose and Springdale, in Dane county, 17 miles southwest from Madison. It is a flourishing village, with a healthy situation, in the valley of Sugar River, surrounded by a fine farming country producing grain of all kinds in great abundance, and well adapted to grazing and wool growing; and occupied by an industrious and enterprizing population. It has several good hydraulic powers, an excellent stone quarry, and good material for making brick. Taking into consideration the many advantages of this place, and the distance to other villages, together with the fact, that the land in the county is owned by actual settlers, it is destined, ere long, to assume an important place among the rapidly growing towns of Wisconsin.

MUD, *Lake*, a small lake in the town of Shields, Dodge county.

MUD, *Lake*, in Columbia county, a widening of the Neenah river, 5 miles below the Portage.

MUDDY, *Creek*, a branch from the north of Chippewa river, in town 26 N., of range 12 W.

MUDDY, *Creek*, a small stream entering the Mississippi, at Cassville, Grant county.

MUKWA, *P. V.* and *C. H.*, on section 20, town 22 N., of range 14 E., on Wolf river, in Waupacca county.

MUKWA, *Town*, in county of Waupacca.

MUKWANAGO, *P. V.*, situated on section 26, in town of same name, Waukesha county, 16 miles south from Waukesha, and 70 miles east from Madison, near the entrance of the Mukwanago creek into the Fox (Pishtakee) river. It is on the Milwaukee and Janesville plank road, and is the market town of an excellent farming region of land. The population is about 500, with 75 dwellings, 2 hotels, 5 stores, a large flouring mill, and a variety of mechanics.

MUKWANAGO, *Town*, in county of Waukesha, being town 5 N., of range 18 E.; centrally located, 10 miles south from Waukesha. Population in 1850 was 1,094. It has 8 school districts.

MUKWANAGO, *Lake*, an expansion of Pishtakee river, about two miles in length, in Waukesha county.

MULLET, *River*, rises in a small lake in Fond du Lac county, and running easterly into Sheboygan river, in Sheboygan county, it enters just above the Falls.

MUSCODA, *Town*, in the county of Grant, being the north half of town 7 N., of range 1 W., and all of the country embraced in towns 8 and 9 N., of ranges 1 and 2 W.; centrally located, 22 miles northeast from Lancaster. It has 2 school districts. This town was organized in 1852.

MUSCODA, *P. V.*, Grant county, in town of same name, is located on section 1, town 8 N., of range 1 W., on the southern bank of the Wisconsin river, being in the northeast corner of the town and county. It possesses a good site for a town, being on a beautiful prairie, heretofore known as English prairie, 10 feet above the level of high water mark. The river bank is composed of sand stone from the base to within seven feet of the top. The soil is a black vegetable loam, very productive. It is located 30 miles northeast from Lancaster, and 80 miles west from Madison, 45 miles from the mouth of the Wisconsin, and 25 below Helena. Population 250, with 50 dwellings, 3 stores, 2 hotels, and various branches of industry.

MUSKEGO, *P. V.*, in town of same name, Waukesha county, town 5 N., of range 20 E.

MUSKEGO, *Town*, in county of Waukesha, being town 5 N., of range 20 E.; centrally located, 10 miles southeast from Waukesha. The population in 1850 was 1,111. It has 8 school districts.

MUSKEGO, *Creek*, Waukesha county, rises in lake of the same name, and empties into Fox River at Rochester.

MUSKEGO, *Lake*, in town of same name, in the southeast part of Waukesha county, is nearly four miles long, and more than a mile wide.

MUSKEGO, *River*, is a tributary from the west of the Menomonee river, which it enters near Big Quinesec Falls.

MUSQUEWOC, *Lake*, in the west part of West Bend, in Washington county, is about 3½ miles long, and three-fourths of a mile wide.

MUSKOS, *River*, is a tributary from the west of the Menomonee river, which it enters near Big Quinesec Falls.

NAGAWICKA, *Lake*, is mostly on section 17 of the town of Delafield. It is about 3 miles long, and three-fourths of a mile wide; at the outlet are the mills and the village of Delafield. This lake has Bark river for its inlet and outlet, and contains a small and beautiful island.

NAMEBIN, *Lake*, La Pointe county. See Megilcheque lake.

NARROWS, *Creek*, is a tributary from the southwest of Baraboo river, which it enters about half way between Baraboo and Reedsburg.

NASHOTAH, *House*, the oldest institution of learning in the State, is located on the eastern bank of the upper Nashotah Lake, in the town of Summit, Waukesha county. It was chartered in 1847, and has all the powers and privileges of a University. At present the only department in operation is the Theological, which numbers about 30 students. The Board of Instruction consists of 3 Professors and 2 Tutors. It has a library of about 4,000 volumes. It is an institution of the Protestant Epispocal Church, and endeavors are now being made to place it upon a permanent foundation, which promises to be successful.

NASHOTAH, *Lake*, (Twin Lakes,) are in the eastern part of the town of Summit, Waukesha county, between which the old stage route from Madison to Milwaukee passes. The lakes are connected by a small brook, and each contains a periphery of two miles—the lower being a trifle the largest. The lower lake approaches within a short distance of the Upper Nemahbin.

NECADA, *River*, rises in the north part of Adams' county, and runs southerly, emptying into Yellow river about 6 miles above the Wisconsin river, in Adams' county.

NEENAH, *P. V.*, in town of same name, Winnebago county, on south side of the outlet of Winnebago lake, opposite Menasha, in town 20 N., of range 17 E.

NEENAH, *Town*, in county of Winnebago. Population in 1850 was 1,420. It has 7 school districts.

NEENAH, *River*, see Fox river of Green Bay.

NEKIMI, *Town*, in county of Winnebago. Population in 1850 was 910. It has 6 school districts.

Nekimi, *P. V.*, on section 20, town 17 N., of range 16 E., in Winnebago county. It is 95 miles northeast from Madison, and 15 southwest from Oshkosh, county seat, and is on the main road from Oshkosh to Milwaukee. Population 600, with 150 dwellings, 2 stores, 4 hotels, and 3 churches—Free Will, Baptist, and Methodist congregations.

Nelson's *Landing*, in Chippewa county, at mouth of Chippewa river, town 22 N., of range 14 W.

Nemahbin, *Lakes*, are in the southeastern part of Summit, Waukesha county, through which Bark river passes transversely. These lakes are separated from each other by a small strip of land, across which the road passes from Delafield west, through Summit centre. The Upper Nemahbin is but a short distance south of Nashotah, and about a mile and a half west of Nagawicka Lake. The lower lake contains a beautiful island, known as "Fairservice's," which was never surveyed, and is now claimed by the Hon. O. Reed. It is covered with a noble growth of maple. These lakes are about 3 miles long from north to south.

Nemadji, *River*, La Pointe county. See Gauche river.

Nemahkum, *P. O.*, in Marquette county, 11 miles from Montello.

Nemandy, *River*, (Emandiga,) in western part of La Pointe county, a tributary from the north of St. Croix river.

Nemayacum, *River*, see Mechan river.

Neosha, *P. O.*, in town of Rubicon, Dodge county, on section 30, town 10 N., of range 18 E., on the Rubicon.

Nepenski, *P. V.*, town 17 N., of range 14 E., Winnebago county. It is 20 miles southwest from Oshkosh, and 90 miles north from Madison, 6 miles from Ceresco, and 6 miles from Berlin. In the vicinity is Rush Lake, 7 miles long, and 3 miles wide, with an unimproved water power at the outlet. Population 95.

Nepeuskum, *P. O.* in county of Winnebago.

NEPEUSKUM, *Town*, in county of Winnebago. Population in 1850, was 361. It has 5 school districts.

NESHKORA, *Town*, in county of Marquette. It embraces sections 4, 5, 6, 7, 8, 9, 16, 17, 18, in town 17, of range 12 E., and sections 1, 2, 3, 4, 5, 6, 7, 8, 9, 10, 11, 12, 13, 14, 15, 16, 17, 18, 19, 20, 21, 22, 23, 24, 25, 26, 27, 28, 29, 30, 31, 32, 33, 34 and 35, in town 17 N., of range 11 E., and sections 2, 3, 4, 5, 6, 7, 8, 9, 10 and 11, in town 16 N., of range 11 E.

NESHKORO, *P. V.*, on section 8, town 17 N., of range 11 E., of Marquette county. It is 18 miles from Marquette, and 80 miles north from Madison, in a fine farming country, with sufficient water power for 10 run of stones, on the main road from Milwaukee to the Wisconsin and Black river pineries, and from Sheboygan to La Crosse. Population 200, with 27 dwellings, 4 stores, 2 hotels, 1 grist mill, 1 saw mill, 1 turning lathe, and Presbyterian and Methodist denominations.

NESHONOE, is the name of a new town in the county of La Crosse.

NEVADA, *P. V.*, on section 25, town 2 N., of range 8 E., in Green county, 9 miles from Monroe, on the main road from Janesville to Galena, 1 mile north of the surveyed route of the S. W. R. R. The advantages for farming are not to be surpassed by any part of the State. The denominations are Baptist, Methodist, and Christian.

NEWARK, *V.*, (Barton *P. O.*) in Washington county, on section 1 and 2 of town of same name. It is 18 miles west of Ozaukee, and 75 miles northeast from Madison, on the direct route from Milwaukee, 36 miles; to Fond du Lac, 28 miles. It is pleasantly situated on the Milwaukee river, in the midst of a highly productive country, with 150 inhabitants, 40 dwellings, 4 stores and 2 hotels, several mechanical shops and religious denominations.

NEWARK, *Town*, in county of Washington, being part of towns 11 and 12 N., of range 19 E. It has 6 school districts.

NEWARK, *Town*, in county of Rock, being town 1 N., of range 11 E.; centrally located, 13 miles southwest from Janesville. Population in 1850 was 798. It has 9 school districts.

NEWARK, *P. V.*, in town of same name, Rock county, town 1 N., of range 11 E.

NEW BERLIN, *P. V.*, in town of same name, Waukesha county, town 6 N., of range 20 E.

NEW CALIFORNIA, *P. V.*, on section 27, in town of Clifton, Grant county, being town 5 N., of range 1 W., 12 miles east from Lancaster, and 75 miles westerly from Madison.

NEW BERLIN, *Town*, in county of Waukesha, being town 6 N., of range 20 E.; located six miles east from Waukesha. Population in 1850 was 1,293. It has 10 school districts.

NEW BUFFALO, *Town*, in county of Sauk. It is north of Baraboo.

NEWBURG, *P. V.*, on sec. 12, town 11 N., of range 20 E., being in the town of Trenton, Washington county, 10 miles west from Ozaukee, and 80 miles northeast from Madison; on the Milwaukee river, 30 miles northwest from the city of Milwaukee. The place is new, it being but five years since the first location. Population 100, with 15 stores, 2 hotels, 1 flouring mill, 1 saw mill, and several mechanical shops.

NEW DIGGINGS, *P. V.*, on section 26, of town 1, range 1 E., in Lafayette county. It is in the heart of the lead mines, and has 5 smelting furnaces. It is 6 miles southwest from Shullsburg, and about 80 southwest from Madison, and has 5 stores, 3 hotels, 1 mill, and 3 religious denominations.

NEW GLARUS, *P. V.*, on section 14, town 4 N., of range 7 E., in Green county. It is 15 miles north from Monroe, and about 25 miles south from Madison. Population 120, with 25 dwellings, 2 stores, 1 hotel, and 1 German reformed church.

NEW GLARUS, *Town*, in county of Green, being town 4 N., of range 7 E.; centrally located, 14 miles north from Monroe. Population in 1850 was 321.

NEW GRANT, *Diggings*, a mining settlement in town 4 N., of range 4 E., in Grant county.

NEW HOLSTEIN, *Town*, in county of Calumet. It has 2 school districts.

NEW MEXICO, *Town* & *Village*, name changed to Monroe, Green county.

NEWTON CORNERS, *P. O.*, on section 7, in town 7 N., of range 13 E., being town of Lake Mills, Jefferson county. It is 15 miles northwest from Jefferson, and 20 east from Madison, at the junction of the State road from Janesville to Portage city with the Madison and Milwaukee mail route. It has 4 dwellings, 20 inhabitants, 1 hotel, and a saw mill near, on Koskonong creek.

NICHOL'S, *Creek*, a small branch of Black river from the north, opposite Robinson's creek.

MIDJIKWE, *Lake*, the most eastern of the sources of the St. Croix river, in La Pointe county.

NIP-AND-TUCK, *Diggings*, a mining point on section 30, of town 4 N., of range 4 W., in Grant county.

NIPPISING, *Creek*, is a small stream in the southeast corner of Walworth county, runs southerly into the State of Illinois.

NIPPISING, *Lakes*, two lakes in the southwest corner of the town of Wheatland, in Kenosha county, the most southern of which is about 2 miles long, the other nearly 1 mile. The road from Kenosha to Beloit passes between them. They discharge their waters into Fox River, (Pishtaka.)

NORTH, *Lake*, is about half way between Okauchee and Tuck-Kipping lakes, and directly north of Pine Lake. It has an area of over 500 acres, and is near the centre of the town of Merton, Waukesha county.

NORWAY, *Town*, in county of Racine, being town 4 N., of range 20 E.; centrally located, 18 miles west from Janesville. Population in 1850 was 870. It has 3 school districts.

NORWAY, *P.O.*, in town of same name, Racine county; being town 4 N., of range 20 E.

NORWICH, *Town*, in county of Waushara; name changed to Oasis.

OAK CREEK, *P.O.*, in town of same name, Milwaukee county, town 5 N., of range 22 E.

OAK, *Creek*, a small tributary of Lake Michigan, from near the town line between the towns of Lake and Oak Creek, in Milwaukee county.

OAK CREEK, *Town*, in county of Milwaukee, being town 5 N., of range 22 E.; centrally lacated, 10 miles from Milwaukee. The population in 1850 was 1,289. It has 7 school districts.

OAKFIELD, *Town*, in county of Fond du Lac, being town 14 N., of range 16 E., centrally located, 10 miles southwest from Fond du Lac. The population in 1850 was 588. It has 8 school districts.

OAKFIELD, *P. O.*, in town of same name, on section 27, in Fond du Lac county, 12 miles southwest from Fond du Lac, and 80 northeast from Madison, on the head waters of Rock river, in a good farming region.

OAK GROVE, *P. V.*, in town of same name, Dodge county, on sections 31 and 32, town 11 N., of range 15 E.

OAK GROVE, *Town*, (formerly Fairfield), in county of Dodge, being town 11 N., of range 15 E. Population in 1850 was 1,143. It has 10 school districts.

OAK HILL, *P. V.*, in Jefferson county.

OAK LAND, *Town*, in county of Jefferson, being town 6 N., of range 13 E.; centrally located, 8 miles west from Jefferson. Population in 1850 was 806. It has 4 school districts.

OASIS, *Town*, in county of Waushara, being town 20 N., of ranges 8 and 9; centrally located, 25 miles northwest from Sacramento.

OASIS, *P. V.*, on section 33, in town of same name, being town 20 N., of range 9, in Waushara county; 30 miles northwest from Sacramento, and 80 miles north of Madison, on the stage road from Madison, *via* Fort Winnebago, to Plover Portage.

OCHA-SUN-SEPA, *River*, a tribntary from the northeast of Courtœrille river, in La Pointe county.

OCKEE, *Creek*, rises in Lowville, Columbia county, and runs nearly west, emptying into the Wisconsin.

O'CLAIR, *River*, L'eau St. Claire, in Chippewa county, a branch of Chippewa river from the E., in town 27 N., of range 9 W.

OCONOMOWOC, *Town*, in county of Waukesha, being town 8 N., of range 17 E.; centrally located, 20 miles northwest from Waukesha. Population in 1850 was 1,218.

OCONOMOWOC, *P. V.*, on section 33, in town of same name, 18 miles northwest of Waukesha, and 50 east from Madison, on the great mail route from Milwaukee to Galena; also on the Milwaukee and Watertown plank road. Population 250, with 50 dwellings, 10 stores, 3 hotels, 1 grist mill, 1 saw mill, 1 oil mill, 2 turning lathes, 1 saleratus factory, and a good supply of mechanics and professional men; also 1 Methodist and 1 Episcopal church. It is beautifully situated on a neck of land between La Belle and Fowler's Lakes, and is surrounded by a fertile farming district.

OCONOMOWOC, *Creek*, rises in the town of Polk, Washington county, and running southwest, passes through a succession of small and beautiful lakes, enters Rock river in the south part of Ixonia, Jefferson county.

OCONOMOWOC, *Lake*, is on the river and in town of same name, about half way between the village of Oconomowoc and Okauchee. It is nearly 2 miles long.

OCONTO, *County*, is bounded on the north by the State line, on the east by the middle of Green Bay and a portion of Brown, on the south by Brown and Outagamie, and on the west by

Waupacca and Marathon. It was set off and established from Brown, February 6, 1851, and organized for county purposes April 7, 1852. The principal rivers are Pishtego, Oconto, Pensaukee, and Little Suamico. The judicial connection of Oconto is with Brown, and representative with Outagamie. The chief product of this county, thus far, has been pine lumber, which is produced in great quantities; but little is known of its agricultural advantages.

OCONTO, *Town*, including the whole of Oconto county. It has 5 school districts.

OCONTO, *Bank*, near the mouth of Oconto river, in Green Bay.

OCONTO, *River*, rises near the head waters of Wolf river, and running southeast, enters Green Bay in town 28 N., of range 22 E.

OENCA, *P. O.*, in Jefferson county.

OGALLA, *P. V.*, at the mills near the mouth of the Eau Galla river, in Chippewa county.

OKAUCHEE, *Lake*, (or Kauchee), is on the Oconomowoc creek, in the eastern part of town of Oconomowoc, at the outlet of which are mills and a settlement formerly known as "Reed's Mills," "Hurd's Mills," and "McCormack's Mills."

OKAUCHEE, *P. V.*, at outlet of lake of same name, in Oconomowoc, Waukesha county.

OMRO, *P. V.*, on section 17 and 18, in town of Bloomingdale, Winnebago county, at the junction of the Manitowoc and Menasha, (extended), and the Waupun and Liberty Prairie plank roads. It is pleasantly situated on the south side of the Neenah river, 11 miles west from Oshkosh, and 75 miles northeast from Madison. It has a heavy body of timber on the north, with a rich soil of openings and prairie on the south, and has excellent facilities by water for obtaining pine logs from the immense pinery of Wolf river, a great quantity of which is here manufactured into lumber. Population 600, with 100 dwellings, 5 stores, 2 hotels, 3 mills, and 4 religious denominations. A Company has been organized and is now completing the proper buildings for the manufacture of glass.

Omro, *Town*, (formerly Bloomingdale,) in county of Winnebago, being town 18 N,, of range 18 E.

Oneida, *P. V.*, in Brown county, on Duck creek, near centre of Oneida Reservation.

O'Neil's, *Creek*, a small tributary of Black river from the east, in town 24 N.

One Mile, *Creek*, a tributary in Sauk county, of the Lemonwier river.

Oneonta, *P. O.*, in Sauk county.

Onion River, *P. V.*, in county of Sheboygan.

Onion, *River*, rises in Holland, Sheboygan county, runs northerly, and unites with Sheboygan river, just below the Falls.

Ontario, *Town*, in the county of Waushara, being town 20 N., of ranges 11, 12 and 13, north of Sacramento.

O'Plaine, *River*, rises in the southern part of Racine county, and runs southerly, through the county of Kenosha, into the State of Illinois, uniting with Kankakee river of Indiana, at Dresden and the Pishtaka at Ottawa, forms the head waters of the Illinois river. The Indian name is She-shik-ma-o.

Oregon, *Town*, in county of Dane, being town 5 N., of range 9 E.; centrally located, 12 miles south from Madison. Population in 1850 was 638. It has 9 school districts.

Oregon, *P. V.*, on section 12, in town of same name, 12 miles south from Madison, on Janesville stage road, on the head waters of Badfish creek, equidistant from Sugar and Catfish rivers. It has 55 inhabitants, 9 dwellings, 1 store, 1 hotel, and 3 religious denominations—Presbyterian, Methodist and and United Brethren.

Orion, *P. V.*, in the town of Richmond, Richland county, being town 9 N., of range 1 E.

OSBORN, *P.O.*, in town of Porter, Rock county, on section 31, town 4 N., of range 11 E.

OSHAUKUTA, *P. V.*, (Hill's Corners), on section 10, town 11 N., of range 9, in Columbia county. It is 7 miles from Fort Winnebago, and 30 miles from Madison. Population 100, with 12 dwellings, 1 store, 1 hotel, and 1 religious denomination.

OSCEOLA, *Town*, in county of Fond du Lac, being town 14 N., of range 19 E. It has 3 school districts.

OSHKOSH, *Town*, in county of Winnebago, being town 18 N., of range 16 E.

OSHKOSH, *P. V.*, on section 24 of town of same name, and county seat of Winnebago county. It is 84 miles north from Madison, 8 miles below the junction of Fox and Wolf rivers, and where these waters empty into Lake Winnebago. The State Land Offices are located at this place. Population, 2,500; with 6 hotels, 6 mills, 1 candle factory, 1 foundry, 1 threshing machine factory, 3 butchers, 2 breweries, 1 pump manufactory, 2 barrel and 2 waggon shops, 1 shingle and 2 sash factories, 1 tannery, 5 blacksmiths, 9 dry goods, 1 drug, 2 hardware, 2 clothing, and 4 boot and shoe stores, 10 groceries, 2 bakeries, 5 warehouses, 1 book-bindery, 1 academy, and 3 newspapers. There are 3 religious denominations—Episcopal, Methodist and Catholic.

OSHTIGWAN, *Lake*, in Marathon county, tributary to the Little Wisconsin, a few miles above its mouth. It is near the 45° 30' north latitude.

OSHTIGWAN, *River*, near the outlet of Lake of the same name.

OSSIN, *River*, rises in Washington county, and runs W., emptying into Lake Horicon, in Dodge county.

OTSEGO, *P. V.*, in town of same name, in Columbia county, on section 22, town 11 N., of range 11 E.

OTSEGO, *Town*, in county of Columbia, being town 11 N., of range 11 W.; centrally located, 15 miles southeast from Portage. Population in 1850 was 420. It has 5 school districts.

OTTAWA, *P. V.*, in town of same name, on section 34, Waukesha county.

OTTAWA, *Town*, in county of Waukesha, being town 6 N., of range 17 E.; centrally located, 15 miles west from Waukesha. Population in 1850 was 793. It has 6 school districts.

OTTAWA, *Lake*, La Pointe county, see Lake Court-eoreille.

OTTER, *Creek*, a branch from the south of L'eau Claire river, in town 27 N., of range 9 W.

OTTER, *Creek*, in Bad Ax county, is a small tributary of Kickapoo river.

OTTER, *Creek*, is a small stream rising near Mineral Point, in Iowa county, running southerly, emptying into the Peckatonnica at Otterborne, in the northwest corner of town 2 N., of range 4 E.

OTTER, *Creek*, rises in town 11 N., of range 8 E., and running south, enters the Wisconsin about 4 miles below Lower Sauk.

OTTER, *Creek*, rises in the town of Lima, Rock county, and runs northwest, enters Koskonong lake.

OTTER, *Lake*, is a small lake in the northeast corner of the town of Sugar Creek. It is about 2 miles long.

OUTAGAMIE, *County*, is bounded on the north by Oconto and a portion of Waupacca, east by Brown, south by Calumet and Winnebago, and west by Waupacca, and is 24 miles north and south by 27 miles east and west. It was established Feb. 17, 1851, from Brown, to which it remained attached for judicial purposes until March 15, 1852, when it was completely organized. The boundaries were defined March 4, 1852. The seat of justice is about half way between the villages of Appleton and Grand Chute, and about a mile from each. The general surface of the county is level and covered with a heavy growth of timber, such as maple, elm, ash and hickory, with but little or no waste lands. The soil is good, but the agricultural existence of the county is so recent, little can be said of its capabilities. All the crops that have been tested here have succeeded beyond the expectations of the farmer. The population, now numbering about 4,000, is composed of good, rural, and industrious settlers, mostly from New England and New York. It is watered by the Lower Fox on the southeast, and by Wolf river on the west, and Duck Creek on the northeast. This county belongs to the fourth judicial circuit, to the second senate, and to the third congressional districts, and with Oconto, constitutes an assembly district. County Officers for 1853 and 1854: Judge, Perry H. Smith; Sheriff, A. B. Everts; Clerk of Court, H. S. Eggleston; Attorney, A. S. Sanborn; Register of Deeds, J. S. Buck; Clerk of Board of Supervisors, G. W. Gregory; Treasurer, Robert Morrow; Surveyor, Chas. Turner; Coroner, Patrick Hunt.

OXFORD, *Town*, in county of Marquette, being town 15 N., of range 8.

OZAUKEE, *C. H.* & *P. V.*, see Port Washington.

OZAUKEE, *County*, was set off from Washington at the session of the legislature in January 1853. It comprises all of that portion of said county east of range 20. For a description of this county, see Washington county.

PACKWAUKEE, *P. V.*, on section 20, town 15 N., of range 9 E., in Marquette county, 35 miles northwest from Dartford, and 50 miles north from Madison. It is situated on the north side of Buffalo Lake, on a direct line from Portage to Stevens' Point, 18 miles north from the former place. Being on the navigable waters of the Neenah river, it is supposed that this place will command the river trade of a large portion of good farming lands in Adams and Waushara counties. Population 300, with 75 dwellings, 3 stores, 2 hotels, 1 mill, and 3 religious denominations.

PACKWAUKEE, *Town*, in county of Marquette. It has 12 school districts.

PAINT, *Creek*, a branch of Chippewa river from the southeast, in town 28 N., of range 8, in Chippewa county.

PAKWEYORRA, *Lake*, a widening of Chippewa river near its source.

PALMYRA, *Town*, in county of Jefferson, being town 5 N., of range 16 E.; centrally located, 12 miles southeast from Jefferson. Population in 1850 was 997. It has 8 school districts.

PALMYRA, *P. V.*, on section 22, in town of same name, 15 miles southeast from Jefferson, and 45 miles southeast from Madison. It is situated on Scupernong creek, on the M. & M. R. R. 40 miles from Milwaukee. It has a fine water power, and is surrounded by a good farming district, comprising prairies, openings, and wood land.

PALMYRA, *Lake*, a small lake about three quarters of a mile southeast of Palmyra village, in Jefferson county.

PARDEEVILLE, *P. V.*, in town of Wyocena, Columbia county, on Neenah river, in section 3, town 12 N., of range 10 E.

PARIS, *P. V.*, in town of same name, Kenosha county, being in town 2 N., of range 21 E.

PARIS, *Town*, in county of Kenosha, being town 2 N., of range 21 E.; centrally located, 10 miles northwest from Kenosha. Population in 1850 was 947. It has 9 school districts.

PARIS, *Town*, in county of Grant, being town 2 N., range 2 W.; centrally located, 15 miles southwest from Lancaster. It has 4 school districts.

PATCH, *Diggings*, a mining town in Grant county, being town 2 N., of range 1 W.

PATCH GROVE, *Town*, in county of Grant, being all of said county embraced in towns 5, 6, and 7 N., of range 5, 6, and 7 W.; centrally located, 20 miles northwest from Lancaster. It has 11 school districts.

PATCH GROVE, *P. V.*, in town of same name, being on section 4, in town 5 N., of range 5 W., Grant county.

PATTENWELL, *Peak*, in Adams county, on west bank of Wisconsin river, in town 18 N., of range 4.

PATRIDGE, *Lake*, is about 4 miles long and 2 broad, in the town of Weyauwegan, Waupacca county, its outlet being at Wolf river.

PAU-WAI-CON, *Lake*, is a large expansion of Wolf river, a few miles above its mouth. It is about 10 miles wide from east to west, and 3 miles long.

PECKATONICA, *Forks*, of river of same name, at Wiota.

PECKATONICA, *River*, rises a few miles west of Mineral Point, in Iowa county, and running southeast through the counties of Lafayette and Green, empties into Rock river, at Rockton, Illinois.

PEMENEE (ELBOW) *Falls*, of the Menomonee river. At this place the water falls about 9 feet in the distance of 800 feet; the water is contracted to 50 feet in width.

PENSAUKEE, *River*, rises in town 25 N., of range 18 E., in Oconto county, and runs northeast, entering Green Bay in town 7 N., of range 21 E.

PEN YANN, *P. O.*, in the county of Racine.

PEQUOT, *P. V.*, on the Brothertown Reservation, at the mouth of a small stream on Lake Winnebago, in Calumet county, about 90 miles northeast from Madison.

PERRY, *Town*, in county of Dane, being town 5 N., of range 6 E. It is 25 miles southeast from Madison. It is unorganized, but attached to Primrose.

PESHTIGO, *Shoals*, on western shore of Lake Michigan, at the mouth of river of the same name.

PESHTIGO, *River*, the largest tributary of Green Bay, between the Menomonee and Neenah. It enters the Bay about half way between the Oconto and Menomonee rivers.

PEWAUKEE, *Town*, in county of Waukesha, being town 7 N., of range 19 E.; centrally located, 4 miles north of Waukesha. Population in 1850 was 1,093. It has 11 school districts.

PEWAUKEE, *P. V.*, on section 9, in town of same name, in Waukesha county; situated at the foot of Pewaukee Lake, 6 miles northwest from Waukesha, on the Milwaukee, Watertown, and Madison plank road. Population 120, with 25 dwellings, 2 stores, 2 hotels, 1 saw mill, 1 flouring mill, tannery, a Baptist and a Congregational church.

PEWAUKEE, *Lake*, mostly in town of same name, in Waukesha county, is about 5 miles long and nearly a mile wide. It is fed mostly by springs, and discharges its waters at the east end, into the Pishtaka river, at which Pewaukee village and mills are located.

PHEASANT BRANCH, *P. O.*, in east part of Middleton, Dane county, being town 7 N., of range 8 E.

PHEASANT BRANCH, a small tributary of Fourth Lake, in Middleton, Dane county.

PICKARDEE, *Creek*, enters the Mississippi in town 8 N., Crawford county.

PIERCE, *Town*. A new town in county of La Crosse.

PIERCE, *County*, includes all that part of St. Croix county south of the north line of town 27, and was set off from St. Croix, March 16, 1853. It therefore is bounded on the west by St. Croix river, by which it is separated from the Territory of Minnesota. This county holds out very great inducements to immigrants, a large amount of the 500,000 acre grant, given by Congress to the State for schools, is in this county, and is sold at one dollar and twenty-five cents per acre, the settler being allowed thirty years pre-emption. The lands are about half prairie and half timber—the prairies a black loam, producing as great a yield of wheat, oats, corn, and other grain, as any other part of the West. The timber is of an excellent quality, oak, ash, butternut, black walnut, sugar maple, &c.

Steam boats pass up, during the season of navigation, near to the homes of the inhabitants. It is to be fully organized at once, and is attached to the sixth judicial circuit, and to the same representative districts as St. Croix, Polk and La Pointe.

PIERCEVILLE, *P. V.*, in town of Sun Prairie, Dane county, on section 26, town 8 N., of range 11 E.

PIGEON, *Creek*, rises near Lancaster, and enters Grant River in Beetown, Grant county.

PIGEON, *Creek*, is a small stream rising in Sheboygan county, unites with Stony Creek in Farmington, Washington county.

PIGEON GROVE, *P. O.*, in Columbia county.

PIKE, *River*, is a small stream rising about 6 miles west of the city of Kenosha, taking a circuit of about 15 miles to the north, enters Lake Michigan at Kenosha.

PIN HOOK, *P. O.*, in Grant county.

PINE BLUFF, *P. O.*, in town of Cross Plains, Dane county, town 7 N., of range 7 E.

PINE, *Creek*, a small stream uniting with Skillet river, enters the Baraboo river about 3 miles west of the village of Baraboo.

PINE, *Creek*, enters the Kickapoo river from the west, in Crawford county.

PINE, *Lake*, is a small lake between Red Cedar and Birch Lakes, in Chippewa county, on the east branch of Red Cedar river.

PINE, *Lake*, a widening of Red Cedar River, below Birch Lake on the same.

PINE, *Lake*, is of the Oconomowoc Group, lying in the south part of Merton, Waukesha county, immediately north of Nagawicka, and of the same size. It is surrounded by scenery, which, for beauty, is unsurpassed, while the land is excellent for agricultural purposes. Several beautiful villas have been built upon its borders.

PINE RIVER, *Town*, in county of Waushara, being towns 19 and 20, of range 13 E.

PINE RIVER, *P. O.*, in Waushara county.

PINE, *River*, rises in town 20 N., of range 10 E., in Waushara county, and running east, enters the west end of Lake Pauwaicun.

PINE, *River*, rises in Bad Ax county, and runs southerly into the Wisconsin river, at the range line between ranges 1 and 2 E.

PINE, *River*, a tributary from the north of St. Croix river, La Pointe county.

PINE, *River*, (of the Menomonee), see Muskos river.

PINE VALLEY, *Town*, in county of La Crosse, being all of said county, between towns 16 and 23 N.

PIPE, *Creek*, rises near Dodgeville, Iowa county, and runs northerly, emptying into the Wisconsin river at Helena.

PIKE, *Creek*, a small stream entering Lake Michigan, at Kenosha.

PIKE, *Lake*, in town 27 E., of Portage county, the source of Big Plover river.

PIKE, *Lake*, a small lake in town of Hartford, Washington county.

PISHTAKA, *River*, see Fox River of Illinois.

PRIVABIK, *River*, of Lake Superior, see Iron river.

PLATTE, *Mounds*, two conical shaped hills on either side east and west of Belmont, Lafayette county, about 12 miles southwest from Mineral Point, and 62 miles from Madison. They are three miles apart, and have a small mound half way between them.

PLATTE, *River*, rises in Wingville, Grant county, runs southerly, and empties into the Mississippi, in Grant county.

PLATTEVILLE, *Town*, in county of Grant, being town 3 N., of range 1 W.; centrally located, 15 miles southeast from Lancaster. It has 8 school districts.

PLATTEVILLE, *P. V.*, is situated near the Rountree branch of Little Platte river, being on section 15, town 3 N., of range 1 W., 16 miles southeast from Lancaster, and 70 southwest from Madison. It is in the immediate vicinity of some excellent bodies of mineral. It was settled in 1827 by General John H. Rountree, and a post office was established in 1830. The village was incorporated in 1841, and contains an academy incorporated in 1839. Platteville has a population of about 1,200, with 3 hotels, 2 smelting furnaces, a large academical building, built of stone, several churches, and other public buildings.

PLEASANT PRAIRIE, *P. V.*, in town of same name, Kenosha county, being town 1 N., of range 22 E.; centrally located, 7 miles southwest from Kenosha. Population in 1850 was 959. It has 9 school districts.

PLEASANT SPRING, *Town*, in county of Dane, being town 6 N., of range 11 E.; centrally located, 12 miles southeast from Madison. Population in 1850 was 732. It has 6 school districts.

PLOVER, *Town*, in county of Portage, being town 23 N., of ranges 5, 6, 7, 8 and 9.

PLOVER, *P. V. & C. H.*, on section 22, town 23 N., of range 8 E., in town of same name, in Portage county, being the county seat. It is 120 miles northwest from Madison. Population 200, with 35 dwellings, 2 stores, 2 hotels, 1 grist and 1 saw mill.

PLUM, *Creek*, a small stream in Brown county, entering Fox river from the south at Bridgeport.

PLUM, *Creek*, rises in town 26 N., of range 15 W., in Chippewa county, runs southeast into Chippewa river.

PLUM, *Creek*, empties into the Kickapoo river from the west, in Crawford county.

PLUM, *Island*, a small island at the junction of Green Bay with Lake Michigan, south of Pottowottomee.

PLYMOUTH, *Town*, in county of Rock, being town 2 N., of range 11 E.; centrally located, 10 miles southwest from Janesville. Population in 1850 was 511. It has 4 school districts.

PLYMOUTH, *P. V*, in county of Sheboygan, being on section 22, in town of same name 15 N., of range 21 E.

PLYMOUTH, *Town*, in county of Sheboygan, being town 15 N., of range 21 E.; centrally located, 12 miles west from Sheboygan. It has 8 school districts.

POINT, *Creek*, in Manitowoc county, a small tributary of Lake Michigan, into which it empties about 10 miles southwest from Manitowoc.

POINT DETOUR, in La Pointe county, opposite the Twelve Apostle Islands, between Chegwamegon Bay and Bank Pointe.

POINTE SABLE, a point of land extending into Green Bay, in north-east corner of town 24 N., of range 21 E.

POLK, *County*. By an act of the legislature approved March 14, 1853, all that portion of St. Croix county lying north of the line between township 31 and 32, was set off into a separate county, to be called and known as the county of Polk. It is therefore bounded on the north by La Pointe, on the east by Chippewa, on the south by Chippewa and St. Croix, and on the west by the Territory of Minnesota, from which it is separated by the river St. Croix. It is mostly a lumber country, though the southern part contains a large area of excellent farming lands. The village of St. Croix Falls, the county seat, situated at the head of steamboat navigation on St. Croix river, is surrounded with excellent agricultural lands, and with the business naturally centreing there of the extensive pineries above, must be a town of considerable importance. This county is to be fully organized during the present year, and will form a part of the sixth judicial circuit. The representation will continue as before the division of St. Croix.

POLK, *Town*, in county of Washington, being town 10 N., of range 19 E.; centrally located, 20 miles southwest from Ozaukee. Population in 1850 was 1,344. It has 9 school districts.

PORTAGE, *County*, is bounded on the north by Marathon, on the east by Waupacca, on the south by Waushara and Adams, and on the west by La Crosse, and is 30 miles north and south, by 54 miles east and west. It was set off from Brown, Dec. 7, 1836, at which time it embraced about the present county of Columbia. By an act of the legislature, approved March 14, 1841, the territory forming the present counties of Adams, Portage and Marathon was annexed to Portage county, which was organized for county purposes, the judicial connection being with Dane. The county seat was established at the Wisconsin Portage, and the county was fully organized Jan. 31, 1844; as now organized, it does not contain any of its original limits. The eastern boundary of the county was extended one range February 27, 1851. Plover, a little east of the centre of the county, is the seat of justice. The Wisconsin river passes about contrally through the county from the north, and with its branches afford many good water powers which are, at present, chiefly used for working up pine timber, with forests of which the country is covered. This county is connected with the third judicial circuit, and with the second senate and second congressional districts, and, with Marathon, sends one member to the assembly. The population, as organized in 1840, was 1,623; 1842, 646; 1846, 931; 1847, 1,504; 1850, 1,267. At the last date, including Marathon, there were 13 farms, 30 manufactories, and 280 dwellings. County Officers for 1853: Judge, Enoch S. Bean; Sheriff, Aaron Drake; Clerk of Court, C. Shekels; District Attorney, Luther Hanchett; Clerk of Board of Supervisors, Matthias Mitchell; Treasurer, Ames M. Dunton.

PORTAGE CITY, *P. V. & C. H.*, on section 5 and 8 of town 12 N., of range 9 E., in Columbia county. It is 40 miles north from Madison. Population 2,000; with 12 stores, 7 hotels, 1 steam saw mill, 2 harness makers, 4 waggon makers, 6 blacksmiths, 3 cabinet, 3 paint, 8 shoe, 3 tin and sheet iron, 3 butchers, 6 millinery and 4 tailor's shops, 2 breweries, 2 livery stables, 2 jewelry stores, 2 drug stores, 1 brick yard, 1 iron foundry, 1 blind and sash factory, 1 chair factory and 1 tannery; 12 lawyers and 5 doctors; 3 district and 2 select schools; 1 church building and 2 denominations. It is finely situated on a bluff between the Fox and Wisconsin rivers at the point where they are connected by a ship canal. The Wisconsin is navigable to this place, and the commerce on the river is considerable and constantly increasing. Two steamers ply constantly between this place and Galena during the summer. The number of mills on the Wisconsin, and its tributaries, is about 100; the lumber from which seeks a market between this place and St. Louis. The amount of lumber sent below is almost beyond calculation. In addition to which, numerous mills are starting on the river at different points below the pinery, and logs are rafted to them. The amount of square timber rafted exceeds millions of feet annually, shingles and bolts, lath, pickets, &c. The Wolf river pinery is beginning to pour its vast amounts of the finest lumber in the State, through the Fox river, which stream also is navigable for small steamboats. When the projected State improvement is finished, inter-communication will be established between the upper Lake country and the Gulf of Mexico, and the carrying trade will produce a large revenue to the State. The importance of Portage City, as a commercial point, is beyond doubt very great. It commands 200 miles north where the pine forests nourish a large population, and are continually pouring their products south, and will for years to come.

Portage, *Lake*, is a small body of water in the north part of Marathon county, tributary to the Chippewa river.

Portage Prairie, *Town*, in county of Columbia, being town 12 N., of range 12, 18 miles east of Portage city. Population in 1850 was 455. It has 4 school districts.

Port des Morts, see Death's Door.

Porter, *Town*, in county of Rock, being town 4 N., range 11 E.; centrally located, 12 miles northwest from Janesville. Population in 1850 was 881. It has 7 school districts.

Port Hope, *Town*, in county of Columbia. Population in 1850 was 603. It has 4 school districts.

Port Hope, *P. V.*, in town of same name, on section 3 on the Neenah river, at the junction of French creek, 7½ miles north from Portage city, and 48 miles north of Madison, at the natural head of steamboat navigation on the Neenah river, and on the stage and mail route from Fort Winnebago to the Wisconsin pinery. It is beautifully located, in a good farming district. Population about 30; 5 dwellings, 1 store, 1 hotel, 1 Baptist, and an organized church of Methodists, and has a good hydraulic power unimproved.

Portland, *Town*, in county of Dodge, being town 9 N., of range 13 E.; centrally located, 14 miles southwest from Junea. Population in 1850 was 523. It has 6 school districts.

Port Washington, *Town*, in county of Washington, being town 11 N., range 22 E. See Ozaukee. Population in 1850 was 1,373. It has 5 school districts.

Port Washington, *V.*, (Ozaukee *P.O.*), on section 28, in town of same name, in Ouzaukee county. It is the county seat, and is situated 80 miles northeast from Madison, on the lake shore, half way between Milwaukee and Sheboygan. Population, 2,500; with 300 dwellings, 10 stores, 5 hotels, 3 mills, 2 breweries, 1 foundry, 5 blacksmiths, 4 waggon-makers, 6 shoe-makers, and 5 tailors' shops; 2 good piers, 1 church, and 5 denominations.

Poplar, *Creek*, a small stream in the eastern part of Pewaukee, Waukesha county, being a tributary to the Pishtaka.

Poplar, *River*, a tributary of Lake Superior, in La Pointe county.

POTOSI, *P. V.*, on section 34, in town 3, of range 3 W., 12 miles south of Lancaster, and 80 miles southwest from Madison. It is at the head of a ravine about 2 miles from the Mississippi river, near the mouth of Grant river, and embraces the town plats of Lafayette, Van Buren, and Dublin. This place was formerly known as Snake Hollows, at which improvements were commenced as early as 1836.

POTOSI, *Town*, in county of Grant, being fractional town 2, and town 3 N., of range 3 W.; centrally located, 10 miles south from Lancaster. It has 8 school districts.

POTTAWOTTOMEE, *Island*, in towns 33 and 34 N., of range 30 E., in Door county; contains about 35 square miles.

POTTER, *Lake*, a small lake in the east part of East Troy, Walworth county.

POWACK, *Lake*, a small body of water in the northern part of the town of Muskego, in Waukesha county.

POYNETTE, *P. V.*, on section 34, town 11 N., of range 9 E., in Columbia county, 12 miles south from Portage city, and 21 miles north from Madison. It is situated in a rich farming district of cultivated lands, on Ockee creek, and has a good hydraulic power unimproved. It contains 150 inhabitants, 32 dwellings, 1 store, and 1 hotel.

PRAIRIE DU CHIEN, *P. V. & C. H.*, is situated on section 6, town 6 N., of range 6 W., upon an elevated prairie, averaging one mile in width, and is about 8 miles in length, extending from the mouth of the Wisconsin river, northward, along the bank of the Mississippi. It has one of the best landings on the river, is very healthy; and all who have visited the place concur in the opinion that its location gives it a commanding commercial importance.

PRAIRIE DU CHIEN, *Town*, in county of Crawford, including the same. Population in 1850 was 1,407. It has 14 school districts.

Poysippi, *P. O.*, in Waupacca county.

Prairie du Lac, (Lake Prairie), is a large prairie in Rock county, near the foot of Lake Koskonong.

Prairie du Sac, *P. V.*, in town of same name, Sauk county, on section 36, town 10 N., of range 6 E.

Prairie du Sac, *Town*, in county of Sauk, south of Baraboo. It has 5 school districts.

Prairie La Crosse, is the name given to the beautiful prairie at the mouth of La Crosse river, it was formerly an Indian trading station, and was frequented by them for the purpose of playing their favorite game of ball, from which fact the river now known as La Crosse river, derived its original name of Ball river.

Prairie La Crosse, *Village*, see La Crosse *P. V.*

Pratt's, *Creek*, rises in the north part of town of Oak Grove, in Dodge county, and runs southwest, emptying into the Crawfish, in the town of Shields.

Prescott, *Town*, (formerly Elizabeth), in county of Peirce, being all of said county, south of town 27 N. It is southeast of Willow river.

Prescott, *P. V.* & *C. H.*, of the new county of Peirce. It is at the junction of the St. Croix and Mississippi, having a number of public houses, stores, warehouses, &c. It must eventually be an important depot for the St. Croix and its tributaries, as well as for Minnesota.

Prideaux Fork, *Creek*, a branch of Grant river from the northwest, in Beetown, Grant county.

Primrose, *P. V.*, on section 9, in town of same name, Dane county; 22 miles southwest of Madison. It contains 250 inhabitants, 50 dwellings, 1 store, 1 Baptist, and 1 Freewill Baptist church.

PRIMROSE, *Town*, in county of Dane, being town 5 N., of range 8 E.; centrally located, 18 miles southwest from Madison. It has 6 school districts.

PRINCETON, *P. V.*, in Marquette county, being on section 24, town 16 N., of range 11 E.; 10 miles from Montello.

PRINCETON, (formerly Pleasant Valley), in Marquette county.

PROSPECT HILL, *P. V.*, on section 29 of New Berlin, Waukesha county. It is 6 miles from Waukesha, and 70 miles southeast from Madison, at the junction of the Milwaukee and Janesville plank road with the Racine and Waukesha stage route. It has 40 inhabitants, 6 dwellings, 1 store, 1 tavern, and a steam grist and steam saw mill, 1 blacksmith and 1 waggon shop.

PUCKAWAY, *Lake*, in Marquette county, is an expansion of the Neenah river, about 2 miles wide, and 7 miles long.

PULASKI, *Town*, in county of Iowa, being towns 8 N., of ranges 1 and 2; centrally located, 10 miles northwest from Mineral Point. It has 3 school districts.

PULASKI, *P. V.*, in town of same name, in northwest corner of Iowa county, on the Wisconsin river.

PYKI, *River* and *Lake*, upper tributaries of St. Croix river, in La Pointe county.

QUAVER, *Rapids*, on Menomonee river, between Sturgeon and Pemenee Falls.

QUITQUIOC, *Village*, is situated upon the Mullet river, a branch of the Sheboygan and in the township of Plymouth, county of Sheboygan. It contains a fine hotel, a saw mill, several stores, blacksmith shops, &c. The river, upon which it is located, is named after General Mullet, and not, as many suppose, from the species of fish of that name. The amount of attention which this village has received from the legislature, and the peculiarity of its name, have given it an importance which it would not otherwise have attained.

Etymologists have puzzled their heads very much over the word Quitquioc. By some it has been supposed to be a corruption of *hic*, *haec*, *hoc*, but this, like many other suggestions from the same source, is too absurd to merit consideration. The real derivation of the word is from the Menomonee, *Quitlztlqueouowouwoc*, which signifies a sulphur or mineral spring. A spring of this character is said to exist there, and this, together with the romantic beauty of the scenery in that vicinity—it being upon the border of that belt of *Moraines* denominated the "Potash Kettles"—may make it hereafter the Saratoga of Wisconsin.

RACCOON, *River*, in Bad Ax county, head waters in the south part of La Crosse county, runs southwest, and empties into the Mississippi in town 14 N.

RACINE, *City*, is situated on the western shore of Lake Michigan, at the mouth of Root river, and comprises fractional sections 9 and 16 of town 3 N., of range 23 E. It was first settled in 1835, incorporated as a village in 1841, and received a city charter in 1848. The city is principally built upon a plain or table land elevated some thirty or forty feet above the waters of the lake, forming a beautiful site for a city. It is laid out in regular lots and blocks with wide streets, and is justly entitled to the appellation of "La Belle City of the Lakes." It is the county town of Racine county, situated 16 miles north of the State line, and 25 south of Milwaukee. Its beautiful and healthful location, combined with its commercial advantages, early attracted the attention of adventurers and capitalists; and it has had a rapid, continuous, and healthy growth, as will be seen by the following statement of annual enumeration of its inhabitants: In 1840 the population was 337; 1844, 1,100; 1847, 3,004; 1849, 4,002; 1850, 5,111; 1851, 5,897; and it is now supposed to be nearly 7,000. Racine has one of the best, if not the very best harbor on the western shore of the lake. Over $60,000 have been expended in its construction by the citizens, of their own means, raised by voluntary taxation. This enterprize is justly considered one of the most important ever projected and carried out to a successful completion by so small a community, and furnishes a fair index to the character of her population for enterprize. In addition to the amount raised by this means, Congress has appropriated $12,500, which has been expended, and $10,000 are now appropriated to be expended the present season. The harbor is now sufficient to accommodate the entire shipping of the lake, and being protected by the high banks of the river is entirely safe. The city of Racine is also distinguished among western towns for the number and beauty of its public buildings. Over $125,000 are now invested in them. Fourteen churches have been erected, to wit: 1 Presbyterian, 1 Congregational, 1 Baptist, 1 Freewill Baptist, 1 Episcopal, 1 Methodist, 1 Lutheran, 2 Welch, 1 German Evangelical, 1 German Lutheran, 1 Universalist, 2 Catholic—1 German and 1 Irish. Racine college, an Episcopal institution, is located at this point. A beautiful college edifice, of brick, has been erected, which, together with the college grounds, are valued at $15,000. This amount was contributed by the citizens. The institution is under the management of Rev. Roswell Park, D. D. The first session of the college commenced last fall, and now numbers over 20 pupils. The board of education of the city are now engaged in erecting a central high school edifice for the more advanced scholars of the common schools. The building and furniture cost $6,000, exclusive of the lot. The facilities afforded by the harbor and other commercial advantages of the place, have attracted a large amount of capital. There are ten warehouses in the city valued at $53,000, and two bridge piers valued at $7,000. Three ship yards are constantly employed in the building and repairing of vessels, and five new vessels are now being built in them. The citizens of the city own in whole, or in part, between thirty and forty different vessels, with a tonnage of over 4,000 tons, consisting of propellers, schooners, brigs and sloops, which are engaged in the carrying trade between the upper and lower lakes, and in the lumber trade on lake Michigan. There are now 126 mercantile stores in the various branches, 1 steam flouring mill with four run of stone, and 2 water mills just out of the limits of the corporation; there are 7 different mechanics shops, with steam engines and their furnaces. The bank of Racine is in successful operation, issuing bills and doing a general banking business. There are 3 plank roads extending into the country from the city—the Racine and Rock River road, leading west through the villages of Rochester, Burlington, Spring Prairie, Elkhorn and Delavan, a distance of 56 miles, completed—the Racine and Raymond road, leading northwest from the city 15 miles, nearly completed—and the Racine and Wilmot road leading southwest, a distance of 16 miles, now in process of construction. Speed's and O'Reilly's telegraph lines both have offices in the city, and the Racine and Rock River telegraph company have a line completed from Racine to Beloit, touching at all the intermediate villages. The Racine, Janesville, and Mississippi rail road has been surveyed and located from Racine to Beloit, and the contracts are now let for the whole distance and the work in process of construction, and will be completed by September 1854. Considering the natural advantages of Racine—its importance as a commercial point—the character and enterprize of its inhabitants—its institutions of learning—its size, being second only to Milwaukee in population among the places of the State—and, above all, its beautiful and healthful location—no place in the State offers more inducements to those seeking a home in the West, either as a pleasant residence or a place of business.

RACINE, *College*, was chartered by the legislature in 1852, and is located in the city of Racine, where fine college buildings have been erected. It is the diocesan college of the Protestant Episcopal church of Wisconsin.

RACINE, *County*, is bounded on the north by Waukesha and Milwaukee, on the east by the State line in Lake Michigan, on the south by Kenosha, and on the west by Walworth. It was organized from the limits of Milwaukee Dec. 7, 1836. The seat of justice is at the city of Racine, on the lake shore. This county has a proper proportion of prairie and timber, and is well adapted to agriculture. Its productions are various. Besides other branches of agriculture, the raising of fruit and keeping of cattle and sheep are successfully carried on. There is also a large amount of capital profitably employed in various branches of manufacture. A large portion of the county is well settled and improved. Though small in extent, it possesses advantages unsurpassed by any county in the State. Its soil is well adapted to all the products of the climate, and being contiguous to the lake, it has good and convenient markets both at Racine and other lake ports. Its principal streams are O'Plaine and Root rivers. It is in the first judicial circuit, the first congressional district, and forms the seventh senate district, and sends four members to the assembly, as follows: 1. City of Racine; 2. Towns of Racine, Mount Pleasant and Caledonia; 3. Towns of Yorkville, Dover, Raymond and Norway; 4. Towns of Burlington and Rochester. The population in 1838 was 2,054; 1840, 3,475; 1842 6,318; 1846, 17,983; 1847, 19,583; 1850, 14,971. It has 947 farms, 2,578 dwellings, and 99 manufactories.

RACINE, *Town*, in county of Racine, being fractional towns 3 and 4 N., of range 23 E., in which is located the city of same name. The population of the town in 1850 was 777. It has 7 school districts.

RANDOLPH, *P. V.*, in town of same name, Columbia county, on section 24, town 13 N., of range 12 E.

RANDOLPH, *Town*, in county of Columbia, being town 13 N., of range 12 E.; centrally located, 18 miles northeast from Portage city. Population in 1850 was 618. It has 5 school districts.

Random, *Lake*, see Cold Spring lake, Washington county.

Rapide de Croche, *Rapids*, of the Neenah river, 4 miles below the Grand Kaukalin. At this place the river has a descent of a little over a foot in 1,300 feet, and there is a very short elbow in the river, making the natural navigation very difficult.

Raspberry, *River*, (Framboise), enters Lake Superior, opposite the island scalled the Twelve Apostles, in La Pointe county, 15 miles west from Isle St. Michael, and 6 east from Sandy river.

Rathbun, *P. V.*, in county of Sheboygan, being in the town of Mitchell, town 14 N., of range 20 E.

Rat, *River*, is an eastern tributary of Wolf river.

Rattle Snake, *Creek*, a branch of Grant river, from the west, in Grant county.

Rattle Snake, *Diggings*, in town 4 N., of ranges 4 and 5 west, in Grant county.

Raymond, *Town*, in county of Racine, being town 4 N., of range 21 E.; centrally located, 12 miles northwest from Racine. Population in 1850 was 820. It has 7 school districts.

Raymond, *P. V.*, on section 10 of town of same name, in Racine county, 15 miles northwest from the city of Racine, and 90 miles southeast from Madison. Population, 600; with 150 dwellings, 1 store, 1 hotel, and Baptist and Congregational churches.

Readland, residence of Hon. Geo. Read McLane, on the border of Pine Lake, in towns of Merton and Delafield, Waukesha county.

Red Cedar, *Lake*, is the lowermost lake on the east branch of Red Cedar river.

Red Cedar, *Lake*, is about one mile west from the centre of the town of Oakland, Jefferson county, and covers an area of over 500 acres. It is about one mile south of Ripley lake, in the same town and county. It empties, through a small stream running southeasterly, into Lake Koskonong.

RED, *Banks*, name given to the south shore of Green Bay, in town 25 N., of range 22 E.

RED, *River*, in Door county, enters Green Bay, in town 26 N.

REEDSBURGH, *Town*, in county of Sauk, being all of said county, in towns 11, 12, and 13 N., of ranges 2, 3, and 4; centrally located, west from Baraboo. It has 5 school districts.

REEDSBURG, *P. V.*, near the geographical centre of Sauk county, on section 10, town 12 N., of range 4 E., 18 miles northwest from Baraboo, and 50 miles northwest from Madison. It is surrounded by good farming lands, abounding in mineral wealth of iron and copper ore. Population 250, with 60 dwellings, 4 stores, 1 hotel, 4 mills, and 4 religious denominations.

RHINE, *Town*, in county of Sheboygan, being town 16 N., of range 21 E.; centrally located, northwest from Sheboygan, and was organized in 1852. It has 6 school districts.

RICHFIELD, *Town*, in county of Washington, being town 9 N., of range 19 E.; centrally located, 22 miles southwest from Ozaukee. Population in 1850 was 869. It has 14 school districts.

RICHLAND, *County*, is bounded on the north by Bad Ax and Sauk, on the east by Sauk, on the south by Iowa, and on the west by Bad Ax and Crawford, and is about 24 miles square. It contains 16 townships in a square form, and some fractional ones on the Wisconsin river, which constitutes its southern boundary. It was set off from Iowa county 15th Feb. 1842, remaining attached thereto for judicial purposes until Feb. 7, 1850. The seat of justice has been established at Richland Centre. The county is connected with the second congressional district, the fifth judicial circuit, and the fifteenth senate district, and constitutes an assembly district. It is divided into five towns, as follows:—Buena Vista on the east side, comprising towns 9, 10, 11, 12 N., of range 2 E., and one tier of sections from the east side of town 9 N., of range 1 E.—Richland, town 10 N., of range 1 E.—Rockbridge, town 12 N. of range 1 E., and 11 and 12 N. of range 1 W.—Richwood, town 9, 10, 11, and 12 N. of range 2 W., and 2 tiers of sections from the west side of towns 9 and 10, of range 1 W.—Richmond, 4 eastern tiers of sections from towns 9 and 10, of range 1 W., and 5 tiers of sections from the western part of town 9 N., of range 1 E. There are 4 considerable mill streams running from north to south through the county, emptying into the Wisconsin—Bear Creek, in the east part—Pine River, running through the central—Eagle Creek, more westerly—and Knapp's Creek, in the extreme west. These streams, with their tributaries, supply the county abundantly. The water is invariably soft. There are some pretty prairies surrounded by groves of heavy timber. The face of the country is diversified by hills and valleys. Fishes—pike, pickeral, codfish, mullet, suckers, and speckled trout are in abundance. Plenty of the best timber such as maple, butternut, walnut, bass, ash, elm and oak of different kinds, with pine and poplar. Lead and copper have been discovered in the southern part. A marble quarry has been opened in the valley of the Bear Creek. All the stone is found in quarries—none scattered on the surface. There are many large tracts of well-watered and rich land in the county—hence the name. The county is settling rapidly with an intelligent and enterprizing population, almost wholly Americans. Its agricultural, mineral and lumbering resources, together with its proximity to an extensive mining country, and its facilities for market, serve as great inducements to settlement and cultivation. There are many thriving villages. Perhaps there is no greater natural curiosity in the West than the natural bridge of the Pine river, located on the middle of the northwest quarter of section 10, town 11 N., of range 1. It is a rock from 40 to 60 feet high, and over 1½ miles long, and extends into a level country, with a beautiful arch, sufficiently large for the waters of the Pine river in times of flood. The rock is solid for 30 feet above the water, and is covered with a beautiful grove of thrifty pines. It is a species of sand stone, four rods wide and perpendicular (except where it projects over) its entire length. This forms a great water power, and also shelter for man and beast. The Indians used to assemble here in great numbers to worship, the chief or principal speaker standing upon the top of the rock whilst his audience remained below. Another curiosity is a warm cave, which sends forth a warm current of air at all seasons. Population in 1850 was 903, now about 3,000; with 76 farms, 175 dwellings, and 4 manufactories.

RICHLAND, *P. V.* and *C. H.*, is the county seat of Richland, being in town 10, of range 1 E. It is 7 miles above Sextonville, on Pine Creek, situated on a prairie, surrounded by beautiful groves and shade trees. It possesses an excellent water power, and mills are being erected.

RICHLAND CITY, *P. V.*, on the north side of Wisconsin river, at the mouth of Pine creek, Richland county. It has a good landing, the banks being about four feet above high water. It is a very flourishing village, and in a good section of farming lands.

RICHMOND, *P. O.*, in town of same name, Walworth county, being in town 3 N., of range 15 E.

RICHMOND, *Village*, late county seat of Richland county, on bank of the Wisconsin river.

RICHMOND, *Town*, in county of Walworth, being town 3 N., of range 15 E.; centrally located, 8 miles northwest from Elkhorn. Population in 1850 was 756. It has 9 school districts.

RICHMOND, *Town*, in county of Richland. For bounds see Richland county. It has 7 school districts.

RICHWOOD, *Town*, in county of Richland. It has 2 school districts. For bounds, see Richland county.

RIDGEWAY, *Town*, in county of Iowa, being part of towns 5, 6 and 7 N., of ranges 3, 4 and 5 E.; centrally located, northeast from Mineral Point. It has 8 school districts. It is on the east side of the county, and embraces one of the Blue Mounds and also Porter's Grove. A small village, called Moundville, lies at the foot of the mounds. Both prairie and timber meet the eye in every direction. It is abundantly watered by springs and streams.

RIDGEWAY, *P. V.*, on section 14, town 6 N., of range 4 E., in Iowa county; 14 miles northeast from Mineral Point, and 35 miles west from Madison. It has 1 store, 3 hotels, 1 grist and 1 saw mill; 1 Presbyterian, 1 Methodist, and 1 Congregational church. It is in a well-watered region and of good soil.

RIPLEY, *Lake*, is near the northwest corner of the town of Oakfield, Jefferson county. It is nearly 2 miles long, and covers nearly 500 acres. Its waters run westerly into Dane county, and thence southeast into Lake Koskonong.

RIPON, *P. V.*, on section 21, town 16 N., of range 14 E., in Fond du Lac county, 22 miles west from Fond du Lac, and 64 miles northeast from Madison; on inlet to Green Lake, which falls 100 feet in distance of one mile. Water power is improved to half its capacity. Brockway college, a Presbyterian institution, is located at this place. There are Episcopal, Methodist, and Presbyterian congregations. There are sash, chair, cabinet and woollen factories. At this point the following highways cross each other:—from Watertown to Fox River and the Menomonee country—from Madison to Oshkosh and Green Bay—and from Fond du Lac to La Crosse.

RISING, *Prairie*, is east of Beaver Dam, in Dodge county.

ROARING, *Creek*, emptying into Lake Pepin, a small stream in Chippewa county.

ROBINSON'S, *Creek*, a small tributary from the east, in La Crosse county, of Black river, into which it enters, being in town 20 N., of range 4 W.

ROCHE-A-GRIS, *River*, rises in northeast corner of Adams county, and runs southwest, emptying into the Wisconsin, in town 18 N.

ROCHESTER, *P. V.*, in town of same name, Racine county, on sections 2 and 11; it is 23 miles west from Racine and 75 miles southeast from Madison, at the junction of the Muskego and Fox rivers, and has a good water power on each river, both of which are improved and have machinery in operation on them. It is on the Racine and Rock River plank road. The plank road from Racine intersects the Racine plank road, and terminates at this place. It has a daily eastern and western mail, and weekly mails from Waukesha and Milwaukee. The place is surrounded by a rich farming country, settled by an intelligent and enterprising population. It contains about 500 inhabitants, with 62 dwellings, 5 stores, 3 hotels, 3 mills, 2 plough, 2 harness, 1 boot and shoe, 1 fanning mill, 1 waggon and carriage, and 1 tin and copper shops, 1 foundry, and 1 saleratus factory; 1 Presbyterian church, and 2 good school houses.

ROCHESTER, *Town*, in county of Racine, being town 4 N., of range 19 E.; centrally located, 24 miles northwest from Racine. Population in 1850 was 1,672. It has 11 school districts.

ROCKBRIDGE, *Town*, in county of Richland. It has 5 school districts. For bounds, see Richland county.

ROCK, *County*, is bounded on the north by Dane and Jefferson, on the east by Walworth, on the south by the State of Illinois, and on the west by Green. The county seat is at Janesville, on Rock river. It was set off from Milwaukee, Dec. 7, 1836, and fully organized Feb. 19, 1839. The county is about equally divided between prairie and oak openings, with no large bodies of heavy timber. It is situated on both sides of Rock river, the valley of which is as rich soil as can be found in any part of the country. The prairies are some of them quite large, but beautifully undulating, and productive in the highest degree, and are being settled and cultivated to the very centre. The different varieties of soil—upland, bottom land, prairie and openings, afford facilities for cultivating all the productions of the climate to the greatest advantage—wheat upon the rolling prairies and openings—the coarser grains upon the bottom lands—and tame and wild grasses upon the low prairies and marshes, flourish best, though each class of soil is adapted more or less to all these products. It is watered by Rock river and its branches. The principal villages are Janesville, Beloit, Fulton, and Milton. The county is in connection with the first judicial circuit, the second congressional district, and is entitled to the following representation:—17th Senate district, consists of the towns of Rock, Fulton, Porter, Centre, Plymouth, Newark, Avon, Spring Valley, Magnolia, and Union.—18th Senate district, consists of the towns of Beloit, Turtle, Clinton, Bradford, La Prairie, Harmony, Johnstown, Lima and Milton.—1st Assembly district, Beloit, Turtle and Clinton.—2d Assembly district, Milton, Harmony, Lima, Johnston, Bradford, and La Prairie.—3d Assembly district, Janesville, Rock Centre, and Fulton.—4th Assembly district, Porter, Union, Magnolia, Spring Valley, Plymouth, Newark and Avon. Its population in 1840 was 1,701; 1842, 2,867; 1846, 12,405; 1847, 14,720; 1850, 30,717. Square miles, 720. It has 3,631 dwellings, 1,975 farms, and 126 manufactories. County Officers for 1853 and 1854: Judge, James Armstrong; Clerk of Court, George W. Crabb; Sheriff, William H. Howard; District Attorney, Wm. S. Rockwell; Clerk of Board of Supervisors, C. P. King, Register, Samuel A. Martin; Treasurer, Robert F. Frazer; Coroner, Calvin Chapin.

Rock, *Creek*, is the outlet of Fish lake, in town of Deerfield, Dane county, runs northeast through the town of Waterloo, Jefferson county, emptying into Waterloo creek, in Portland, Dodge county.

Rock, *Town*, in county of Rock, being town 2 N., of range 12 E.; centrally located, 6 miles southwest from Janesville. Population in 1850 was 553. It has 8 school districts.

Rock, *Island*, lies near the northeast corner of Pottowottomee Island, at the connection of Green Bay with Lake Michigan. It is about 5½ miles in circumference.

Rock, *Island*, is in the Wisconsin, at the mouth of Copper Rock river. It is 30 feet high from the water.

Rock, *Lakes*, are two lakes, Upper and Lower, just above Trout Lake, on the most eastern branch of the Manidowish river. They are 300 yards apart—the Lower is half a mile, and the Upper a mile in diameter.

Rock, *Lake*, is about 3 miles long and 1¼ wide, in the eastern portion of the town of Lake Mills, Jefferson county, covering an area of 1,650 acres. It discharges its waters into the Crawfish through Keyes creek, entering near the village of Milton.

Rock, *Mounds*, on section 1, town 14 N., of range 6 W., in Bad Ax county, also on section 33, town 17, of range 4 W., in La Crosse county, on line between towns 16 and 17 N., near the east side of range 7 W.

Rock, *River*, rises in Fond du Lac county, and runs south through Dodge, Jefferson and Rock counties, into Illinois.

Rock Prairie, *P. O.*, in town of Harmony, Rock county, being town 3 N., of range 13 E.

Rock River, *P.O.*, in Fond du Lac county.

Rock River, *West Branch*, see Crawfish river.

Rock River, *Woods*. This name has been given to the whole of the timbered lands on the borders of Rock river. It includes the northeastern towns of Jefferson county, and the eastern portions of the town of Milford.

ROCK HILL, *P.O.*, in town of Kingsboro', Marquette county, being on section 29, town 14 N., of range 11 E.; 14 miles from Montello.

ROCK VALLEY, *P. O.*, in Rock county.

ROCKY, *Lake*, a small lake in the southwest corner of Portland, Dodge county.

ROCKY RUN, *Creek*, a small stream entering the Wisconsin from the northeast corner of Lowville, at Dekorra.

ROCKY RUN, *P.O.*, on section 5, in town of Lowville, Columbia county; 10 miles southeast from Portage, and 28 miles north from Madison, on a creek of the same name, having at this point an unimproved water power sufficient to carry ten run of stone most of the year. It is within a good farming region, cultivated by industrious and intelligent people.

RODMAN, *River*, rises in Osceola, Fond du Lac county, and runs southeast into Milwaukee river.

ROME, *P. V.*, on section 17, in town of Sullivan, Jefferson county, on Duck creek, 10 miles east from Jefferson, and 40 miles east from Madison. This place is in the fertile and timbered lands of Jefferson county. Population, 130; with 30 dwellings, 2 stores, 1 hotel, and 2 mills, with a good water power.

ROOT CREEK, *P. O.*, in town of Greenfield, Milwaukee county, on section 26. It is on the Janesville and Milwaukee plank road.

ROOT, *River*, rises in the town of Muskego, Waukesha county, and runs southeast, entering Lake Michigan at the city of Racine, being about 35 miles in length.

ROSE, *Lake*, mostly on section 29, in town and county of Jefferson. It is about 1½ miles in length.

ROSENDALE, *Town*, in county of Fond du Lac, being town 16 N., of range 15 E.; centrally located, 13 miles westerly from Fond du Lac. Population in 1850 was 714. It has 5 school districts.

Rosendale, *P. V.*, in county of Fond du Lac, on section 35, in town 16 N., of range 15 E. It is 11 miles from Fond du Lac city, and 70 miles northeast from Madison. It is located on a small stream running east and west, with a prairie country on the north, and openings on the south, and is noted for the health and salubrity of the climate. Population, 150; with 25 dwellings, 3 stores, 2 hotels, 5 manufactories, and 2 denominations.

Roslin, *P. V.*, in Marquette county, being on section 23, town 14 N., of range 9 E., 10 miles from Montello.

Round, *Lake*, in town of Summit, Waukesha county, 2 miles west of Nemahbin.

Rountree, *Creek*, a branch of Platte river, in Grant county.

Roxbury, *Town*, in county of Dane, being fractional town 9 N., of ranges 6 and 7 E.; centrally located, 18 miles northwest from Madison. It has 6 school districts.

Roxo, *P. V.*, in Marquette county, being on section 13, town 15 N., of range 9 E.; 2 miles from Montello.

Rubicon, *Town*, in county of Dodge, being town 10 N., of range 17 E; centrally located, 12 miles southeast from Juneau. It has 10 school districts.

Rubicon, *River*, rises near Schleisingerville, in Washington county, and runs west into Rock river, in town of Hustisford, Dodge county.

Rushford, *Town*, in county of Winnebago, being towns 17 and 18 N., of range 14 E.; centrally located, 15 miles from Oshkosh. Population in 1850 was 514. It has 4 school districts.

Rush, *Lake*, in town of Rushford, Winnebago county. It is about 5 miles long and 2 broad. Its outlet has several good water powers, the principal of which is at Waukau village. It discharges its waters northerly into Neenah river, a short distance west of Omro village.

RUSH RIVER, *Town*, in county of St. Croix, being towns 27 and 28 N., of ranges 16, and east half of 17; centrally located, southeast from Willow river. It has 1 school district.

RUSH, *River*, rises in St. Croix county, and running southerly into Lake Pepin, in town 24 N., of range 16 W.

RUSH RIVER, *P. O.*, at head of river of same name, in St. Croix county.

RUSSELL'S CORNERS, *P. O.*, in town of Flora, Sauk county, town 12 N., of range 7 E.

RUTLAND, *P. O.*, in southwest corner of town of same name, Dane county.

RUTLAND, *Town*, in county of Dane, being town 5 N., of range 10 E.; centrally located, 14 miles southeast from Madison. Population in 1850 was 759. It has 8 school districts.

SACRAMENTO, *P. V. & C. H.*, on section 35, town 18, of range 13 E., Waushara county, on south side of Fox river, being in southeast corner of the county. It has a healthy and pleasant location in the openings, on an inclined plane, above the banks of the river, and is the only river town in the county. It was laid out in 1851, by Thomas J. Townsend, Esq., since which time it has increased very rapidly. It is surrounded by a country of excellent farming lands. Population 250, with 40 dwellings, 3 stores, 3 hotels, a warehouse, timber yard, &c. It commands the river trade of a large section of country.

SALEM, *P. O.*, in town of same name, in the county of Kenosha.

SALEM, *Town*, in county of Kenosha, being town 1 N., of range 20 E.; centrally located, 16 miles west from the city of Kenosha. Population in 1850 was 1,123. It has 8 school districts.

SALT, *Licks*, at the southern bend of Mullet river, in Sheboygan county.

SANDY, *Creek*, a small stream rising near Patch Grove, Grant county, running southwesterly into the Mississippi.

SAND, *Creek*, in La Pointe county, see Foul river.

SAND PRAIRIE, *P. O.*, in county of Richland, being in town 9 N., of range 2 W., town of Richwood.

SANDY *Portage*, at a rapid of the Menomonee river, with a perpendicular fall, about a mile in extent.

SANDY, *River*, a tributary of Lake Superior, 6 miles west of Raspberry river, and 3 miles east of La R. Gauche.

SARABOO, a branch from the southwest of Kewaunee river, near which it enters in town 24 N., of range 24 E.

SAPPAH, *River*, see Black river.

SAUK, *County*, is bounded on the north by Adams, on the east by Columbia, on the south by Iowa and Dane, and on the west by La Crosse, Bad Ax, and Richland. It was set off from Crawford in 1839; established, and annexed to Dane for judicial purposes, January, 1840, and fully organized in 1844. The boundaries were changed March 6, 1849, and further changed 1853. The seat of justice is at Baraboo, on river of the same name, a few miles southeast from the centre of the county. It is connected with the third judicial circuit, the second congressional, and the twenty-third senate district, and, with Adams, sends one member to the assembly. The number of square miles is about 800. The soil, in every part where cultivation has been attempted, produces well, and seems peculiarly congenial to wheat. The timber, except on the Baraboo Bluffs, is oak in its different varieties. There is an almost inexhaustible body of heavy timber, consisting of sugar maple, elm, basswood, iron wood, hickory, butternut, oak, cherry, &c. The surface of the country is generally undulating—in some places level, in others hilly—presenting, perhaps, as great a variety as any county in the State. Its leading geological formation is old red sand stone. On the higher points there are occasionally found the remains of the carboniferous lime stone, so abundant in the northwest. The Baraboo Bluffs are sometimes considered as a formation peculiar to themselves; but as geologists do not seem to agree as to what they are, the opinion is ventured that they belong to the same class as the prevailing strata, but that by the action of some powerful agency of a vitrifying or igneous nature, their density has been increased, and their general appearance somewhat changed. They are harder, finer grained, and often much more highly colored, than the common sand stone. Large masses of conglomorate are often found among them, especially on the higher portions. These masses are composed of sand and smooth round stones of almost all sizes, from that of a pin head to several feet in diameter. In the diluvial deposites, along the banks of the river, are found masses of conglomerate in a transition state, a part firmly consolidated, a part only slightly so. No trace of fossil remains have yet been discovered, except in the carboniferous lime stone. There are no mines in the county worked at present with any degree of profit, though there are strong indications of copper, and a considerable quantity (five tons) was once dug on Copper Creek, near Reedsburg. Small fragments, weighing from an ounce to several pounds, are often found in different parts of the county, and there is at least a possibility that extensive mines may yet be found. A beautiful article of purple freestone occurs on the Baraboo bluffs, and a good quality of marble near the southwest part of the county, though neither yet has been much explored. The principal streams are the Wisconsin and Baraboo rivers, Honey, Dell and Narrows creeks. The Wisconsin river has as yet only been used for the purpose of navigation, though at present attention is being called to the construction of a dam across it at the Dells. Dell creek is a good sized stream for mill purposes; is about 15 miles long, and remarkable for the deep gulches through which it runs. There are several interesting caves in the sand stone rock in the vicinity of this stream. Narrows Creek is about twelve miles long, and affords several good mill sites. There is one mill in operation on the stream, and at its mouth is laid out the town of Excelsior. Honey Creek is about 25 miles in length, together with the rapidity of its current, renders it peculiarly serviceable as a water power. Several mills are already in operation upon the stream, and others are in process of erection. The Baraboo river, however, is the most important stream as a water power in the county, if not in the State. It is some 80 miles in length. There are already seven dams across it, each propelling from 1 to 3 mills. The rapids of this river at Baraboo are about two miles in length. The bed of the stream is rock; the amount of water is about 4,500 inches; the amount of fall, 50 feet. There are already in operation, along these rapids, 4 saw mills, running 5 saws; 1 flouring mill with 2 run of stone; (another, with 2 runs, was burned in the fall of 1852); 4 lath and picket factories, 1 carding machine, 1 iron foundry, 1 machine shop, 1 bark mill, and several turning lathes, and but a small portion of water is used. Other machinery is in process of erection along the stream, and many good mill sites yet lie untouched. Devil Lake is, perhaps, the only lake in the county worthy of notice. It occupies about a square mile, is situated a little over two miles south of the foot of the Baraboo rapids, and about three miles from Baraboo village. On the east, south and west of the lake, the rough, rocky banks rise from the edge of the water, almost perpendicularly, to the height of 150 or 200 feet. The smooth crystal water, and the steep, craggy rocks, presenting the most perfect contrast. On the north, the land gradually rises for a short distance, and then as gradually slopes away to the Baraboo river. Although several attempts have been made, the depth of the lake has never been fathomed. The purity and beauty of this body of water, together with its surrounding romantic scenery, never fail to excite the admiration of all who visit it. Of the Prairies, Sauk Prairie is much the largest. It is about 16 square miles in area. It is bounded on the north by the Baraboo bluffs, a chain of high steep bluffs also extend along its western side, and on the south and east is the Wisconsin river. Its surface is undulating, soil good, and a considerable portion is cultivated. It is based (as we suppose all genuine prairies must be) upon a diluvial strata. There are several other smaller prairies in the county, from one to five miles in extent, but as there is such a great uniformity, it is unnecessary to go into detail. The following is a pretty accurate detail of the hotels, stores, manufactories, &c., in the county: 13 taverns, 22 stores, 5 groceries, 4 drug stores, 7 tailors, 3 distilleries, 1 brewery, 2 steam saw mills, 4 grist mills, 1 foundry, 1 furniture, 1 machine, 9 shoe, 15 blacksmiths, 6 waggon, 4 coopers, 5 tinners, and 3 jewellers shops, 1 carding machine, 6 lath and picket factories, 1 pottery, and 1 tannery; 302 farms, 7 manufactories, and 821 dwellings; 4 district school houses, 3 select schools, and 3 churches. Population in 1840 was 102; 1842, 393; 1846, 1,003; 1847, 2,178; 1850, 4,372. County Officers: Judge, J. M. Clark; Sheriff, Daniel Munsen; Clerk of Court, George Mertons; District Attorney, J. B. Quinley; Register, Edwin P. Spencer; Clerk of Board of Supervisors, James T. Moseley; County Treasurer, Curtis Bates; County Surveyor, Wm. H. Canfield; Coroner, Royal Gendall.

Sauk, *Creek*, is a tributary of Lake Michigan, which it enters at Ozaukee. It rises in south part of Sheboygan county.

Saukville, *P. V.*, in town of same name, county of Washington, being town 11 N., of range 21 E.; located 4 miles west from Ozaukee.

Saukville, *Town*, in county of Washington, being town 11 N., of range 21 E.; 6 miles west from Ozaukee. It has 8 school districts, and possesses an excellent improved water power. Population in 1850 was 1,796.

Scarboro, *Creek*, rises near the source of Twin rivers, and runs northeast, entering Kewaunee river in northwest corner of town 24 N., of range 24.

SCHLEISINGERVILLE, *P. V.*, in town of Polk, on section 18, in Washington county, 25 miles west from Ozaukee, and easterly from Madison 80 miles. It derives its name in honor of Hon. B. Schleisinger Weil, State senator from the fourth district, whose residence is near this place, and who laid it out in 1845. Population, 125; with 25 dwellings, 3 stores, 3 hotels, 1 mechanical shop, 1 tannery, and 1 church edifice. It is on the Milwaukee and Fond du Lac road, possessing a healthy climate and good soil of farming lands.

SCOTT, *P. V.*, in county of Sheboygan, being in town 13 N., (Scott), of range 20 E.

SCOTT, *Town*, in county of Sheboygan, being town 13 N., of range 20 E.; centrally located, 22 miles southwest from Sheboygan.

SCOTT, *Town*, in county of Columbia, being town 12 N., of range 11 E.; centrally located, 12 miles from Portage city. Population in 1850 was 395. It has 4 school districts.

SCUPERNONG, *Creek*, rises in the south part of the town of Delafield, and running southwest, (affording a mill site at Waterville and one in Ottawa), through Summit and Ottawa, enters Bark river in Cold Spring, Jefferson county.

SEARGENT, *P. O.*, is in the southeast part of town of Oasis, Waushara county, being town 20 N., of range 9 E.; 30 miles northwest from Sacramento, and 80 miles north from Madison, on the stage route from Berlin to Stevens' Point.

SECOND *Lake*, the second from below of the chain of Four Lakes, in the towns of Blooming Grove and Dunn, 6 miles southeast from Madison. It is 2 miles wide and 3½ long.

SEELEY'S, *Creek*, rises in the southwest corner of town 11, range 7 E., runs northeast, emptying into the Baraboo river, by its course, about 10 miles above the village of Baraboo.

SEVEN MILE CREEK, *P. O.*, in town of Lemonweir, Sauk county.

SEXTONVILLE, *P. V.*, on section 7, town 9, of range 2 E., in Richland county, 5 miles above Richland city, on Pine creek, at the mouth of Willow creek. It is 56 miles west from Madison. Population 130, with 21 dwellings, 2 stores, 1 hotel, 2 mills, and 2 excellent water powers.

SHAGWAMIGON, *Bay*, (Chegoimegon and Chagwamigon), south of the Twelve Apostle Islands, in La Pointe county, Lake Superior.

SHAGWAMIGON, *River*, empties into bay of the same name, in La Pointe county, 6 miles west from Bad river.

SHAKWEYA, *River*, (or NEW WOOD), enters the Wisconsin from the west at Lynch's Trading House, 4 miles below Grand Father Bull Falls.

SHARON, *P. V.*, on section 13, in town of same name, Walworth county, 12 miles southwest from Elkhorn, and 60 miles southeast from Madison, in a fine farming country. Population, 110; with 15 dwellings, 1 store, 1 hotel, and 1 catholic church.

SHARON, *Town*, in county of Walworth, being town 1 N., of range 15 E.; centrally located, 13 miles southwest from Elkhorn. Population in 1850 was 1,169. It has 10 school districts.

SHAWANA, *County*, was established at the January session of the legislature in 1853, most of its limits were taken from Oconto. The seat of justice is at Shawana village, near the outlet of the lake of same name.

SHAWANA, *Lake*, in town 27 N., of ranges 16 and 17; is about 6 miles long and 2 in width, discharging its waters through an outlet into Wolf river.

SHAWANA, *P. O.*, near lake of same name, in Shawana county.

SHEBOYGAN, *County*, is bounded on the north by Calumet and Manitowoc, on the east by the State line in Lake Michigan, on the south by Washington, and on the west by Fond du Lac. It was set off from Brown Dec. 7, 1836; organized for county purposes Dec. 17, 1838; and attached to Fond du Lac for judicial purposes; and fully organized January 22, 1846. The whole surface of the county is covered by a dense growth of timber, among which pine is found in considerable quantities along the margin of the principal streams. The seat of justice is at the village of Sheboygan, on the lake, centrally from the north and south boundaries of the county. It is watered by the Sheboygan river and its tributaries. It is connected with the fourth judicial circuit, the third congressional and the first senate districts, and sends two members to the assembly as follows: 1st. Towns of Sheboygan, Wilson, Lima and Holland; 2d. Towns of Sheboygan Falls, Harmony, Rhine, Plymouth, Greenbush, Abbott, Mitchell, Scott and Lynden. Population in 1840 was 133; 1842, 227; 1846, 4637; 1847, 5,580; 1850, 8,836. There are 1,790 dwellings, 581 farms, and 30 manufactories. County Officers for 1853 and 1854: Judge, Chas. E. Morris; Sheriff, J. D. Murphy; Clerk of County Court, A. H. Edwards; District Attorney, Edward Elwell; Register, Charles Adolphi; Clerk of Board of Supervisors, J. T. Kingsbury; Treasurer, Geo. H. Wordan; County Surveyor, Horace Cleves.

SHEBOYGAN, *Town*, in county of same name, being towns 15 and 16 N., of range 23 E. It has 7 school districts.

SHEBOYGAN, *P. V.*, the county seat of county of same name, is situated on the lake shore, near the middle of the county, and at the mouth of Sheboygan river, a stream about 400 feet wide, and from 12 to 15 feet deep. The town plat is a dry, level and sandy plain, about 40 feet above the level of lake Michigan. In 1846 this village contained about 400 inhabitants, and had no churches, newspapers, or roads. At present it has a population of 2,000; 7 good churches, viz. Episcopal, Baptist, Presbyterian, Congregational, Methodist, German Reformed and Roman Catholic, and 4 weekly newspapers, viz., Mercury, Lake Journal, Republicaner, and The Niewsbode. During the past year the county has raised $20,000, and the General Government has appropriated $10,000 for the purpose of constructing a harbor at the mouth of the river. The work was commenced last spring, and has been vigorously prosecuted during the summer and fall. It will be finished during the coming season, which will give Sheboygan the best and most accessible harbor on the lake. One of the best plank roads in the State runs from this place to Taycheda, a thriving village on Lake Winnebago. There are four stage and mail routes running from here: one north, to Manitowoc and Two Rivers; one west, to Fond du Lac, Menasha, and Green Bay; one southwest, to Cascade, Mayville, &c.; and one south, to Milwaukee and Chicago.

SHEBOYGAN, *Falls*, is 6 miles above the mouth of Sheboygan river, in county of same name, at the crossing of the U. S. road.

SHEBOYGAN FALLS, *P. V.*, on section 36, town 15 N., of range 22 E., in town of same name, and county of Sheboygan, 6 miles from the county seat, 115 miles from Madison via Fond du Lac, and 150 miles from the same place via Milwaukee. The village was first settled 15 years ago, a saw mill erected, and one or two buildings. The plat was laid out and named Rochester. The real commencement of creating a village was made seven years ago, and since, its growth has been constant. The soil in the vicinity is well adapted to the growth of wheat and other kinds of grain. It is located on both sides of the river, which has a fall of 30 or 40 feet in half a mile. A bed of lime stone underlies the whole village a few feet below the surface. Lime made from it is of the finest quality. Large quantities of pine and oak timber are cut along the banks of the river during winter. The Sheboygan and Mayville plank road will pass through the village, and the Sheboygan and Fond du Lac plank road passes through the north part of it. Population 800, with 200 dwellings, 12 stores, 4 hotels, 2 grist mills, 1 foundry, 2 turning lathes, 2 cabinet shops, 1 printing office, and 3 churches.

SHEBOYGAN FALLS, *Town*, in county of Sheboygan, being towns 14 and 15 N., of range 22 E. It has 9 school districts.

SHEBOYGAN, *River*, rises in Fond du Lac county, near the southern extremity of Lake Winnebago, and runs southeasterly, emptying into Lake Michigan at the village of Sheboygan. It drains about 400 square miles of surface.

SHEBOYGAN, *Lake*, a small lake in town of Rhine, Sheboygan county.

SHELL, *Lake*, see Pewaukee lake.

SHELL, *River*, see Kayesikang river.

SHIELDS, *Town*, in county of Marquette, being town 16 N., of range 16 E.

SHIELDS, *Town*, in county of Dodge, being town 9 N., of range 14 E.; centrally located, 14 miles southwest from Juneau. Population in 1850 was 590. It has 6 school districts.

SHOPIERE, *P. V.*, in county of Rock, in town of Turtle, being on section 3, town 1 N., of range 13 E. It is 9 miles southeast from Janesville, and 54 from Madison, on the Turtle creek, which gives a water power here of 9 feet head and fall, and is a very reliable stream for supply of water. The flouring mill is of stone, 4 stories high, running three pairs of burrs, and is completely finished throughout. From the north side of the Turtle stretches Rock Prairie; on the south side commences a timbered tract, extending some 7 miles. Abundance of excellent lime stone for building purposes is found in the vicinity, which suggested the name—a corruption of the French Chaux (Sho) Pierre. Turtleville flouring mill is one mile below, on the same stream. Population 200, with 38 dwellings, 3 stores, 1 hotel, 2 mills, 1 plough manufactory, 1 congregational church.

SHULLSBURG, *P. V.*, and county seat of Lafayette county, in town 1 N., of range 2 E., head waters of an eastern branch of Fevre river. It is 16 miles from Galena, and 75 southwest from Madison. The business and trade of a large portion of country is concentrated at this place, where an excellent and ready market is found for mineral and all of the products of industry, which is paid for in *gold* and *silver* coin—bank bills and coppers having long since been repudiated in the lead mines. It contains 2,500 inhabitants, with 5 hotels, 12 dry good and grocery, 1 drug, 1 jewelry, and 1 tin and iron stores; 2 waggon, 5 smiths, 2 cabinet, 4 tailors, 4 shoe, 2 saddle and harness, 6 carpenter, and 1 gunsmith shops; 4 mineral warehouses, 4 church edifices—1 Primitive Methodist, 1 P. E. Methodist, 1 Catholic and 1 Congregational—the latter of which is built of stone. The court house is built of brick, 44 by 60 feet, with offices for county purposes, and the jail of stone.

SHULLSBURG, *Town*, in the county of Lafayette, being a part of town 1, of ranges 2 and 3 E., in which is located the seat of justice of the county. There are 2 furnaces for smelting lead ore in this town. Shullsburg is noted for its inexhaustible mines of lead ore which have been worked for many years, and are the most productive in the mineral district. The Southern Wisconsin rail road is located through the entire length of the town from east to west. The population of the town is 3,500.

SHUNAKEE, *Lake*, see North Lake, Waukesha county.

SILVER, *Creek*, has its source in English Lake, in Manitowoc county, and running easterly, enters Lake Michigan about 10 miles south of Manitowoc.

SILVER, *Creek*, rises in town of Metomon, Fond du Lac county, and runs northwest into Green Lake, Marquette county.

SILVER, *Lake*, in town of Salem, Kenosha county, discharges its waters through a small stream into Fox river, near Salem *P. O.* It is about a mile in diameter.

SILVER, *Lake*, is nearly in the centre of town of Summit, Waukesha county. It is a mile in length.

SILVER, *Lake*, a small lake in eastern part of town of Sugar Creek.

SINSINAWA, *Creek*, rises in Smeltzer, Grant county, and runs southerly, discharging its waters into La Fevre river, in Illinois.

Sinsinawa, *Mound*, is a conical elevation, one mile south of the village of Fair Play, Grant county.

Sioux Portage, *Creek*, in Portage county, is the inlet of Yellow Lake.

Siscoe, *River*, rises in town of Clayton, Winnebago county, and runs southwest into Wolf River, at the head of Lake Pauwaicun.

Sketch, *Lake*, the largest of the lakes forming one of the sources of Red Cedar river.

Skillet, *Creek*, a tributary from the south of Baraboo river, which it enters about 3 miles above Baraboo village.

Skinner's *Creek*, in Green county, a branch of the Peckatonnica, which it enters in the town of Cadiz.

Slawson's *Prairie*, in Dodge county, east of Beaver Dam.

Sleeping Bear, *River*, (Nibegomowin), a tributary from the west of Burnt Wood river.

Smeltzer's Grove, *P. O.*, in town of Smeltzer, being town 2 N., of range 7 W., in Grant county.

Smeltzer, *Town*, in county of Grant, being town 2 N., of range 1; centrally located, 18 miles southeast from Lancaster. It has 5 school districts.

Snail, *Lake*, or Shell Lake, see Pewaukee Lake.

Somers, *Town*, (formerly Pike), in county of Kenosha, being town 2 N., of range 22 E.; centrally located, 5 miles southwest from Kenosha city. Population in 1850 was 680. It has 7 school districts.

Soochera, *River*, see Fond du Lac river.

South Bristol, *P. O.*, in Racine county.

South Genesee, *P. V.*, in town of Genesee, Waukesha county, being town 6 N., of range 18 E.

South Grove, *P. V.*, in town of Walworth, Walworth county, being town 1 N., of range 16 E.

SOUTH *Fork* of Black river, from the east, entering the same in town 23 N., of range 3 W.

SOUTH *Fork*, a tributary of Baraboo river, in Bad Ax county.

SOUTHPORT, *Town*, in county of Kenosha, being fractional towns 1 and 2 N., of range 23 E., on Lake Michigan. Population in 1850 was 363. It has 7 school districts.

SPAFFORD'S *Creek*, a small tributary of the Peckatonnica.

SPENCER, *River*, a small stream in La Pointe county, entering Lake Superior.

SPRING, *Creek*, a branch of Ockee creek in Lodi, Columbia county.

SPRINGDALE, *P. O.*, in town of same name, Dane county, being town 6 N., of range 7 E.

SPRINGDALE, *Town*, in county of Dane, being town 6 N., of range 7 E.; centrally located, 14 miles southwest from Madison.

SPRINGFIELD, *Town*, in county of Dane, being town 8 N., of range 8 E.; centrally located, 10 miles northwest from Madison. It has 6 school districts.

SPRING GROVE, *P.O.*, in town of same name, Green county, being town 1 N., of range 9 E.

SPRING GREEN, *Town*, in county of Sauk, being all of the ranges of town 8 in said county; centrally located, southwest from Baraboo. It has 14 school districts.

SPRING GROVE, *Town*, in county of Greene, being town 1 N., of range 9. Population in 1850 was 703. It has 7 school districts.

SPRING, *Lake*, is a small lake in town of Marion, Waushara county, tributary to the Neenah.

SPRING, *Lake*, in town of Green Lake, Marquette county, with its outlet, forms one of the inlets of Green Lake.

SPRING, *Lake*, is a small lake in the north part of Mukwonago, Waukesha county.

Spring, *Prairie*, town in county of Walworth, being town 3 N., of range 18 E.; centrally located, 6 miles from Elkhorn. Population in 1850 was 1,344. It has 8 school districts.

Spring Prairie, *P. V.*, in town of same name, on section 30, Walworth county, 7½ miles east from Elkhorn, 70 miles southeast from Madison. Population 200; with 20 dwellings, 3 stores, 1 hotel, and one Baptist church.

Springvale, *P.O.*, in Fond du Lac county.

Springvale, *Town*, in county of Columbia, being town 12 N., of range 11 E.; centrally located, 12 miles southeast from Portage city. Population in 1850 was 471. It has 4 school districts.

Springvale, *Town*, in county of Fond du Lac, being town 15 N., of range 15 E.; centrally located, 12 miles southwest from Fond du Lac. Population in 1850 was 588. It has 8 school districts.

Spring Valley, *P. O.*, in town of same name, Rock county, town 2 N., of range 10 E.

Spring Valley, *Town*, in county of Rock, being town 2 N., of range 10 E.; centrally located, 15 miles southwest from Janesville. Population in 1850 was 766. It has 7 school districts.

Springville, *P.O.*, in Bad Ax county, on section 23, town 13 N., of range 5 W.

Squaw Portage, *River*, in La Pointe county, running nearly parallel to Namekagon river, entering the same a few miles above the junction with the St. Croix.

Squirrel, *River*, a tributary from the west of the Little Wisconsin.

State Line, *P. O.*, in town of Sharon Walworth county, being in town 1 N., of range 15 E.

St. Croix, *County*, is bounded on the north by La Pointe, on the east and south by Chippewa, on the southwest and west by the boundary between the State and Minnesota. The county seat is at Hudson, formerly Willow river, at the mouth of a stream of the same name, emptying into Lake St. Croix. It was set off from Crawford, and organized January 29, 1850; was attached to Crawford for judicial purposes April 10, 1843, and again fully organized February 26, 1848. The boundaries were somewhat changed March 16, 1849. It is attached to the third congressional district, to the sixth judicial circuit, and to the nineteenth senate district, and, with La Pointe, sends one member to the assembly. It is one of the largest counties in the State, being 130 miles in length, and 50 in width; presents to the agriculturist, in fertility of soil, well watered and well wooded farms, in the means of access to market through Lake St. Croix and the Mississippi, and in the perfect healthiness and salubrity of climate, advantages which are to be found combined in but few places in the West. The surface is generally undulating north of the Falls of St. Croix. It is mostly timbered with maple and other hard woods, while south of the Falls is a due proportion of prairie and openings. But little attention has yet been paid to the pursuits of agriculture, and the manufactories are confined for the present to pine lumber. It is well watered with fine streams and beautiful lakes. The principal streams are Willow, Kinnickinnic, Vermillion, Isabelle, and Rush river. Population in 1846 was 1,419; in 1847, 1,674; in 1850, 624; with 181 dwellings, 4 farms, and 2 manufactories. In 1846 the census returns included all of the present Territory of Minnesota, east of the Wisconsin river, also the present county of La Pointe. In 1847 it included the same, excepting the county of La Pointe. This is the reason why there appears to be a decrease in the population from 1847 to 1850. County Officers: Judge, S. S. N. Fuller; Sheriff, A. S. Youle; Clerk of Court, Joseph Bowman; District Attorney, Benjamin Allen; Register, William R. Anderson; Clerk of Board of Supervisors, Charles R. Knight; Treasurer, James M. Bailey; Surveyor, William R. Anderson; Coroner, Jonathan Bailey. (See Peirce and Polk Counties.)

St. Croix, *Lake*, is an expansion of the river of same name, commencing 12½ miles above its mouth, and extending to within a few rods of the Mississippi, and is about a mile broad.

St. Croix, *Pinery*. The amount of sawed pine lumer manufactured at mills on the Wisconsin side of St. Croix river, annually, is about 20,000,000 feet, besides shingles, logs, hewed timber and lath, to wit.: Prescott Mills, 3,500,000; Kinnikinnick, 1,500,000; Rush River, 2,000,000; Hudson, 2,000,000; Willow River, 4,000,000; Osceola, 3,000,000; Falls of St. Croix, 4,000,000. Total, 20,000,000.

St. Croix, *River*, rises in upper St. Croix Lake, within two miles of the Bois Brule river of Lake Superior, and enters the Mississippi river a few miles above Lake Pepin, having a descent of about 230 feet. At the different mills on this river are manufactured 26,000,000 feet of lumber. It is about 300 feet wide, and is navigable to the Falls.

Stephens' *Point*, town in county of Portage, being towns 24 and 25 N., of ranges 5, 6, 7, and 8.

Stevens' Point, *P. V.*, in Portage county, on section 32, town 24 N., of range 8 E., 5½ miles north of Plover, and 120 miles north of Madison, on the Wisconsin river. It is the principal depot of the lumbering trade of the Upper Wisconsin, from which most of the lumbermen make their outfits both for the pine forest in the fall, and for St. Louis, with rafts, in the spring; is beautifully situated, is proverbially healthy, and rapidly being built up. It will probably be the first point at which two great thoroughfares will meet—a rail road from Chicago to Ontonagon, of the Lake Superior, and from Green Bay to St. Pauls, of the Mississippi. A plank road is about to be commenced from Green Bay to this place, and another is projected from Berlin. The surrounding country is fast settling, and is adapted to farming equally as the up river country is pre-eminent for lumbering. The land office of the Stevens' Point land district is located here. Population 500; with 84 dwellings, 9 stores, 4 hotels, 3 mills; 1 chair, 1 bedstead, 1 leather, 1 harness, and 1 sash manufactory; 2 tailors, 2 blacksmiths, 2 shoemakers, 1 sleigh and waggon maker, and 3 organized religious societies.

ST. LOUIS, *River*, rises in several small lakes in latitude 48° N., longitude 16° W. from Washington, and enters west end of Lake Superior.

STOCKBRIDGE, *P. O.*, in Calumet county, at mouth of a small stream entering Lake Winnebago.

STOCKBRIDGE, *Town*, in county of Calumet. It has 5 school districts.

STONER'S PRAIRIE, *P.O.*, on section 17, on prairie of same name, in town 6, of range 9 E., being town of Fitchburg, Dane county, 8 miles southwest from Madison.

STONEY *Creek*, is a small stream in the north part of Washington county, in the towns of Fredonia and Farmington, uniting with Pigeon Creek, enters the Milwaukee river in southeast corner of the town of Farmington.

STONEY, *Creek*, rises in town of Clayton, Winnebago county, and runs northeast into the Little Butte des Morts Lake.

STONEY *Hill*, in Marquette county, being town 17 N., of range 9 E., between Montello River and Deer Creek.

STOUGHTON, *P. V.*, in Dane county, on section 8, in town of Dunkirk, being town 5 N., of range 11 E., 16 miles southeast from Madison; is pleasantly situated on the Catfish river, a few miles below the First Lake, and is on the route of the Milwaukee and Mississippi rail road, 20 miles from Janesville, and 18 miles from Milton. It has a good hydraulic power, with a sufficient supply of water, having a head of 9 feet. It is in one of the most productive farming sections of the State. Population 150, with 30 dwellings, 2 stores, 2 hotels, 1 grist and 1 saw mill.

STRAWBERRY *Islands*, Green Bay, between Chamber's Island and Eagle Bay.

STRONG'S LANDING, *Village*, see BERLIN, *P. V.*, (Appendix.)

STURGEON, *Bay*, a long point of water extending from Green Bay across Door county, into within 2 miles of Lake Michigan. It is 6 miles wide, and 15 miles in length, narrowing towards its head, where it receives a small stream.

STURGEON, *Falls*, are falls of the Menomonee river, of 14 feet in the distance of 1,000 feet.

STURGEON, *Portage*, Door county, is the portage from Big Sturgeon Bay to Lake Michigan, about 1¼ miles.

SUGAR, *Creek*, in town of same name, Walworth county, and running southeast unites with Geneva Creek, entering Pishtaka river at Burlington.

SUGAR, *Creek*, a branch of Sugar river, rises in town of Sylvester, Green county, and runs southeast, entering Sugar river opposite to Clareville.

SUGAR CREEK, *P. O.*, in town of same name, Walworth county, in town 3 N., of range 16 E.

SUGAR CREEK, *Town*, in county of Walworth, being town 3 N., of range 16 E.; centrally located, 5 miles northwest from Elkhorn. Population in 1850 was 1,229. It has 7 school districts.

SUGAR, *River*, rises in town of Primrose, Dane county, runs southeast through Green and Rock counties, into the State of Illinois. It empties into the Peckatonnica, in Winnebago county, Illinois.

SUGAR RIVER, *Diggings*, a point of some considerable importance as a mining settlement. It is in town 4 N., of range 8, Green county, and is known by the name of Exeter.

SULLIVAN, *P. O.*, in town of same name, Jefferson county, being town 6 N., of range 16 E.

SULLIVAN, *Town*, in county of Jefferson, being town 6 N., of range 16 E.; centrally located, nine miles east from Jefferson. Population in 1850 was 872. It has 6 school districts.

SULPHUR, *Springs*, in town of Holland, Sheboygan county.

SUMMERVILLE, *P. V.*, Rock county, on sections 1 and 2 of Clinton, being town 1 N., of range 14 E., 15 miles southeast of Janesville, and 60 southeast from Madison, on stage and mail route from Milwaukee to Beloit, at crossing of road from Johnstown to Belvidere, Ill. In a good farming district of prairie, timber, and openings. It has 85 inhabitants, with 17 dwellings, 1 store, 2 hotels, 2 blacksmiths, and 2 organized religious denominations.

SUMMIT, *P. V.*, in town of same name, Waukesha county, 15 miles northwest from Waukesha.

SUMMIT, *Town*, in county of Waukesha, being town 17 N., of range 17 E.; centrally located, 15 miles west from Waukesha. Population in 1850 was 1,008. It has 6 school districts.

SUN PRAIRIE, *P. O.*, in town of same name, Dane county, being town 8 N., of range 11 E.

SUN PRAIRIE, *Town*, in county of Dane, being town 8 N., of range 11 E.; centrally located, 10 miles northeast from Madison. It has 6 school districts.

SUSSEX, *P. V.*, in town of Lisbon, Waukesha county, on section 26, town 8 N., of range 19 E., 10 miles north from Waukesha, and 60 miles east of Madison, 1½ miles north of the Milwaukee and Lisbon plank road, in a fine farming country, well adapted to raising the winter grains. Population 100; with 15 dwellings, 1 waggon shop, 1 shoe shop, 2 blacksmiths, 1 saw mill, 1 school house, and an Episcopal church.

SWAN, *Lake*, Columbia county, an expansion of Fox river above the Portage. It is half a mile wide, and 3½ miles long.

Sylvania, *P. O.*, in Racine county.

Sylvester, *Town*, in county of Green, being in town 2 N., of range 8 E.; centrally located, 8 miles east from Monroe. Population in 1850 was 712. It has 12 school districts.

Sylvester, *P. V.*, Green county, on section 11, town 2 N., of range 8 E., 9 miles northeast from Monroe, and 35 miles southwest from Madison. Population 300; with 70 dwellings, 1 store, 1 hotel, and 3 religious denominations.

Tainter's, *Creek*, enters the Kickapoo from the northwest, in town 10 N., of range 7 W.

Talking Fish, *River*, a tributary of Lake Superior, enters Shagwamigon Bay, south of Magdalen Island, in La Pointe county.

Tamarac, *Creek*, a tributary near its mouth of Trampaleau river from the east.

Taynah, *Creek*, is a small tributary of the Wisconsin, in Columbia county. See Rocky Run.

Taychedah, *P. V.*, near Fond du Lac City, on Lake Winnebago, in Fond du Lac county.

Taychedah, *Town*, in county of Fond du Lac, being the north third of town 15, and south half of town 16 N., of range 18 E.; centrally located, 6 miles from Fond du Lac City. Population in 1850 was 798. It has 5 school districts.

Techora, *P. O.*, in town of Green Lake, Marquette county, being on section 33, town 15 N., of range 13 E.; 14 miles from Montello.

Telungowan, *River*, see Duck River.

Teotsa, *P. V.*, on section 12, town 4 N., of range 13 E., in Rock county; 10 miles north from Janesville, and 30 southeast from Madison. It is on Rock River. Population 100; with 25 dwellings, 1 store, 1 hotel, and 1 mill. Denominations, Seventh-day Baptists and First-day Baptists.

THERESA, *Town*, in county of Dodge, being town 12 N., of range 17 E.; centrally located, 14 miles northeast from Juneau. It has 5 school districts.

THERESA, *P. V.*, in town of same name, on section 10, Dodge county, 15 miles northeast from Juneau, and 64 miles northeast from Madison. It is situated on the old Milwaukee and Fond du Lac road at the crossing of Rock river. Population 200; with 30 dwellings, 2 stores, 2 hotels, 1 grist and 1 saw mill, 1 pearl ash manufactory, and several mechanical shops.

THE SISTERS *Islands*, in Green Bay, near eastern shore, about 5 miles northeast from Eagle Harbor.

THIRD, *Lake*, adjoining and east of Madison, Dane county, is of the Four Lakes group, 6 miles long and 2 miles broad. It is also called Menona.

THOMPSONVILLE, *P. V.*, in county of Racine, being on section 30, in township 4 N., of range 22 E., town of Caledonia. It is 9 miles from Racine, and 90 miles southeast from Madison. It is located on the borders of prairie and timber, at the corners of two public roads, with a plank road to the city of Racine, and on the line between the towns of Caledonia and Raymond. Population 40, with 12 dwellings, 1 store, 2 hotels, with mechanics of various kinds. Name changed to Whitesville.

THORN APPLE, *Creek*, rises in town 23 N., of range 23 E., in Kewaunee county, runs southerly, discharging its waters into East Twin river, in Manitowoc county.

TOKEN, *Creek*, the principal inlet of Fourth Lake, mostly in Windsor and Westport, Dane county.

TOLAND'S PRAIRIE, *P. V.*, in town of Erin, Washington county, being town 9 N., of range 18 E.

TOMAHAWK, *Lake*, in the southeast corner of La Pointe county, discharges its waters into the Mississippi, through Chippewa river.

TREMPELEAU, *Mountain*, see Mount Trempeleau.

TREMPELEAU, *River*, a considerable tributary of the Mississippi, in La Crosse county, enters the same near Mount Trempeleau, about 15 miles northwest from the mouth of Black river.

TRENTON CORNERS, *P. O.*, in town of same name, Dodge county, being town 13, N., of range 14 E.

TRENTON, *Town*, in county of Washington, being town 11 N., of range 20 E.; centrally located, 12 miles west from Ozaukee. It has 6 school districts.

TRENTON, *Town*, in county of Dodge, being town 13 N., and north half of town 12 N., of range 14; centrally located, 14 miles northwest from Juneau. Population in 1850 was 997. It has 11 school districts.

TRENTON, *P. V.*, in town of same name, on section 1, Washington county, 11 miles northwest from Ozaukee, and 90 miles easterly from Madison. Population 75; with 20 dwellings, and 2 mills.

TROUT, *Creek*, enters the Mississippi in town 8 N., in Crawford county.

TROUT, *Creek*, Grant county, a small stream entering the Wisconsin, in town of Fennimore.

TROUT, *Lake*, is near the head of the Manidowish river, in Marathon county. It is a beautiful body of clear water, 8 miles long and four wide, and yields a great quantity of the fine fish from which it is named.

TROY, *P. V.*, in town of same name, Walworth county.

TROY CENTRE, *P. V.*, in town of Troy, Walworth county, being town 4 N., of range 17 E.

TROY LAKES, *P. V.*, in town of East Troy, Walworth county, being town 4 N., of range 18 E.

TRUMBELLE, *River*, rises in town 27 N., of range 18 E., in St. Croix county, and runs south, emptying into the Mississippi, near the head waters of Lake Pepin.

TUCK-KIP-PING, *Lake*, is about 2 miles in length, situated in the northeast corner of the town of Merton.

TURTLE, *Creek*, rises in Turtle Lake, near the northeast corner of Richmond, Walworth county, and runs Southwest into Rock river, at Beloit.

TURTLE, *Lake*, is in the eastern part of Richmond, Walworth county, and falls into Rock river, at Beloit, through Turtle creek.

TURTLE, *Town*, in county of Rock, being town 1 N., of range 13 E.; centrally located, 7 miles east from Janesville. Population in 1850 was 966. It has 7 school districts.

TWELVE APOSTLES, *Islands*, in Lake Superior, La Pointe county, near the 47° N. latitude, and 14° W. longitude from Washington. They embrace in all an area of about 400 square miles, of which one half is water. The soil in some portions is good, but in the major part difficult to clear and cultivate. The waters about these islands afford excellent white fish, siscorret and trout. In regard to health, no portion of the Continent surpasses the Apostle Islands. In the summer months they present to residents of the south the most cool and delightful resort that can be imagined, and for invalids especially; such as are effected in the liver and lungs, the uniform bracing atmosphere produces the most surprising and beneficial results.

TWIN, *Creek*, a tributary from the north of Baraboo river, in Sauk county, which it enters in town 13 N., of range 4 W.

TWIN, *Lakes*, see Nashotah Lakes.

TWIN, *Rivers*, (Nashotah Rivers), E. and W., have their sources, the one in Kewaunee, the other in Brown county, and run nearly parallel to the southeast, uniting, and enter Lake Michigan at the village of Two Rivers, Manitowoc county.

TWO RIVERS, *P. V.*, is situated on the shore of Lake Michigan, at the mouth of Twin Rivers, on section 1, town 19, of range 24 E., 6 miles northeast from Manitowoc. It is quite an important place, and does a large trade in lumber, fish, leather, &c.

Ulao, *P. O.*, in Washington county.

Union Grove, *P. O.*, in Racine county.

Union, *P. V.*, in town of same name, Rock county, being town 4 N., of range 10 E.

Union, *Town*, in county of Rock, being town 4 N., of range 10 E.; centrally located, 16 miles northwest from Janesville. Population in 1850 was 1,050. It has 9 school districts.

Upper St. Croix, *Lake*, is on the St. Croix river, in La Pointe county. It is about 12 miles long and nearly 3 wide, and is noted for the depth and clearness of its water, and a small island near its outlet.

Ursine, *P. O.*, in Grant county.

Utter's Corners, *P. V.*, Walworth county, on section 6, town 3 N., of range 15 E., being town of Richmond, 15 miles northwest from Elkhorn, and about 50 miles southeast from Madison. It has a store, hotel, and Methodist church, and is surrounded by a good farming country.

Utica, *Town*, in county of Winnebago, being town 17 N., of range 15 E.; centrally located, 12 miles southwest from Oshkosh. Population in 1850 was 630. It has 6 school districts.

Vaseaux, *Lake*, head of the northwest branch of the Neenah.

Vermillion, *River*, rises near the head waters of the Kinnikinnic river, and runs southerly, entering the Mississippi.

Vernon, *P. V.*, is located on section 9 in town of same name, Waukesha county, 8 miles south from Waukesha, and 70 miles southeast from Madison. It is situated in a well timbered and watered vicinity. Population 40; with 11 dwellings, 1 store, 1 hotel, 1 blacksmith and waggon shop, and 2 organized religious denominations.

Vernon, *Town*, in county of Waukesha, being town 5 N., of range 19 E.; centrally located, 9 miles south from Waukesha. Population in 1850 was 889. It has 11 school districts.

VERONA, *P. O.*, in town of same name, Dane county, on Badger prairie, town 6 N., of range 8 E.

VERONA, *Town*, in county of Dane, being town 9 N., of range 9 E.; centrally located, nine miles southwest from Madison. It has 9 school districts.

VIENNA, *P. V.*, in town of Spring Prairie, Walworth county, being in town 3 N., of range 18 E.

VIENNA, *Town*, in county of Dane, being town 9, of range 9 E.; centrally located, 12 miles north from Madison.

VIEUX DESERT, *Lake*, see Kattakittekin.

VINLAND, *P. O.*, in Winnebago county.

VINLAND, *Town*, in county of Winnebago. Population in 1850 was 756. It has 6 school districts.

WABANGI ONIGOM, *Portage*, see Plover Portage.

WABINCK, *River*, rises near the centre of Waupacca county, and runs southeast, entering Wolf river a mile north of the mouth of the Waupacca river.

WABIZIPINIKAN, *River*, see Willow river.

WALDWIC, *P. O.*, in Iowa county.

WALDWIC, *Town*, in southeast corner of Iowa county, intersected by the east Peckatonnica and Yellowstone creek. It possesses both prairie and timber, is sparsely settled, and is adapted both to mining and farming.

WALLACE, *P. O.*, in Iowa county.

WALNUT SPRINGS, *P. O.*, in Green county.

WALWORTH, *County*, is bounded north by Jefferson and Waukesha, east by Racine and Kenosha, south by the State of Illinois, and west by Rock. It was set off Dec. 7, 1836, from Milwaukee, to which it was attached for judicial purposes, and was fully organized January 17, 1838. The county seat is at Elkhorn, the centre of the county. The surface is for the most part undulating, but through its whole extent there are small bodies of level prairie or meadow land, and abrupt and irregular hills or knobs. A chain of these enters the county, about the middle of the northern line, and runs through the northwestern corner. The greater portion of the county consists of oak openings. There are some 12 or more prairies of limited size, exclusive of low lands and marshes. There are also a few small bodies of heavy timber. Of soil, there are many varieties. The prairie—high and low; the openings—of white, black, and burr oak; all have their peculiarities of soil, and are all fitted in a high degree to the different productions of the country. The most considerable streams are the Geneva Outlet, Sugar and Honey Creeks, running eastward into Fox river and Turtle and Whitewater creeks, running westward into Rock river. These all head in the county, and are fed by springs. The population of the county consists mainly of people from the New England and other Eastern States. It ranks among the very first counties of the State for its intelligence, enterprize, fertility and wealth. The principal villages are Geneva, Delavan, Whitewater, Elkhorn and East Troy. Population in 1838, 1,019; 1840, 2,611; 1842, 4,618; 1846, 13,439; 1847, 15,039; 1850, 17,866; with 1,960 farms, 3,092 dwellings, and 82 manufactories. It belongs to the first judicial circuit, the first congressional district, forms the twelfth senate district, and sends five members to the assembly, as follows: 1. Towns of Whitewater, Richmond and La Grange. 2. Towns of Sugar Creek, Lafayette and Troy. 3. Towns of East Troy and Spring Prairie. 4. Elkhorn, Geneva and Hudson. 5. Delavan, Darien and Sharon. 6. Walworth, Linn, and Bloomfield. County Officers: Judge, William C. Allen; Sheriff, J. C. Crum; Clerk of Court, Wm. H. Pettit; Register, John Perry.

WALWORTH, *P. V.*, near centre of town of same name, on section 17; 11 miles southwest from Elkhorn, and 70 miles southeast from Madison, in a good farming region. Population 60, with 10 dwellings, 1 store, and a Baptist Church.

WALWORTH, *Town*, in county of Walworth, being town 1 N. of range 16 E.; centrally located, 10 miles southwest from Elkhorn. Population in 1850 was 987. It has 7 school districts.

WARNER'S, *Creek*, a small stream entering the Wisconsin, in town 6 N., of range 5 W., Grant county.

WARNER'S LANDING, *P. O.*, (discontinued), in Bad Ax county.

WARREN, *P. O.*, in Rock county.

WARREN, *Town*, in county of Waushara, being town 18 N., of range 12.

WARREN, *Town*, Waukesha county, name changed to Merton.

WARWICK, *P. O.*, in Marquette county.

WASHINGTON, *County*, is bounded on the north by Fond du Lac and Sheboygan, on the east by the State line in Lake Michigan, on the south by Milwaukee and Waukesha, and on the west by Dodge. It was set off from Milwaukee December 7, 1836, was organized for county purposes August 30, 1840, and fully established February 20, 1845. By an act of the legislature, approved in 1853, the portion of the county east of range 20, was set off and organized into a new county, by the name of Ozaukee, and the county seat of the new county was fixed at Ozaukee, (Port Washington), and that of Washington county, at West Bend, near the centre of the county. The surface is rolling, and abounds in living springs and streams of water, and is heavily timbered with oak, beech, maple, ash, &c. A large majority of the farmers are hardy Germans, who cultivate thoroughly. Wheat has been a surer crop for the last few years in this than in any other county in the State. The soil is well adapted to the raising of the grape and to tillage. The county is connected with the third judicial circuit, and with the third congressional district, and its legislative representation is as follows: The towns of Mequon, Cedarburg, Grafton, Port Washington, Saukville, Fredonia and Belgium, constitute the third senate district. The towns of Erin, Richfield, Germantown, Jackson, Polk, Hartford, Addison, West Bend, Newark, Trenton, Farmington, Kewaskum and Wayne, constitute the fourth senate district. First assembly district, towns of Belgium, Fredonia, Saukville, and Port Washington. Second assembly district, towns of Cedarburg, Grafton and Mequon. Third assembly district, towns of Erin, Richfield, Polk, Jackson, and Germantown. Fourth assembly district, Hartford, Addison, Wayne, Kewaskum, Newark, West Bend, Trenton and Farmington. The principal streams are the Milwaukee river and Oconomowoc creek. Population in 1838, 64; 1840, 343; 1842, 965; 1846, 7,473; 1847, 15,447; 1850, 19,476. There are 1,636 farms, 381 buildings, and 7 manufactories.

WASHINGTON, *Town*, in county of Green, being town 3 N., of range 7; centrally located, 8 miles north from Monroe. Population in 1850 was 317. It has 4 school districts.

WASHWAGOWING, *Lake*, see Flambeau Lake.

WASSAWA, *Lake*, see Yellow Lake.

WASSAWA, *River*, see Yellow River.

WATERFORD, *P. V.*, on section 35, in town of Rochester, Racine county; 23 miles northwest from city of Racine, and 80 miles southeast from Madison. It is situated on Fox river (Pishtaka) 25 miles southwest from Milwaukee, and has a fine hydraulic power. Population 500, with 100 dwellings, 4 stores, 2 hotels, 2 flouring mills, 3 saw mills, several mechanical shops, and a woollen factory; with 4 denominations—Baptist, Methodist, Presbyterian and Catholic—the latter having a good church edifice.

WATERLOO, *Town*, in county of Jefferson, being town 8 N., of range 13 E.; centrally located, 12 miles northwest from Jefferson. Population in 1850 was 831. It has 6 school districts.

WATERLOO, *Town*, in county of Grant, being fractional town 2 and 3 N., of range 4 W.; centrally located, 12 miles southwest from Lancaster. It has 2 school districts.

WATERLOO, *P. V.*, on section 8, in town of same name, Jefferson county, being the most northwest town in said county. It is 16 miles northwest from Jefferson, and 25 miles east from Madison. The location is on a creek of the same name, with a good hydraulic power sufficient for three mills now in operation. Population 200, with 60 dwellings, 4 stores, 2 hotels, 1 church, 1 pump and 1 fanning mill manufactory, 1 cabinet, 2 waggon, 1 plough and 3 blacksmith shops.

WATERLOO, *Creek*, rises in Bristol, Dane county, runs southeast into Jefferson county, thence northeast, emptying into Crawfish river in Portland, Dodge county.

WATERTOWN, *City*, is situated on both sides of Rock river, at the line between Dodge and Jefferson county, on the old stage route, half way (40 miles) between Madison and Milwaukee, and 12 miles north of Jefferson. It is connected with Milwaukee by a plank road, and is a point in the charters of several rail roads. The location of Watertown, in the heart of an excellent farming country, its good hydraulic power, access to market, and the energy and spirit of its inhabitants, cannot fail to have it continue, as it now is, one of the largest and most important inland towns in the State. The following are some of the statistics of the place taken in May, 1853:—Watertown now contains 4,000 inhabitants; with 6 dry good, 11 grocery, 2 drug, and 3 hardware stores, 15 taverns, 1 tobacconist, 2 bakeries, 3 meat markets, and 2 livery stables, 7 blacksmith, 6 waggon, 2 joiner, 2 jewelry, 4 tin, 6 cabinet, 1 chair, 1 machine, and 5 shoe shops; 1 fork and hoe, 1 plough, 1 door and sash, and 1 saleratus factory; 3 flouring and 4 saw mills; 1 fanning mill and 2 harness maker's shops; 2 book stores, 2 barber's shops, 1 gunsmith, 1 tannery, 1 furnace, 1 pottery, 1 oil mil, 1 carding machine, 1 rake and cradle, factory, 1 woollen and yarn factory, 2 printing offices, 6 school houses, 2 select schools, Jones's Exchange bank, and several lawyer's offices.

WATERTOWN, *Town*, in county of Jefferson, being town 8 N., of range 15 E.; centrally located, 11 miles north of Jefferson. Population in 1850, including village of same name, was 1850. It has 14 school districts.

WATERVILLE, *P. V.*, in east corner of Summit, Waukesha county.

WAUKAU, *P. V.*, on section 36, in town of Rushford, Winnebago county, 12 miles southwest from Oshkosh, and about 60 miles northeast from Madison, 2½ miles south of Neenah river, on the outlet of Rush Lake, with 30 feet fall of water, in a good and productive section of farming land. Population 500, with 150 dwellings, 7 stores, 3 hotels, 5 mills, and considerable water power unoccupied.

WAUKESHA, *County*, is bounded on the north by Dodge and Washington, on the east by Milwaukee, on the south by Walworth and Racine, on the west by Jefferson, and is 24 miles square. It was set off from Milwaukee and fully organized January 31, 1846. The eastern portion of the county is heavily timbered, while the western is divided between oak openings, prairie and marsh. The soil is good and well adapted to tillage and grazing. The county is distinguished for its numerous and beautiful lakes, there being probably more than 30 within its limits. It is watered by the Fox, (Pishtaka), Menomonee, Ashippin and Bark rivers, and Oconomowoc, Scupernong, Poplar, White and Mukwonago creeks. Population in 1846 was 13,793; 1847, 15,866; 1850, 19,324. It has 2,561 dwellings, 1,743 farms, and 78 manufactories. The county of Waukesha is in the first congressional district and the second judicial circuit, and its legislative representation is as follows: Ninth senate district, towns of Oconomowoc, Merton, Lisbon, Summit, Menomonee, Delafield, Pewaukee, and Brookfield. Tenth senate district, towns of Ottawa, Genesee, Waukesha, New Berlin, Muskego, Vernon, Mukwonago and Eagle. The assembly districts are as follows: 1st. towns of Merton, Delafield, Summit and Oconomowoc. 2nd. towns of Pewaukee, Lisbon, Menomonee and Brookfield. 3d. towns of Ottawa,

Genesee, Mukwonago and Eagle. 4th. towns of Waukesha, Vernon, Muskego and New Berlin. County Officers for 1853 and 1854: Judge, Martin Field; Clerk of Court, Lemuel White; Register, William R. Williams; Sheriff, Charles B. Ellis; Clerk of Board of Supervisors, Benjamin E. Clark; District Attorney, John E. Gallagher; Surveyor, John O. Reedsburg.

WAUKESHA, *Lake*, is a small lake in northwest corner of Norway, Racine county, about one mile in diameter and three quarters of a mile west of Wind Lake.

WAUKESHA, *P. V.* and *C. H.*, is located on section 3, town 6, of range 19 E., in town and county of the same name, 18 miles west of Milwaukee and 70 east of Madison. It is situated on Fox river, (Pishtaka), near the head of a beautiful prairie from which it derived its former name of Prairieville. It is situated on the Milwaukee and Mississippi railroad. This place was incorporated in 1852, and has about 1,500 inhabitants, 1 flouring, 1 saw, and 1 carding mill, 1 iron foundry, 1 machine and car shop, 3 blacksmiths, 2 coopers, 2 wheelwrights, 6 shoemakers, 2 cabinet makers, and 4 saddle and harness makers, 4 hotels, 8 dry good, 2 drug, 3 hardware and 7 grocery stores, 1 printing office, 6 churches, 1 academy, and is the seat of Carroll College, incorporated in 1846. It has a stone court house and jail built of the celebrated *Waukesha limestone*, and the several societies of Masons, S. of T., I. O. of O. F., D. of T., and B. of U.

WAUKESHA, *Town*, in county of same name, being town 6 N., of range 19 E.; centrally located, 3 miles south from village of Waukesha, the county seat. Population in 1850 was 2,314. It has 10 school districts. It is a good township of mostly prairie, and well watered, &c.

WAUPACCA, *P. O.*, in Waupacca county.

WAUPACCA, *Town*, in county and on river of same name, west of Mukwa.

WAUPACCA, *County*, is bounded on the north and northeast by Oconto, on the east by Outagamie, on the south by Winnebago and Waushara, and on the west by Portage. It was set off from Winnebago and established February 17, 1851, and attached thereto for judicial purposes. It is watered by the Wolf, Waupacca, Wabunk, Embarrass and Little Wolf rivers, and contains some of the best pine timber in the State. It being new, but little is known of its agricultural capacities. The county seat is at Mukwa, on Wolf river. Waupacca county belongs to the fourth judicial circuit, to the second senate and third congressional district, and with Outagamie and Oconto, sends one member to the assembly.

WAUPACCA, *Falls*, on river of same name, at which place is a descent of 7 feet.

WAUPACCA, *River*, rises near Plover, Portage county, and runs southeast, entering Wolf river near Mukwa.

WAUPUN, *P. V.*, in county of Fond du Lac, being on section 32, town 14 N., of range 15 E., 18 miles southwest from Fond du Lac city, and 50 miles northeast from Madison. The village is divided by the county line between Dodge and Fond du Lac counties. Population 500, with 100 dwellings, 9 stores, 2 hotels, 2 mills, and 1 distillery; Presbyterian and Baptist churches. The States Prison is located at this place.

WAUPUN, *Town*, in county of Fond du Lac, being town 14 N., of range 15 E.; centrally located, 15 miles southwest from Fond du Lac. Population in 1850 was 882. It has 5 school districts.

WAUSAU, *P. V. & C. H.*, on sections 25, 35, 26 and 36, of town 29 N., of range 7 E., in Marathon county, at Big Bull Falls, on the Wisconsin. It is 150 miles north from Madison. Its location is good for manufacturing and agricultural interests—combining fertility of soil, unsurpassed in the north—water power sufficient to supply the State, if properly distributed—and large quantities of pine for future use. The place is new, having had a *P. O.* but two years. The interest lumbering chiefly; but recently attention has been paid to the cultivation of some of the maple ridges, which are very numerous, and found to repay the laborer largely. It has a migratory population of about 300; with 5 stores, 4 hotels, 4 mills with 12 run of stones, and 9 saw mills.

WAUSHARA, *County*, is bounded on the north by Portage and Waupacca, east by Winnebago, south by Marquette, and west by Adams, and is 18 miles north and south by 36 miles east and west. It was established February 15, 1851, from Marquette, remaining in judicial connection therewith, until February 16, 1852, when it was completely organized. The seat of justice is at Sacramento, in the southeast corner of the county, on Fox river. This county embraces what has been familiarly known recently as the "Indian Lands" of Marquette county. It belongs to the third judicial circuit. County Officers for 1853 and 1854: Sheriff, Nathaniel Boyington; Clerk of Court, Allyn Boardman; District Attorney, C. M. Seely; Register, James S. Bugh; Clerk of Board of Supervisors, Augustus P. Noyes; Treasurer, Charles N. Shumway; Surveyor, S. W. Hall; Coroner, George Marshall.

WAUSHARA, *Town*, in county of same name, being town 18, of range 13; in the southeast corner of which is Sacramento, the county seat.

WAUSHARA, *P. V.*, is situated on section 26, town 13 N., of range 13 E., in Dodge county, 17 miles northwest from Juneau, and 43 miles northeast from Madison. Population 400; with 60 dwellings, 6 stores, 3 hotels, 2 mills, 2 blacksmiths, 1 waggon maker; and 2 churches, with 5 denominations. It is on the Watertown and Fort Winnebago road, and the United States road from Fond du Lac to Fort Winnebago.

WAUTOMA, *P. O.*, in town of same name, Waushara county, on section 34, town 19 N., of range 10 E.

WAUTOMA, *Town*, in county of Waushara, northwest from Sacramento.

WAUWATOSA, *P. V.*, in town of same name, in Milwaukee county, 5 miles west from Milwaukee, with which it is connected by the M. & M. R. R., and 2 plank roads. It is near the centre of the township, and has 4 stores, 2 hotels, 1 flour mill, 1 saw mill, various mechanics, and 2 churches, belonging to the Congregational and Baptist denominations, costing respectively $2,500 and $2,000, and a good school house.

WAUWATOSA, *Town*, in county of Milwaukee, being town 7 N., of range 21 E.; centrally located, 5 miles from Milwaukee city. Population 2,500. It has 11 School districts. The surface of the country is rolling, with a good soil, presenting fine situations for residences, many good ones having been already erected. The social, educational, and religious advantages are of a superior order.

WAYAKOMING, *Lake* and *River*, form the head waters of the St. Croix river.

WAYNE, *Town*, in Lafayette county.

WAYNE, *Town*, in county of Washington, being town 12 N., of range 18 E.; centrally located, 24 miles northwest from Ozaukee. Population in 1850 was 714. It has 10 school districts.

WEBSTER, *Island*, a small island in Fox Lake, Dodge county, in town 13 N., of range 13 E.

WEDGER, *Creek*, a small branch of Black River, in La Crosse county, from the north, being in town 23 N., of range 2 W.

WELAUNEE, *P. O.*, in Winnebago county.

WELCH *Fork*, a branch from the north of Grant river, in Beetown, Grant county.

WESACOTA, *River* (Brule or Wood River of Menomonee), is a branch of the Menomonee, forming a portion of the boundary line between Wisconsin and Michigan. It rises in Lake Brule, and is about 100 feet in width.

WEST BEND, *Town*, in county of Washington, being town 12 N., of range 19 E.; centrally located, 20 miles northwest from Ozaukee. Population in 1850 was 672. It has 4 school districts.

WEST BEND, *P. V.* and *C. H.*, on section 14, in town of same name, Washington county. It is 17 miles west from Ozaukee, and 90 miles northeast from Madison, on the Milwaukee river, with an excellent water power and good general advantages. The county seat of Washington county was established at this place in 1853. Population 500, with 200 dwellings, 7 stores, 2 hotels, 2 mills, 10 mechanical shops, 1 church and 3 denominations. It is on the road from Ozaukee to Fort Winnebago, at its junction with the Milwaukee and Fond du Lac plank road, and is a point on the air line railroad from Milwaukee to Fond du Lac.

WESTFIELD, *P. O.*, in town of same name, Marquette county.

WESTFIELD, *Town*, in county of Marquette, being towns 16 and 17 N. of ranges 8 and 9 W.

WEST *Fork* OF MONTREAL *River*, a small tributary from the southwest, of Montreal river, in La Pointe county.

WEST POINT, *Town*, in the county of Columbia, being town 10 N. of range 7 E.; centrally located, 17 miles southwest from Portage. Population in 1850 was 197. It has 4 school districts.

WESTPORT, *Town*, in county of Dane, being town 8 N. of range 9 E.; centrally located, 8 miles north of Madison. It has 3 school districts.

WEST ROSENDALE, *P. O.*, in Rosendale, Fond du Lac county.

WEYAUWEGO, *P. V.*, in Waupacca county.

WEYAUWEGO, *Town*, in county of Waupacca, being town 21 N. of range 13; situated west from Mukwa.

WHAYPAW, *River*, is a tributary, from the west, of the Wisconsin, in Marathon county.

WHEATLAND, *P. V.*, in town of same name, Kenosha county.

WHEATLAND, *Town*, in county of Kenosha, being town 1, and S. one-third of town 2 N. of range 19 E.; centrally located, 22 miles southwest from Kenosha city. Population in 1850 was 1,193. It has 11 school districts.

WHITE, *Creek*, a tributary of the Wisconsin, in Adams county.

WHITE, *Creek*, a tributary from the west of Fox river, in Waukesha county.

WHITE ELK, *Lakes*, are four in number, forming the most northeastern head waters of the Chippewa river into which they run through the Manodowish. They are severally called Lower White Elk Lake, and Second, Third and Fourth White Elk Lakes.

WHITE FISH, *Bay*, on western shore of Lake Michigan, in Door county.

WHITE FISH, *Lakes*, emptying into Little Wisconsin river in 45° 45′ north latitude, about half-way between Wisconsin and Little Wisconsin rivers.

WHITE, *Lake*, in the north part of town 25 N. of range 17 E., in Oconto county, discharges its waters southwesterly into Wolf river.

WHITE, *Rapids*, are shoals of Menomonee river, below Penemee Falls.

WHITE, *River*, rises in the western part of Waushara county, and runs southeast, entering Fox river, in town 17 north.

WHITE OAK SPRINGS, *P. V.*, on section 32, town 1 N., of range 2 E.; being in county of Lafayette, and distant 5 miles from Shullsburg, and 80 miles southwest from Madison. Population 100; with 26 dwellings, 4 stores, and 1 hotel. Its location and advantages are as favorable as any village in the West. Lead ore abounds in large quantities in its vicinity, and forms no inconsiderable item in the pursuit of its inhabitants.

WHITE OAK SPRINGS, *Town*, of same name in Lafayette county, on the State line.

WHITEWATER, *Creek*, rises in town of same name, Walworth county, and running northwest, enters Bark river, about 5 miles above Fort Atkinson, in Jefferson county.

WHITEWATER, *P. V.*, is situated on sections 4 and 5, in town of same name, in the northwest corner of Walworth county; it derives its name from Whitewater creek which passes through it. It was settled about the year 1839. The village has a population of about 1,000, derived mostly from New York, New England and Ohio. There are four well finished churches, and the fifth—the Catholic—is erected and partly completed. The buildings are generally neat, and in good taste, and the grounds finely planted with trees and shrubbery, which contribute to give the place an attractive rural air. It is one of the pleasantest of our interior villages, and will continue to be a desirable place of residence. It is the principal point between Waukesha and Janesville, on the Milwaukee and Mississippi rail road, and is made the point of intersection of that road and the proposed Wisconsin Central rail road, for which a company has been recently chartered, and just organized. The construction of this road, which is confidently anticipated, would render Whitewater a very central location, on the junction of the main east and west, and north and south rail road lines of the State, and connect it, by direct communication with Chicago, at 90 miles distance. It has now a considerable business in the purchase of produce and the sale of lumber, induced by the rail road. It contains 2 grist mills, 1 saw mill, 1 iron foundry, 1 manufactory of pottery ware, and the usual variety of stores and mechanic shops, &c. The location of the village is on a soil of sandy loam, which secures dry streets and side-walks, and eligible building sites.

WHITEWATER, *Town*, in county of Walworth, being town 4 N., of range 15 E.; centrally located, 13 miles northwest from Elkhorn. Population in 1850 was 1,252.

WHITEWATER, *Lakes*, are 2 small lakes, forming the source of Creek of same name, in south part of town of same name.

WHITNEY'S *Mills*, on the Wisconsin, in south part of Portage county.

WIGOBIMIS, *Lake*, is in the northwest part of St. Croix county, discharging its waters through a river of same name into St. Croix river.

WIGOBIMIS, *River*, is the outlet of Lake of same name, in St. Croix county.

WILLET, *P. O.*, in town of Adams, Green county.

WILLIAMSTOWN, *Town*, in county of Dodge, being town 12 N., of range 16 E.; centrally located, 8 miles northeast from Juneau. It has 6 school districts.

WILLOW CREEK, *P. O.*, in Marquette county.

WILLOW, *Creek*, rises in northeast corner of Richland county, and running southwest, enters Pine river, at Sextonville.

WILLOW, *Creek*, rises in town of Wautoma, Waushara county, and running east, enters the west end of Lake Pauwaicun.

WILLOW, *Prairie*, Waushara county, contains about 2,000 acres of land. It is in the centre of town 20 N., of range 8 E.

WILLOW RIVER, *P. O.*, St. Croix county. See Hudson.

WILLOW RIVER, *Town*, (formerly Beuna Vista,) being town 29 and 30, and west half of town 28 N., of range 19 W., in which is located the county seat of St. Croix county. It has 3 school districts. Name changed to Hudson in 1852.

WILLOW, *River*, rises in the eastern portion of St. Croix county, and runs southwest, entering Lake St. Croix, about 18 miles above the mouth of St. Croix river, into the Mississippi.

WILLOW SPRINGS, *P. O.*, in town of same name, Lafayette county.

WILLOW SPRINGS, *Town*, Lafayette county.

WILMOT, *P. V.*, in town of Salem, Kenosha county, being in town 1 N., of range 20 E.

WILSON, *Town*, in county of Sheboygan, being towns 13 and 14 N., of range 23 E.; centrally located, 6 miles south from Ozaukee. It has 5 school districts.

WINCHESTER, *Town*, in county of Winnebago, being town 20 N., of range 15 E.; centrally located, 15 miles northwest from Oshkosh. It has 1 school district.

WIND, *Lake*, is in the northern part of the town of Norway, Racine county, and is 2 miles long and 1½ miles wide.

WINDSOR, *P. V.*, on section 34, of town of same name, Dane county, in a good farming district, on Token Creek, 10 miles northeast from Madison, on road to Portage city.

WINDSOR, *Town*, in county of Dane, being town 9 N., of range 10 E.; centrally located, 12 miles northeast from Madison. It has 7 school districts.

WINGVILLE, *Town*, in county of Grant, being town 6 N., of range 1 W.; centrally located, 15 miles northeast from Lancaster. It has 7 school districts.

WINGVILLE, *Village*, Grant county. See Montfort *P. O.*

WINNEBAGO, *County*, is bounded on the north by Outagamie, east by Calumet, (from which it is separated by Lake Winnebago), on the south by Fond du Lac, and on the west by Waushara and Marquette. It was set off from Fond du Lac and Brown counties, January, 1843. It was organized for county purposes, (its judicial connection being with Fond du Lac,) Feb. 20, 1842, and was fully organized Feb. 8, 1847. The seat of justice has been established at Oshkosh, near the entrance of Fox river (Neenah,) into Lake Winnebago. The surface of the county is generally level or slightly undulating, and well diversified with openings, prairie, marsh, timber, and springs of pure cold water. The soil produces all kinds of grain, and is well adapted to grazing. The county is comparatively new, and its agricultural advantages have never been fully developed. It is believed, however, that it will be more distinguished for its dairying, the growing of stock, and its manufactures, than for the raising of grain. The principal streams are the Fox and Wolf rivers. It is connected with the fourth judicial circuit, with the third congressional district, and constitutes the twenty-first senate district, and is divided into two assembly districts, viz: 1st. Towns 17 and 18, ranges 14, 15, 16 and 17. 2d. Towns 19 and 20, ranges 14, 15, 16 and 17. Population in 1840 was 135; in 1842, 143; in 1846, 732; in 1847, 2,748; in 1850, 10,167. County Officers for 1853 and 1854: Judge, Edwin Wheeler; Clerk of Court, E. R. Baldwin; Sheriff, Alex. F. David; Register, Edwin R. Rowley; Clerk of Board of Supervisors, J. H. Osborn; Treasurer, Jonathan Dougherty.

WINNEBAGO, *Island*, at mouth of lake of same name. See Doty's Island.

WINNEBAGO, *Lake*, is situated between the counties of Calumet and Winnebago, having its head in Fond du Lac. It is nearly 30 miles in length from north to south, and about 12 miles wide at the mouth of the Neenah, at Oshkosh. This lake forms a portion of the navigation of the Fox and Wisconsin river improvement, and is about 160 feet above the level of Lake Michigan, and 63 feet below the Wisconsin Portage. It is navigable its whole length for small steam boats, which ply regularly upon it during the summer season. It covers an area of about 90 square miles.

WINNEBAGO, *Marsh*, Dodge county. See Horicon lake.

WINNEBAGO, *Rapids*, on Neenah river, at the outlet of Lake Winnebago, has a descent of 7½ feet in a distance of 7,700 feet.

WINNEBAGO, *Town*, in county of Winnebago. Population in 1850 was 1,647. It has 4 school districts.

WINNEÇONNA, *P. V.*, on east side of Wolf river, in town of same name, Winnebago county.

WINNECONNA, *Town*, in county of Winnebago, town 19 N. of range 15 E.; centrally located, 10 miles northwest from Oshkosh. Population in 1850 was 1948. It has 3 school districts.

WIOTA, *Town*, in county of Lafayette.

WISCONSIN *River*, is the most important in Wisconsin, rising in Lake Vieux Desert, on the northern boundary and extending completely across the State, in a southwesterly direction, enters the Mississippi, by its course, 90 miles from the line of Illinois. Its head waters are surrounded by extensive forests of pine timber, with plenty of waterfall for its economical manufacture into lumber, and a good channel and current to transport the same to market. It is navigable for steamboats to the Portage of the Fox river, 114 miles, from its mouth, and even above for small boats. The trade of this river in lumber and mineral (lead) is quite extensive, and gradually increasing, and at the completion of the Fox and Wisconsin Rivers Improvement, the trade in all branches of commerce will be great.—The following account of this river was made by Marquette and Joliet, who descended it from the Portage in 1673: "The river upon which we embarked is called Mescousin (Wisconsin); the river is very wide, but the sand bars make it very difficult to navigate, which is increased by numerous islands, covered with grape vines. The country through which it flows is beautiful; the groves are so dispersed in the prairies that it makes a noble prospect; and the fruit of the trees shows a fertile soil. These groves are full of walnut, oak, and other trees unknown to us in Europe. We saw neither game nor fish, but roebuck and buffaloes in great numbers. After having navigated 30 leagues, we discovered some iron mines; and one of our company, who had seen such mines before, said these were very rich in ore. They are covered with about three feet of soil, and situate near a chain of rocks, whose base is covered with fine timber. After having rowed ten leagues further, making forty leagues from the place we embarked, we came into the Mississippi, on the 17th June.

WISCONSIN, *State.* See Introduction, page 4.

WISSAKUDE, *River*, of Lake Superior, see Bois Brule or Burnt Wood river.

WISCONSIN, *Pinery*, is all of that section of country, north of Dell Prairie, tributary to the Wisconsin river, producing yearly 70,000,000 feet of pine lumber, beside shingles, timber, &c. The following statement shows the location of the several mills, the number of saws, and the amount of lumber manufactured annually by each, commencing at the lowest point on the river:—Dell Creek, 2 saws, 1,000,000 feet.—Lemonwier, 5 saws, 2,700,000 feet.—Yellow River, 7 saws, 3,700,000 feet. Pointe Bausse, 3 saws, 200,000 feet.—Grand Rapids, 15 saws, 8,000,000 feet.—Crooked Rift, 1 saw, 600,000 feet—Mill Creek, 5 saws, 2,400,000 feet.—Little Plover River, 1 saw, 600,000 feet. Conant Rapids, 3 saws, 2,000,000 feet.—Big Plover River, 2 saws, 1,200,000 feet.—Stevens' Point, 5 saws, 3,000,000 feet. Little Aux Plaines, 2 saws, 2,400,000 feet.—Little Eau Claire, 2 saws, 1,500,000 feet.—Big Aux Plaines, 2 saws, 2,000,000 feet.—Little Bull Falls, 8 saws, 6,000,000 feet.—Junior Bull Falls, 1 saw, 600,000 feet.—Big Eau Claire, 8 saws, 6,000,000 feet.—Little Rib, 2 saws, 1,000,000 feet.—Big Bull Falls, 22 saws, 19,000,000 feet.—Trap, 2 saws, 900,000 feet.—Pine River, 4 saws, 2,000,000 feet.—Jenny Bull Falls, 4 saws, 4,000,000 feet.—Making a total of 105 saws, and 70,000,000 feet. This statement does not include lumber manufactured at several places below the Dells, the logs for which come from above that point.

WISCONSIN, *Natural History Association.* This Society was organized at Madison, the capital of the State in 1852. Its object is to collect and procure in a *Museum*, the Fauna and Flora of the State, books, papers, and documents relating to the physical sciences, and the social, political, and natural history of the Great West. Soon after the organization of the Association a large and very valuable collection of specimens in natural history, prepared by Samuel Sercomb, Esq., who has resided 15 years in the West, collecting the same, was purchased. This, together with several valuable donations, has placed the Association upon a substantial basis. It is now constantly receiving additions by contributions, purchase, and exchange, and the catalogue embraces quadrupeds, birds, reptiles, fishes, molusca, crustacea, insects, geological and botanical specimens, Indian relics, curiosities of nature and art, books, papers, documents, &c. The circular of the Society solicits correspondence with the Secretary in relation to any thing of interest that can be obtained, by exchange or otherwise, in different parts of this and other western States. The following are the Officers: President, Leonard J. Farwell; Secretary, William Dudley; Taxidermist, Samuel Sercomb.

WISCONSIN, *State Agricultural Society*. This Society was organized on the fifth day of March, A. D. 1851, at a meeting of some of the leading agriculturists of the State, held at the Capitol, in Madison. At that meeting a constitution was adopted and officers chosen, consisting of a President, three Vice-Presidents, (one to be located in each congressional district), a Recording Secretary, a Corresponding Secretary, and a Treasurer, who, together with five additional members, chosen from the Society at large, constitute an Executive Committee, which forms the executive and administrative power of the Society. By a standing resolution of the Executive Committee, the President, Secretaries and Treasurer constitute a Standing Committee, with power in the recess of the Executive Committee to transact such minor business as may be necessary. The Standing Committee meets monthly, on the first Wednesday in each month, at the rooms of the Society, in the Capitol, at Madison, for the transaction of business. The Executive Committee meets quarterly, or at the call of the Corresponding Secretary, at which meetings the proceedings of the Standing Committee are re-viewed, for confirmation or otherwise. The

Society meets annually, on the third Wednesday of January in each year. It possesses ample and commodious rooms in the Capitol, which are elegantly fitted up, and placed in charge of the Corresponding Secretary. The first volume of the Society's Transactions was issued in the spring of 1852, and was a large and elegant volume, well stored with valuable reading, and showing evident marks of advancement in agricultural science and scientific investigation. The second volume is now in press, and will shortly be issued. The great and unparalleled success which has attended the labors of this Society may be traced almost entirely to the intelligent enterprize and active energy of the officers who have hitherto had the direction and management of its affairs. To their judicious management, wise counsels, and zealous labors so uniformly and freely bestowed, our State is, and must ever be, greatly indebted for that advancement which is now so rapidly taking place in our agricultural and industrial interests. In this respect the Society has been most fortunate. The first Annual Cattle Show and Fair of the Society was held at Janesville, in the month of October, 1851, and was a most brilliant exposition of the condition of the rural arts in Wisconsin. The show of cattle, sheep, horses, and swine, was such as to astonish and delight all; while the domestic manufactures, and the products of the dairy exhibited, gave ample proof of the skill and industry of the exhibitors—nor were the treasures of Ceres and Pomona wanting to give variety to the scene—but all alike admirably blending, each in due proportion, gave promise of the future high rank which Wisconsin must attain, amid the peaceful walks of husbandry. The Show at Milwaukee, in the fall of 1852, amply sustained the proud position of the Society, and demonstrated the certainty of its success. The Fair for the present year is to be held at the city of Watertown, on the 4th, 5th, 6th, and 7th days of October next. Ample arrangements have been made for the accommodation of the immense throngs that will be in attendance, and no pains will be spared to make this, the most brilliant and successful of all the exhibitions of the Society. The Officers, for the current year, are as follows: President, Elisha W. Edgerton, Summit. Vice Presidents, Bertine Pinkney, Rosendale; Jeremiah E. Dodge, Potosi; and Nathaniel B. Clapp, Kenosha. Recording and also Corresponding Secretary, Albert C. Ingham, Madison. Treasurer, Simeon Mills, Madison.—Additional Members of the Executive Committee: Hiram Barber, Juneau; Henry M. Billings, Highland; Martin Field, Mukwonago; Sam. S. Daggett, Milwaukee; and Mark Miller, Janesville. All communications for the Society should be addressed to the Corresponding Secretary at Madison, Wisconsin.

WISCONSIN *University*. The buildings of this Institution are situated one mile west of the Capitol in Madison, on a beautiful eminence commanding an extensive view of the basin of the Four Lakes. The site comprises, within the enclosure, about 50 acres; on which, in accordance with the plan adopted by the Regents, it is proposed to erect five collegiate structures, namely: the main edifice, on the crown of the hill, at the head of a wide avenue leading through the grounds in the direction of the Capitol; and the four subordinate buildings, on a line, several rods in advance of the main edifice, two on either side of the avenue. The main edifice is intended to contain all the public rooms, the observatory, and two dwelling houses. The other buildings are to be divided into dormitories for the residence and accommodation of students. The first dormitory building, on the north side of the avenue, was completed in the summer of 1851; and the Collegiate Department was opened in it on the third Wednesday of the same year. The corresponding building, on the south side of the avenue, is in process of erection, to be followed, next in order, by the construction of the main edifice. The organic law of the University provides for the establishment of the four Faculties, namely: of "Science, Literature and

Arts;" of "Law;" of "Medicine;" and of the "Theory and Practice of Elementary Instruction." Of these, the former has been organized by the Regents, and the following chairs having been created by ordinance: 1. Of Ethics, Civil Polity, and Political Economy; 2. Of Mental Philosophy, Logic, Rhetoric, and English Literature. 3. Of Ancient Languages and Literature. 4. Of Modern Languages and Literature. 5. Of Mathematics, Natural Philosophy and Astronomy. 6. Of Chemistry and Natural History. The Chair of Ethics, &c., is occupied by the Chancellor of the University, who, together, with the other Professors, and the requisite number of Tutors, will constitute the Faculty of Science, Literature, and Arts. The University was originally endowed by act of Congress, granting seventy-two sections of land to be selected by the State for that use. Under the appraisal of 1852, the capital fund derived from the sale of these lands, amounts to $170,000. They are now open to private entry, at the appraised value, in the office of the Commissioners of School and University Lands at Madison. They are selling off rapidly, and it is believed that the whole will be converted into a productive fund within a short period. The University of Wisconsin, like the community whose institution it is, is still young. It has gone into operation with appointments amply sufficient to answer all present educational demands, while the condition of its finances justifies the confidence, that its increasing capabilities will keep pace with the future growth of the State, and make it an attractive gathering point for the scholars of the West.

WISSAUNA, *Lake*, see Golden Lake, of Waukesha county.

WISHICONI, *Lake*, is a small body of water, in Marathon county, tributary to the Chippewa.

WOLF, *Creek*, a small tributary of the Peckatonnica, into which it empties at Gratiot, Lafayette county.

WOLF, *River*, (Pauwaicun,) east of the Wisconsin, and running southeast, unites with Neenah river just above Great Butte des Morts Lake, at which place it is much larger than the Neenah. It is navigable, for over 100 miles from its mouth, for small steamers, and furnishes the best pine lumber in the State.

WOLF RIVER, *Pinery*, as it is called, is the extensive evergreen district on Wolf river and its tributaries, Rat, Pine, Little, Waupacca, Little Wolf, Embarass, and Shawana rivers. Some of these are large streams, and afford excellent hydraulic power. The annual manufacture of lumber, besides shingles and timber, will be partially shown by the following list which contains nothing but the estimated amount of sawed lumber : Appleton, 2,000,000 ; Menasha and Neenah, 3,000,000 ; Oshkosh, 5 mills, 4,000,000 ; Algoma, 2 mills, 1,000,000 ; Butte des Morts, 2 mills, 1,000,000 ; Winneconna, 1 mill, 500,000 ; Little river, 1 mill, 500,000 ; Little Wolf, 4 mills, 5,000,000 ; Shawana, 2 mills, 1,000,000 ; Red river, 1 mill, 500,000 ; Clark's, 2 mills, 1,000,000 ; Fox river above mouth of Wolf, 6,000,000. Making a total of 25,500,000.

WORTH, *P. O.*, in Sheboygan county.

WRIGHTSTOWN, *Town*, in Brown county.

WYALUSING, *P. V.*, on section 1, town 5 N., of range 7 W., Grant county, 25 miles northwest from Lancaster, and about 100 miles west from Madison. It is beautifully situated on the Mississippi river, and has an excellent steam boat landing. The vicinity is well supplied with timber and water, and good hydraulic powers, and is well adapted to all the pursuits of agriculture. Population 30 ; with 2 stores and 1 hotel.

WYOCENA, *P. V.*, in town of same name, Columbia county, being on sections 21 and 22, town 12 N., of range 10 E.

WYOMING, *P. O.*, in town of same name, Iowa county.

WYOMING, *Town*, in county of Iowa, being part of towns 7 and 8 N., of ranges 3 and 4. It has 4 school districts.

YELLOW, *Lake*, is the source of a river of the same name, a small tributary of the St. Croix, in La Pointe county, from the south.

YELLOW, *River*, rises in the south part of Portage county, and runs southerly, emptying into the Wisconsin river, in southeast corner of town 17 N., of range 4 E., Adams county.

YELLOW, *River* and *Lake*, in La Pointe county. See Massawa River and Lake.

YELLOW, *River*, Chippewa county, rises in Marathon county, and runs southwesterly into the Chippewa river, about 5 miles above the falls.

YELLOW STONE, *Creek*, is a tributary from the northwest of Dodge's branch or east branch of the Peckatonnica river, into which it empties, in the town of Argyle, Lafayette county.

YORK, *P. O.*, Dane county, on section 21, of town of same name. It has 1 store, 3 hotels, and is 22 miles northeast from Madison.

YORK, *Town*, in county of Dane, being town 9, of range 12 E.; centrally located, 19 miles northeast from Madison. It has 6 school districts.

YORK, *Town*, in county of Greene, being town 4 N., of range 6; centrally located, 16 miles northwest from Monroe. Population in 1850 was 191. It has 2 school districts.

YORKVILLE, *P. O.*, town of York, Racine county, being in town 3 N., of range 21 E.

YORKVILLE, *Town*, in county of Racine, being town 3 N., of range 21 E.; centrally located, 10 miles west of Racine. Population in 1850 was 997. It has 10 school districts.

YOUNG HICKORY, *P. V.*, in town of Jackson, Washington county, being in town 10 N., of range 20 E.

APPENDIX.

ALMOND, *Town*, in county of Portage.

ANCIENT, *P. O.*, in Dane county.

ARGYLE, *P. O.*, in Lafayette county.

ARGYLE, *Town*, in Lafayette county.

ASHTON, *P. O.*, in Dane county.

BADGER, *P. O.*, in Fond du Lac county.

BEAULIEUX, *Rapids*, are in the Wisconsin river, seven miles above the mouth of Pine river. See Jenny Bull Falls.

BELMONT, *Town*, in Lafayette county.

BENTON, *P. O.*, in Lafayette county.

BERLIN, *P. V.*, is situated on sections 3 and 4, on the east side of Fox river, in town 17 N., of range 13 E. It was laid out in 1849 by N. H. Strong, Esq., from whom it derived the name of Strong's Landing, by which it is sometimes called. It is a place of considerable business, has a good river trade, and is in the centre of a large agricultural district. It has two newspapers, and various mercantile and mechanical establishments.

BENTON, *Town*, in Lafayette county.

BIG FOOT PRAIRIE, *P. O.*, in town of Walworth, Walworth county.

BRISTOL, *P. O.*, in town of same name, in the county of Kenosha.

BYRON, *P. O.*, in Fond du Lac county.

CENTREVILLE, *Town*, in Manitowoc county.

CENTRE, *Town*, in Lafayette county.

COLLINS, *P. O.*, in Manitowoc county.

COON PRAIRIE, *P. O.*, in Crawford county.

COPPER ROCK, *River*, is a tributary from the west of Wisconsin river, which it enters, at Rock Island, 10 miles below Grand Father Bull Falls.

COTTAGE INN, *P. O.*, in Lafayette county, on stage route from Madison to Galena, 60 miles southwest from Madison.

DEPERE, *Town*, in Brown county.

DUNKIRK, *P. O.*, in Dane county.

EDSON, *Town*, in Manitowoc county.

ELK GROVE, *P. O.*, in town of same name, Lafayette county.

ELK GROVE, *Town*, in Lafayette county.

EOLIA, *P. O.*, in Dane county.

FAYETTE, *Town*, in Lafayette county.

FLORENCE, *P.O.*, in town of Portage Prairie, Columbia county, on section 6, town 12 N., of range 12 E., at head of Duck Creek.

FOND DU LAC, *City*. This place was one of the earliest located towns in Wisconsin, a paper city, laid out and platted several years in advance of the progress of civilization. But the past ten years has wrought a change which few Western towns can rival. The city is located at the head of Lake Winnebago, on section 10, town 15, of range 17 E. The principal business portion is situated about three-quarters of a mile from the lake, on the Fond du Lac river, whose mouth forms a convenient port of entry for the steam boats and other water crafts which run between this place, Oshkosh, Wolf river, and Upper and Lower Fox rivers. The river, at the upper part of the city and a short distance above, furnishes several very fair mill powers for the manufacture of lumber, flour, &c., and on which an oil mill is also being erected. The principal part of the city is built upon a level prairie on the east side of the river. On the west side was formerly a beautiful sugar maple grove, which affords one of the most inviting and pleasant retreats that could well be desired, and in which are erected a large number of private residences, which are destined to be the most desirable in the city. The place is backed up and sustained by one of the richest and most productive farming counties in the State. One of the most inviting features of this place, is the pure water with which it is supplied, from the large number of never-failing fountains, or artesian wells, which brings the water to the surface of the earth, and yields a most bountiful supply of as pure water as can be found in the State, and to which may be attributed, in a great degree, the extensive healthfulness of the place. The streets are wide, the lots of convenient size, and laid out with much uniformity and taste—with several public squares, which, when properly improved, will add much to the beauty of the place. About 3 miles of double plank road has been constructed within the limits of of the city. A large amount of money has also been expended in building side-walks throughout the entire city, which are mostly of plank, and of very convenient width. The present population of the city is estimated at about 4,000, and is rapidly increasing by the influx of business men and capitalists from the East. It was first incorporated as a village in 1847, and a city charter granted in the winter of 1852. There are in the city 9 hotels, 2 exchange or banking houses, 12 dry goods, 15 grocery and provision, 4 clothing, 4 wine and liquor, 8 boot and shoe, 2 hat and cap, 4 harness and leather, 3 stove and tin ware, and 1 iron and hardware stores; 2 jeweller, 5 cabinet, 5 blacksmith, 3 paint, 2 gun, 3 waggon, and 3 milliner shops; 4 warehouses, 4 lumber yards, 5 saloons, 3 livery stables, 6 bakeries, 1 foundry, 3 sash and blind factories, 4 meat markets; 1 cigar, 1 car, and 1 cradle manufactory; 1 book bindery, 2 planing mills, 3 nursery establishments, 1 auction store, 2 daguerrean galleries, 3 printing offices, 16 law offices, 9 physicians and surgeons, 3 barber's shops. In addition to these, there are a large number of small establishments, where various kinds of business are carried on with great success. There are 7 religious denominations.

FRANCIS CREEK, *P. O.*, in Manitowoc county.

FREEDOM, *P. O.*, in Sauk county.

GEORGETOWN, *P. O.*, in Lafayette county.

GRAND FATHER BULL, *Falls*, are the largest rapids on the Wisconsin river. The river at this place is divided into three chutes by two chains of rocks rising fifteen feet above the water.

GREEN BAY, *Town*, in Brown county.

HAMPDEN, *P. O.*, in town of same name, in Columbia county.

HARTFORD, *P. V.*, in Washington county.

HELENA, *P. V.*, see Helena Village.

HOWARD, *Town*, in Brown county.

HORTONVILLE, *P. O.*, in town of Hortonia, on Wolf river, in Outagamie county.

JACKSON, *County*, was set off from La Crosse at the January session of the legislature in 1853, and includes all of said county of La Crosse, north of town 18. The seat of justice is at the village of Black River Falls, on Black river. In this county about 15,000,000 feet of pine lumber is sawed annually. For further particulars, see La Crosse county.

JANESVILLE, *City*, is located on section 1, of town of same name, in Rock county. It is pleasantly situated on both sides of Rock river, 14 miles north of the State line, and about midway between Lake Michigan and the Mississippi river; 40 miles southeast of Madison, and 90 from Chicago, Ill. It was organized into a city government in April, 1853. It is the county seat of Rock county, has two extensive water powers which are but partially developed, and is surrounded by a fertile and farming dairy country, with which it has an extensive trade. Its steady and rapid increase in population and wealth will appear from the following statistics: The first families settled upon the spot where the city now stands in the year 1836. A village was laid out in 1839. In 1843, the population was 333; in 1845, 857; in 1847, 1,458; in 1849, 1,812; in 1850, 3,100; in 1853, about 5,000. Rail roads from Milwaukee, Racine, Kenosha, Chicago, Beloit, Dubuque, Madison, and Fond du Lac, are projected to this city; the first already completed, and the others are under contract to be finished in one or two years. There are 4 flouring mills, within the limits of the corporation, having 10 run of stones; 3 saw mills, 1 woollen factory, 1 mill for manufacturing water lime, and grinding coarse feed for cattle, swine, &c., to which is to be added an oil mill, two foundries, a mill for sawing stone and turning wood, with a large number of mechanic shops of all descriptions; 12 dry good, 17 grocery, 2 hardware, 2 book, 3 drug, several clothing, shoe and variety stores; 2 banks, (Badger State, and Central Wisconsin); 5 hotels, and a sixth being erected, of very large dimensions, on the ruins of one recently burnt down; 4 printing presses, 3 weekly and 1 monthly newspaper, and 1 book bindery. The State Institution for the Blind is located at Janesville, a portion of the buildings are completed in which several children are receiving instruction. Besides the public schools, Janesville has an academy and a female seminary, both excellent institutions; also 6 large churches erected, built of brick or stone.

JENNY BULL, *Falls*, (Beaulieux Rapids), on the Wisconsin river, are in town 31, of range 6. At this place are 4 mills, cutting about 3,000,000 feet of lumber per year.

KEWASKUM, *P. O.*, in Washington county.

KOSSUTH, *Town*, in Manitowoc county.

LAWRENCE, *Town*, in Brown county.

LEROY, *P. O.*, in Fond du Lac county.

LISBON, *P. O.*, in Waukesha county.

LITTLE CHUTE, *P. O.*, on Fox river, in Outagamie county.

MANITOWOC RAPIDS, *P. V.*, is situated at the Rapids of Manitowoc river, in Manitowoc county, 4 miles west from Lake Michigan. The river at this place furnishes a good hydraulic power, which is improved, and used for several manufacturing purposes.

MANITOWOC RAPIDS, *Town*, in Manitowoc county.

MANITOWOC, *P. V.*, is beautifully situated at the mouth of the Manitowoc river, on Lake Michigan, 90 miles below Milwaukee. Its present population is about 2,000, and is rapidly increasing. Its harbor, the best natural one on the lake west, is being improved through an appropriation by Congress. The county seat of the county has been lately located here, and an appropriation made for the erection of county buildings. It has 1 pier, 4 warehouses, 12 stores, 2 steam saw mills, 6 blacksmith and waggon, 3 shoe, and 3 tailor's shops; 2 ship yards, at which ship building is carried on to considerable extent; 4 hotels, and 2 school houses; it has Episcopalian, Presbyterian, Methodist, and Catholic congregations—the first has built a fine church, and the others have arranged for suitable sites, and will soon erect churches. Large quantities of lumber, manufactured on the river above, are sold and shipped here every year, from which considerable revenue is derived yearly. As soon as the plank road, which is being built between this place and Menasha, is finished, Manitowoc will become the depot of considerable trade of the Fox River Valley, and a place of importance as a commercial point. The rail roads projected from this place north and west, connecting with roads in the interior, will undoubtedly be built.

MANITOWOC, *Town*, in Manitowoc county.

MAPLE GROVE, *Town*, in Manitowoc county.

MARCY, *P. O.*, in Waukesha county.

MENASHA, *P. V.*, is situated at the outlet of Lake Winnebago, on the north side of the northern channel. It is now a place of some ten or twelve hundred inhabitants, and possesses all the advantages for a large town. Its hydraulic power is very great, and has been improved with great rapidity. There are now in operation upon it, 2 grist mills, 5 saw mills, 1 large tub and pail factory, which occupies a building 40 by 60 feet, and 3 stories high, 2 cabinet and chair manufactories, 2 sash and blind establishments, 1 large iron foundry, 1 brewery, and there is also an extensive pottery which turns out large quantities of the best kind of ware, pronounced, by those who are conversant with such matters, equal to the best Ohio stone ware—and the clay of which it is made is found in the immediate vicinity in inexhaustible quantities. The place contains 4 taverns, and the usual number of shops and stores. Hon. Curtis Reed commenced the settlement of the place in July, 1849, and has since been the leading spirit of the place. A plank road connects this place with Appleton and Grand Kaukauna; and one is also in progress of construction to Manitowoc, on Lake Michigan, and will be completed during the present season. The State Improvement and U. S. Land Offices are located here; and an appropriation of $5,000 has been made by Congress for the construction of a light house. A daily line of steam boats connect with Fond du Lac, and the Fox and Wolf rivers.

MEEME, *Town*, in Manitowoc county.

MENOMONEE FALLS, *P. O.*, in Waukesha county.

MENTOR, *P. O.*, in Sheboygan county.

MENTOR, *P. O.*, in Waukesha county.

MISHCOTT, *P. O.*, in Manitowoc county.

MONTICELLO, *Town*, in Lafayette county.

MUSCLE, *Lake* and *River*, are on the western head waters of the Wisconsin, in Marathon county.

MUSKEGO CENTRE, *P. O.*, in town of Muskego, Waukesha county.

MUKWA, *P. V. & C. H.*, on Wolf river, in Waupacca county.

NEENAH, *P. V.*, is situated at the outlet of Lake Winnebago, opposite Menasha, on the south side of the south channel. The property was first purchased from the Government by Harrison Reed in 1846. There are now 3 large flouring mills, 2 saw mills, 1 sash and blind manufactory, 1 cabinet shop, 1 planing mill, and an immense hydraulic power yet unoccupied. Some think that time will ultimately connect the two villages of Menasha and Neenah, including the large island between, in one large city, possessing advantages of location and water power rarely equalled.

NEW DIGGINGS, *Town*, in Lafayette county.

NEW HOLSTEIN, *P. O.*, in town of same name, in Calumet county.

NEWTON, *Town*, in Manitowoc county.

NORTH JANESVILLE, *P. O.*, in town of Janesville, Rock county, town 3 N., of range 12 E.

OAKLAND, *P. O.*, in town of same name, in Jefferson county.

ONEONTA, *P. O.*, in Sauk county.

ORIN, *P. O.*, in Richland county.

ONION RIVER, *P. O.*, in Sheboygan county.

OWASCUS, *P. O.*, in Fond du Lac county.

PITTSFIELD, *Town*, in Brown county.

SPRINGVILLE, *P. O.*, in Fond du Lac county.

TURKEY GROVE, *P. O.*, on section 31, town 5, of range 6, 28 miles from Madison, Dane county.

WISCONSIN EMIGRANT AGENCY. For the purpose of promoting emigration to the State, an Emigration Agency has been established, the officers of which are paid by the State, and are interested only to point out the various industrial resources of Wisconsin, its adaption to mercantile and mechanical pursuits—the best location where either wild, government, or improved lands can be procured—and such other general and useful information as is needed by the emigrant. The office of the Agency is at 89, GREENWICH STREET, NEW YORK. The following named gentlemen are connected with this Agency, either of whom will give, free of cost or charge, impartial and reliable informntion, both verbal and documentary, to all wishing to inquire in regard to the State:

HERMAN HAERTEL, Commissioner.

JOHN H. BYRNE, Assistant Commissioner.

THOMAS J. TOWNSEND, Travelling Agent.

NEWSPAPERS IN WISCONSIN.

Place.	County.	Name of Paper.	Publishers.
Appleton,	Outagamie,	Appleton Crescent,	Samuel Ryan, jr.
Baraboo,	Sauk,	Sauk County Standard,	C. H. McLaughlin.
Beaver Dam,	Dodge,	Beaver Dam Republican,	Edgar C. Hull.
Beloit,	Rock,	Beloit Journal,	Briggs & Foster.
Berlin,	Marquette,	Marquette Mercury,	J. H. Wells.
Columbus,	Columbia,	Columbus Reporter,	Huntington.
Elkhorn,	Walworth,	Walworth County Reporter,	Utter & Co.
Delavan,	Walworth,	Walworth County Journal,	Bunner & Co.
Fond du Lac,	Fond du Lac,	Fond du Lac Journal,	E. Beeson.
Fond du Lac,	Fond du Lac,	Fountain City Herald,	R. Buck.
Fond du Lac,	Fond du Lac,	National Democrat,	Amos Reed.
Green Bay,	Brown,	Green Bay Advocate,	Robinson & Brother.
Inmansville,	Rock,	Emigranten, [Norwegian]	C. L. Claussen.
Janesville,	Rock,	Democratic Standard,	Daniel C. Brown.
Janesville,	Rock,	Janesville Free Press,	Joseph Baker.
Janesville,	Rock,	Janesville Gazette,	Alden & Holt.
Janesville,	Rock,	Wisconsin & Iowa Farmer,	Mark Miller.
Jefferson,	Jefferson,	Jeffersonian,	W. M. Watt.
Juneau,	Dodge,	Dodge County Gazette,	R. B. Wentworth.
Kenosha,	Kenosha,	Kenosha Democrat,	G. H. Paul.
Kenosha,	Kenosha,	Kenosha Telegraph,	C. L. Sholes.
Kenosha,	Kenosha,	Kenosha Tribune,	Butts & West.
La Crosse,	La Crosse,	La Crosse Democrat,	Stevens & Rogers.
Lancaster,	Grant,	Grant County Herald,	Cover & Goldsmith.
Madison,	Dane,	Wisconsin Argus & Democrat,	Beriah Brown.
Madison,	Dane,	Wisconsin State Journal,	David Atwood.
Manitowoc,	Manitowoc,	Manitowoc County Herald,	C. W. Fitch.
Monroe,	Green,	Monroe Sentinel,	J. Walworth.
Milwaukee,	Milwaukee,	Milwaukee Free Democrat,	S. M. Booth.
Milwaukee,	Milwaukee,	Milwaukee Sentinel,	R. King & Co.
Milwaukee,	Milwaukee,	Wisconsin,	W. E. Cramer.
Milwaukee,	Milwaukee,	Morning News,	Shaw & Hyer.
Milwaukee,	Milwaukee,	Wisconsin Banner, [German]	Shoeffler & Wendt.
Milwaukee,	Milwaukee,	Volksfreund, [German]	Fratney & Hertzberg.
Milwaukee,	Milwaukee,	See Bote, [German]	A. St. Vincent.

Place.	County.	Name of Paper.	Publishers.
Mineral Point,	Iowa,	Mineral Point Democrat,	O. J. Wright.
Mineral Point,	Iowa,	Wisconsin Tribune,	Bliss & Chaney.
Platteville,	Grant,	Independent American,	J. L. Marsh.
Potosi,	Grant,	Potosi Republican,	Seaton & Paul.
Prairie du Chien,	Crawford,	Crawford County Courier,	Hutchinson & Hurd.
Portage City,	Columbia,	River Times,	John Delaney.
Portage City,	Columbia,	Northern Republic,	W. W. Noyes.
Oshkosh,	Winnebago,	Noerdlicher Anzeiger [German]	Coleman & Co.
Oshkosh,	Winnebago,	Oshkosh Courier,	J. Crowley.
Oshkosh,	Winnebago,	Oshkosh Democrat,	Burnside & Co.
Ozaukee,	Ozaukee,	Washington County Blade,	R. A. Bird.
Racine,	Racine,	Racine Advocate,	C. Clement.
Racine,	Racine,	Racine Democrat,	Hewlett & Carey.
Sheboygan,	Sheboygan,	Sheboygan Journal,	F. J. Mills.
Sheboygan,	Sheboygan,	Democratic Secretary,	J. Quintus.
Sheboygan,	Sheboygan,	Sheboygan Chronicle,	Lyman & Eastman.
Sheboygan,	Sheboygan,	Nieuwsbode, [Dutch]	J. Quintus.
Sheboygan,	Sheboygan,	Phœnix aus Norwesten [Germ.]	Reinholt.
Sheboygan,	Sheboygan,	[German]	A. Marschner.
Sheboygan Falls,	Sheboygan,	Sheboygan Falls Free Press,	J. A. Smith.
Shullsburg,	Lafayette,	Pick & Gad,	Samuel G. Bugh.
Stevens' Point,	Portage,	Wisconsin Pinery,	Chandler & Co.
Watertown,	Jefferson,	Democratic State Register,	E. B. Quiner.
Watertown,	Jefferson,	Watertown Chronicle,	J. A. Hadley.
Waukesha,	Waukesha,	Waukesha Chronotype,	H. D. Barron.

All of the foregoing, except the Wisconsin and Iowa Farmer at Janesville (monthly) are published weekly; and daily editions are also published by all in Madison, Milwaukee, and Racine; and tri-weekly by most of those in Milwaukee.

ERRATA.

Page 7, line 2, for "county" read "country."

„ 10, line 15, for "features" read "feature"; line 22, for "are" read "is."

„ 16, line 15, read "200,000,000."

„ 20, read "Green Bay, 28,000,000; Wisconsin, 70,000 000; Total, 211,000,000;" and for "nearly 400,000,000," read "over 200,000,000."

„ 59, line 16, read "Cadwell Prairie, *P. O.*"

„ 60, line 24, read "Calumet Village, *P. V.*"

„ 95, line 5, for "Town" read "*P. O.*"

„ 98, line 24, for "river" read "line."

„ 130, line 7, for "W." read "E."

„ 249, line 1, for "1," read "36."

www.ingramcontent.com/pod-product-compliance
Lightning Source LLC
LaVergne TN
LVHW010252110826
845151LV00004B/1455